The Market Research Society

With over 8,000 members in more than 50 countries, The Market Research Society (MRS) is the world's largest international membership organization for professional researchers and others engaged in (or interested in) marketing, social or opinion research.

It has a diverse membership of individual researchers within agencies, independent consultancies, client-side organizations, and the academic community, and from all levels of seniority and job functions.

All MRS members agree to comply with the MRS Code of Conduct (see Appendix 9), which is supported by the Codeline advisory service and a range of specialist guidelines on best practice.

MRS offers various qualifications and membership grades, as well as training and professional development resources to support these. It is the official awarding body in the UK for vocational qualifications in market research.

MRS is a major supplier of publications and information services, conferences and seminars and many other meeting and networking opportunities for researchers.

MRS is 'the voice of the profession' in its media relations and public affairs activities on behalf of professional research practitioners, and aims to achieve the most favourable climate of opinions and legislative environment for research.

The Market Research Society (Limited by Guarantee) Company Number 518685

Company Information: Registered offi̇   ᵈ business address:
15 Northburgh Street, London EC1V (
Telephone: 44 20 7490 4911
Fax: 44 20 7490 0608
e-mail: info@marketresearch.org.ul
website: www.mrs.org.uk

MARKET RESEARCH IN PRACTICE SERIES

Published in association with The Market Research Society
Consultant Editors: David Barr and Robin J Birn

Kogan Page has joined forces with The Market Research Society (MRS) to publish this unique series of books designed to cover the latest developments in market research thinking and practice.

The series provides up-to-date knowledge on the techniques of market research and customer insight and best practice in implementing them. It also shows the contribution market research and customer information management techniques can make to helping organisations of all kinds in shaping their strategy, structure, customer focus and value creation.

The series consists of several essential guides that focus on the core skills developed in the MRS training and qualifications programmes (www.mrs.org.uk). It provides practical advice and case studies on how to plan, use, act on, and follow-up, research, and on how to combine it with other sources of information to develop deep insights into customers.

Fully international in scope of content, its readership is also from all over the world. The series is designed not only for specialist market researchers, but also for all those involved in developing and using deeper insights into their customers – marketers in all disciplines, including planning, communications, brand management, and interactive marketers.

Other titles in the series:

Consumer Insight, Merlin Stone
The Effective Use of Market Research, Robin J Birn
Market Intelligence: How and why organizations use market research, Martin Callingham
Market Research in Practice: A guide to the basics, Paul Hague, Nick Hague & Carol-Ann Morgan
Questionnaire Design, Ian Brace

Kogan Page Ltd
120 Pentonville Road
London N1 9JN
Tel: 020 7278 0433
www.kogan-page.co.uk

BUSINESS TO BUSINESS MARKET RESEARCH

UNDERSTANDING AND MEASURING BUSINESS MARKETS

RUTH McNEIL

KOGAN PAGE

London & Sterling, VA

This book is dedicated to Tim Sanders (1975–2004) who would have been a great businessman had he lived.

Publisher's note

Every possible effort has been made to ensure that the information contained in this book is accurate at the time of going to press, and the publishers and authors cannot accept responsibility for any errors or omissions, however caused. No responsibility for loss or damage occasioned to any person acting, or refraining from action, as a result of the material in this publication can be accepted by the editor, the publisher or any of the authors.

First published in Great Britain and the United States in 2005 by Kogan Page Limited

120 Pentonville Road
London N1 9JN
United Kingdom
www.kogan-page.co.uk

22883 Quicksilver Drive
Sterling VA 20166-2012
USA

© Ruth McNeil, 2005

The right of Ruth McNeil to be identified as the author of this work has been asserted by her in accordance with the Copyright, Designs and Patents Act 1988.

ISBN 0 7494 4364 2

British Library Cataloguing-in-Publication Data

A CIP record for this book is available from the British Library.

Typeset by Datamatics Technologies Ltd, Mumbai, India
Printed and bound in Great Britain by Creative Print and Design (Wales), Ebbw Vale

Contents

The editorial board   *vii*

Acknowledgements   *ix*

Introduction   **1**

1. The business to business market research industry   **3**
What is business to business market research? Some definitions 3;
The history of B2B market research 5; The size of the B2B market
research sector 5; The people researched in B2B work 7;
Differences between B2B and consumer research 10; How B2B
research complements other research 13; The types of business
problems B2B research addresses 15; The users of B2B market
research 16; Summary 19

2. Sampling for B2B research   **20**
Sampling characteristics of business markets 20; Putting the study
into action 23; Research practices related to sampling 35; Summary 39

3. Trends in B2B research   **40**
Drivers 40; Specific trends and issues 44; Challenges faced by B2B
research 48; Implications of current trends 49; Summary 53

4. What works and does not work in B2B research   **54**
Possible research approaches or methodologies 54; Relative use of
these approaches in B2B research 58; Deciding on the approach 60;
Summary 68

5. The B2B research process: I Desk research   **69**
The desk research process 70; Resources for desk research 71;
Another type of desk research: data mining 74; Validating data
from desk research 76; Summary 76

Contents

6. **The B2B research process: II Qualitative research** 77
Main types of qualitative research 77; The qualitative process 81;
B2B interviewing and moderating 86; Qualitative analysis and
reporting 96; Summary 106

7. **The B2B research process: III Quantitative research** 107
The quantitative process 107; Questionnaire design 110; Design
issues and project management relevant to particular B2B
methods 124; Administering questionnaires: fieldwork issues 133;
Reporting 151; Summary 159

8. **Costing: guidelines on the cost of projects** 160
First considerations 160; Costing basics – factors influencing
costs 161; Containing project costs 165; Summary 165

9. **Overviews of the business respondent, sectors and research
applications** 166
The business respondent 166; Overview of sectors 169; Applications
of market research 177; Summary 210

10. **Regional differences and comparisons in B2B research** 211
Regional review 211; Summary 219

11. **What it is like being a B2B client and B2B researcher** 221
What it is like being a B2B client 221; What it is like being a B2B
researcher 228; Summary 235

12. **Training, organizations and ethics in B2B research** 236
Training 236; Organizations 237; Ethics in B2B research 242;
Summary 245

Appendix 1: Sources for B2B market researchers 247
Appendix 2: Sample screener questionnaire for in-depth interview 254
Appendix 3: Sample focus group recruitment questionnaire 257
Appendix 4: Research snapshot as a reporting technique 260
Appendix 5: Sample self-completion questionnaire (Business Link) 262
*Appendix 6: Sample customer satisfaction research quantitative
questions* 267
*Appendix 7: Sample communication research quantitative
questionnaire* 270
Appendix 8: Principles of the Data Protection Act 1998 272
Appendix 9: The Market Research Society Code of Conduct 273

Glossary 294
References and further reading 299
Index 302

The editorial board

SERIES EDITORS

David Barr has been Director General of The Market Research Society since July 1997. He previously spent over 25 years in business information services and publishing. He has held management positions with Xerox Publishing Group, the British Tourist Authority and Reed International plc. His experience of market research is therefore all on the client side, having commissioned many projects for NPD and M&A purposes. A graduate of Glasgow and Sheffield Universities, David Barr is a Member of the Chartered Management Institute and a Fellow of The Royal Society of Arts.

Robin J Birn has been a marketing and market research practitioner for over 25 years. In 1985 Robin set up Strategy, Research and Action Ltd, a market research company for the map, atlas and travel guide sector, and the book industry. In 2004 he was appointed Head of Consultation and Research at the Institute of Chartered Accountants of England and Wales. He is a Fellow of The Market Research Society and a Fellow of the Chartered Institute of Marketing, and is also the editor of *The International Handbook of Market Research Techniques*.

ADVISORY MEMBERS

Martin Callingham was formerly Group Market Research Director at Whitbread, where he ran the Market Research department for 20 years and was a non-executive director of the company's German restaurant chain for more than 10 years. Martin has also played his part in the market research world. Apart from being on many committees of the MRS, of which he is a Fellow, he was Chairman of the Association of Users of Research (AURA), has been a council member of ESOMAR, and has presented widely, winning the David Winter Award in 2001 at the MRS Conference.

Nigel Culkin is a Fellow of The Market Research Society and member of its Professional Advisory Board. He has been a full member since 1982. He has been in academia since 1991 and is currently Deputy Director, Commercial Development at the University of Hertfordshire, where he is responsible for activities that develop a culture of entrepreneurism and innovation among staff and students. He is Chair of the University's, Film Industry Research Group (FiRG), supervisor to a number of research students and regular contributor to the media on the creative industries.

Professor Merlin Stone is Business Research Leader with IBM's Business Consulting Services, where he works on business research, consulting and marketing with IBM's clients, partners and universities. He runs the IBM Marketing Transformation Group, a network of clients, marketing agencies, consultancies and business partners, focusing on changing marketing. He is a director of QCi Ltd, an Ogilvy One company. Merlin is IBM Professor of Relationship Marketing at Bristol Business School. He has written many articles and 25 books on marketing and customer service, including *Up Close and Personal: CRM @ Work, Customer Relationship Marketing, Successful Customer Relationship Marketing, CRM in Financial Services* and *The Customer Management Scorecard*, all published by Kogan Page, and *The Definitive Guide to Direct and Interactive Marketing*, published by Financial Times-Pitman. He is a Founder Fellow of the Institute of Direct Marketing and a Fellow of the Chartered Institute of Marketing.

Paul Szwarc began his career as a market researcher at the Co-operative Wholesale Society (CWS) Ltd in Manchester in 1975. Since then he has worked at Burke Market Research (Canada), American Express Europe, IPSOS RSL, International Masters Publishers Ltd and PSI Global prior to joining the Network Research board as a director in October 2000. Over the past few years Paul has specialized on the consumer financial sector, directing multi-country projects on customer loyalty and retention, new product/service development, and employee satisfaction in the UK, European and North American markets. Paul is a full member of The Market Research Society. He has presented papers at a number of MRS and ESOMAR seminars and training courses.

Acknowledgements

First on the list must be my two collaborators in the United States, Dr Kerrie Pinkerton (O'Gallagher) in New York and Jo Ingledew in San Francisco. Kerrie worked effectively as a co-author with me much of the time, working ceaselessly to provide a broader view and bring her experience of working in Australia, Europe and North America to bear. This combination of broad view allied with her attention to detail made Kerrie an ideal workmate. No one could have been more devoted to helping an old colleague. Many thanks to both Kerrie and Jo – living proof that writing a book 'virtually' and across multiple time zones can be effective. Eternal gratitude to e-mail!

My particular thanks also to all those who contributed to this book and provided case studies, in particular the many agencies that provided topical information and to those clients who gave permission for data to be reproduced.

There were those who provided insight on regional perspectives, including and in particular Julia Spink (Asia), Warwick Hoare (Australia and Asia) and Mark Dignam (Australia). There were also those who read through my first draft on sector issues and provided useful additional commentary: my thanks here to Keith Bailey (Nokia) concerning the IT/telecoms sector and to Richard Gilmore (Insight) on the pharmaceutical sector.

Others, too numerous to mention, provided help on particular issues, such as Rebecca Candy of Kudos concerning directories and lists, Neil McPhee, Nuance, on market size information, and Mike Brown, Cobalt Sky for help in converting some data.

One of the most depressing things about writing a book like this is that it becomes out of date as soon as it is written; my thanks to my colleagues on the BIG Conference Committee for encouraging me not to worry too much about this but to labour on! It is not just people who deserve thanks: much published data, such as the supplements produced by The Market Research Society, has provided useful case studies already in the public domain. Others too gave ideas on what they would like to see included in the book via a survey undertaken – I wish I had had room to include all you would have liked to see here.

Yvonne Burr of Reuters came up trumps by giving the book a final read-through before it was finally put to bed – my thanks to her too.

Can acknowledgements be made without mentioning my editors, David Barr and Robin Birn, and Jon Finch of Kogan Page? And the endless patience of my husband who spent night after night on his own while I tapped away at the computer? I will not thank Harry the cat, though, as he enjoyed every minute – his place on my lap assured throughout.

Thank you one and all!

Introduction

This book, *Business to Business Market Research* is written as a stand-alone reference document and as part of the new series of books designed for market researchers, market research students and non-professional researchers who may have an interest in research, or more particularly, business to business research.

The series – under the aegis of The Market Research Society and Kogan Page, the publisher – is intended to help readers learn from others' experience, develop core skills, apply market research effectively and provide the latest information on research techniques, use of market research and global activity.

Over the past 13 years, there has been remarkably little published specifically about business to business research. The last significant publication, *Researching Business Markets: The IMRA handbook of business-to-business marketing research*, edited by Ken Sutherland, published by Kogan Page, appeared in 1991 as an update of a book originally written in 1978, *A Manual of Industrial Marketing Research* edited by Alan Rawnsley, published by Wiley.

Here we intend to provide an up-to-date reference source for all those involved in, or occasionally needing to know about, business to business (B2B) market research, giving case studies demonstrating examples of B2B research in practice, its applications and uses. A lot has happened in the last decade – B2B research is no longer seen as just 'industrial' research but has a wider remit; the internet is revolutionizing the way data are obtained, accessed and reported on; markets are merging; and B2B research and business to consumer research are much closer than before. I hope you will find this book of interest, whether to dip into as needed, or to provide guidance if you are commissioning or undertaking B2B research projects.

Just a short note: I have tended to refer to 'the business respondent' and 'companies' as a catch-all – nevertheless, others who fall frequently within the frame of reference of B2B (such as doctors or those outside the strictly commercial arena such as organizations that are not necessarily profit-driven) are included in these denominations. For simplicity, the terms the 'business respondent' and 'company' have been used.

Although on occasion names of companies and others have been included in the book in order for it to 'come alive' to the reader, no endorsement of any nature is intended. Inevitably, when writing a book such as this one relies on one's own frame of reference and what drops into one's lap as reading matter. When people asked me what book I was writing, as soon as I said *Business to Business Market Research* their faces dropped. My hope is that you will not have long faces when you read, or dip into, the book, but will find something here at least that is worth reading and is not *too* dry.

The author, Ruth McNeil in the UK, and those who collaborated most closely on the book, Kerrie O'Gallagher and Joanne Ingledew on the East and West coasts of the United States respectively, are all active research practitioners and would welcome any contact from those with queries or who are interested in commissioning B2B projects. Their e-mail addresses are as follows:

rmcneil@tiscali.co.uk
chrysalisresearch@earthlink.net
joingledew@msn.com

1 The business to business market research industry

WHAT IS BUSINESS TO BUSINESS MARKET RESEARCH? SOME DEFINITIONS

Business to business (B2B) market research refers to research that is undertaken entirely within the business world: a business – the client – wishes to research its business customers or, less commonly, its suppliers or other parties who are involved in the running of (or who contribute to) its business. Only those in business are involved. B2B research includes all research where the product or service is being used in a business environment.

Business research divides broadly into two types: first, consumer or business to consumer (B2C), and second, B2B research. B2C research includes research where the product or service is being used in a non-business environment: that is, where respondents are (in most cases) using their own money. B2B research includes all research where the product or service is being used in a business environment.

As Andrew McIntosh said when describing business to business research, 'The common element is the fact that our respondents are buying the goods or services we research, not with their own money but with the money of companies or organisations for whom they work.'

In some ways, B2B market research is more easily defined by what it is *not* rather than by what it is. It is not research that involves the general public, the mass market, the normal 'consumer' – this is consumer or B2C research. It is easy to grasp that it is not what we commonly call consumer research (FMCG – fast-moving consumer goods – or CPG – consumer packaged goods – research). The main point for us to remember is that in B2B research, the consumer is the customer in the business context, not the 'man in the street' consumer who may be interviewed in the B2C context.

Here are some examples. Research for a multinational food manufacturer with homemakers regarding frozen yoghurts marketed through a retail store would be consumer (FMCG or CPG) research. On the other hand, research for an oil company with customers visiting its service stations would be B2C research – oil is not deemed a fast-moving consumer good and so this research is B2C, not FMCG. Finally, research for an oil company with those who buy aviation fuel would be B2B research: a business (the oil company) is commissioning the work, the subject under scrutiny (aviation fuel) is not a FMCG, and the people being surveyed are business respondents, answering in their business context not as normal everyday consumers.

Nowadays there is a trend to talk about 'business research' overall, and this embraces both B2C and B2B work. In general there may be more B2C work done (this is almost certainly so), and some would argue that the two are becoming rapidly closer and even merging. For example, with the arrival of the internet, deregulation, and with the increasing speed of change in industry and business environments, and merging of companies and applications, the distinctions between B2B and B2C are somewhat blurred. In particular, due to new generation product innovation with products developed for business and 'advanced' consumers alike, research nowadays is often conducted simultaneously with both business respondents (B2B) and 'advanced' consumers (B2C). In some markets (such as printers, paper and laptops), where products are marketed to both business consumers and household consumers, there is a need for researchers to be skilled at both B2C and B2B methods, and for the integration of information collected from both. For this reason, many in the B2B research area will undertake B2C work also and regard themselves as 'business' researchers.

B2B research may be either domestic or involve international research. It embraces many different techniques including desk research, brainstorming, qualitative and quantitative research – the whole research horizon. Importantly, it should be noted that B2B market research is not only about interviewing the 'big boys' or top decision makers – the directors, chief executive officers or chief financial officers, and very senior managers in large businesses. It is also about interviewing the influencers of the business decisions, the implementers, possibly the ultimate end-users of a product or service, and sometimes industry experts. The respondent base is extraordinarily diverse, encompassing myriad people and occupations – purchasing clerks, heating engineers, welders, small manufacturers, tradespeople, industry experts, inventors, journalists, politicians, business analysts and intermediaries.

The principles on which B2B research is based are those of good research practice everywhere, but there are certain specific areas where B2B research is different from others, and these are what we shall be focusing on in this book.

THE HISTORY OF B2B MARKET RESEARCH

While the specific details of origins of the B2B research industry may vary between countries, the following UK example illustrates a typical history.

With the rise of mass consumer markets and the growth in marketing and advertising of consumer products and services after the Second World War, research budgets were largely taken up with FMCG research. In the UK, the 1960s saw the establishment of the first specialist 'industrial' marketing research company by Aubrey Wilson, and in 1964 the Industrial Marketing Research Association (IMRA) was launched. This set the scene for B2B research, with the early emphasis on 'industrial' – in the classic sense of manufacturing industry, both heavy and light. However, even at this early stage, this term was not a totally accurate description. Much research was undertaken outside the strictly 'industrial' field, which embraced wider sectors including the pharmaceutical, agrochemical, energy, information technology (IT) and telecommunications sectors.

The name change from IMRA to BIG (Business Intelligence Group) in the 1990s signalled, first, the recognition by researchers conducting B2B research that the title of 'industrial' research reflected too narrow a constituency for the modern business world, and second, that for today's B2B researcher, intelligence gathering is now often as much the focus as primary market research.

THE SIZE OF THE B2B MARKET RESEARCH SECTOR

Estimates of the size of the market research industry and B2B's share of this vary substantially, reflecting different data collection and estimation methods, some variations in market definitions, and the lack of information on the splits between B2B and B2C.

Recent data from ESOMAR – the European Society of Opinion and Market Research – (ESOMAR World Market Research Turnover) indicate that the worldwide value of market research is circa US $15,000 million per year. Of this, the organization estimates that Europe's share is around 42 per cent and the US share 40 per cent, with the remaining 18 per cent divided mainly between the Asia–Pacific (13 per cent) and other regions (in particular, South America). According to the British Market Research Association (BMRA), non-consumer research (which embraces both B2B and B2C) accounts for around 10 per cent of the total research market. Laurence Curtis, CEO of The Research Business International, was recently quoted as saying that the global market for B2B was around 6–7 per cent of the total research market. If we take this as a conservative estimate, this would indicate that the worldwide B2B market is worth some US $1,000 million.

This is just an estimate and the size of the strictly B2B market is based more on judgement than hard numbers. What we can say, however, is that the B2B market is smaller than the B2C market in most countries, and that the B2B market varies hugely in size: in some countries it is not inconsiderable, while in others it is very small.

In the UK, for 2001 (the most recent set of figures available), the BMRA estimates the size of the business research market at around £118 million per annum. By far the largest sector in expenditure terms in the UK is financial B2B research (£45 million) with others coming well behind – the travel and transport category at £15 million, with IT, professional services and oil companies all at £9 million each, business and industrial sectors at £5 million, followed by property and construction (£2 million). Other categories (such as distribution) account for the remainder of annual expenditure, but all are around £1 million or under. While pharmaceutical research has an annual expenditure on 'business' research of some £56 million and appears to dwarf other sectors, its research is not always defined as 'B2B' market research (this is discussed later).

In the United States, it is similarly difficult to obtain precise estimates of the value of market research and the B2B share of this. However, ESOMAR quotes the 2002 US expenditure on market research (in total) to be US $6.307 billion and for 2003 to be US $6.66 billion – a 5.6 per cent increase. One published estimate of the B2B component of online research comes from Inside Research. This examines online market research revenue from the top 23 market research firms, and estimates that in 2003 US $155.1 million (19 per cent) of the US $796.6 million online MR revenue could be defined as B2B.

As an example of an individual market, the AMSRS (new name for the Market Research Society of Australia) estimates the size of the local market to be around A $350 million and the B2B component to be around A $100 million. The AMSRS indicates that B2B is faster growing: over a long period, it has outpaced B2C and government research, and still remains a growth market.

THE PEOPLE RESEARCHED IN B2B WORK

Defining the B2B respondent

When traditional consumer research is undertaken, normally definitions of the respondents are relatively easy: for example, 'males aged 16–24 years' or 'regular (more than once a month) purchasers of liquid bath soap'. By contrast, defining respondents and developing practical procedures to easily identify them is more of an issue for B2B researchers. Indeed, respondent definition is key to successful B2B market research.

When defining respondents, there are two big issues for the B2B researcher:

The respondent

First, who is the respondent that we need to speak to in the company? What is his or her title/position/role with respect to the issue under investigation? We must ask ourselves (and the client) questions and determine who has the knowledge we are looking for in an interview. Does the business issue that guides the research require us to talk to decision makers, those who influence the decision, and/or users of the product or service under question? We also need to determine where these people can best be found in the structures of the companies we want to survey.

Representativeness

Second, how many do we people need to speak to in the company (and across the different companies) to get a sample that is representative of the organizational structure and of the number of divisions/sites? This will be examined in greater detail in Chapter 2 on sampling.

Titles

When undertaking a B2B project, researchers ask the commissioning company about the typical titles of people they might want to interview. Sometimes, the company can supply both names and titles (and contact details!) sourced from its databases or its sales department. However, equally frequently it does not have precise details (this is especially relevant when testing a new product or service and the potential market is part of what is being investigated) or the way it thinks about 'customers' is different from the way that a researcher has to go about doing research. In these cases, the researcher must draw on previous experience or not be afraid to ask when telephoning or making contact to arrange an interview, 'Who is in charge of Quality Assurance in your company?' or 'Who looks after supply and logistics issues? What is their title?' A trial series of questions will help to develop an operational way of identifying respondents. Being prepared to ask questions and to be persistent are essential skills for the B2B researcher.

Commonly, the sorts of titles of respondents B2B researchers look to interview include those heading companies or board directors including the CEO (chief executive officer), CFO (chief financial officer), and COO (chief operating officer). Also not uncommon are those heading up, or influencing, key activities such as those in purchasing, supplies and logistics, IT, knowledge and information, finance, manufacturing or production, HR (human resources), marketing or sales, innovation and quality assurance. Titles for these are many and various, but very often directors or managers of these divisions are the ones the B2B researcher is targeting, as they know most and are closest to decision making.

It is not always those leading the company, though, who need to be researched. Very often, if we interview at too high a level, those making the ultimate decisions or formulating strategy will not have been involved in the minutiae of the information gathering or at the sharp end of production successes or failures. (We might have just talked to the cheque signers.) They will have relied on those further down the chain to help them make decisions, and it is these people, who input to decisions, who the B2B researcher must speak to as well.

Often clients think that 10 CEOs or the heads of IT and telecoms (for example) in the top 20 companies in the field will make the best group for researching their ideas. However, often it is our role to point out that these people may head the company but are not necessarily the ones to whom we should be speaking. They may be too remote from the decisions we are researching, and someone with a less exalted title may fit the bill much better.

Let us look at a 2003 study that was conducted in several European countries on behalf of a large international manufacturer of home and personal products concerning its corporate reputation. Often in a corporate reputation study the range of respondents is more diverse than in other types of studies. While some of the sample was provided for this particular study, most had to be 'free found' (that is, their names were not provided and they were sourced and found by the researcher). In order to guide interviewers undertaking the telephone survey, they were given some 'key words' to look for and then examples of the sorts of titles that might come up when they telephoned. Some of the key titles suggested are listed below:

- manager/director of ethical trading;
- manager/director of ethical supply chain;
- manager/director of social and environmental affairs;
- manager/director of global sourcing;
- vendor compliance manager;
- director of organic/sustainability;
- officer/manager/director for corporate social responsibility;
- director of culture;
- director of environmental affairs.

They came from divisions variously named external relations, supply chain, ethical trading, ethical supply, corporate social responsibility, sourcing, logistics, compliance, environmental protection or environmental responsibility, responsible sourcing, vendor compliance, organic, workforce protection, local sourcing, and responsible trading.

A further complication was that companies tend to have a slightly different organizational structure or reporting lines, so that, for example, those to be interviewed could report into a number of different divisions – supply chain, logistics, corporate relations, or even HR. Pinning down the right person was not always easy! It is much easier if you know the role and responsibility of the person you want to speak to and then work out the title, but if you have to go in 'title first', then think about some typical titles that might apply, or some key words that might trigger the receptionist to put you through to the right department without having to 'go round the houses' to find your man (or woman). This is one of the more challenging areas of B2B, and ensures that we must keep on our toes, as fashions for titles and names change quickly. The B2B researcher must be aware of the trends.

The centre of influence

A slightly more difficult question to answer is where the decisions are made, or 'Where is the centre of influence?' within a respondent organization. This will often influence sample selection and composition. Some companies often set strategy and direct operations from their head office or home base. This is often true of companies operating in North America (especially those with global franchises – although it depends what point they are at in the cycle of devolution/centralization). For European companies that often work to a model of giving greater autonomy to individual operating companies, decisions may be taken at more diverse locations and not just at the corporate core, so more widespread interviewing is required.

DIFFERENCES BETWEEN B2B AND CONSUMER RESEARCH

There are major differences between the two fundamental types of research, including:

- respondent differences;
- sample and sample size differences;
- content differences.

Respondent differences

As was stated in the definition, B2B market research involves those who, in their capacity as owners or employees, are involved in decision making or operations on behalf of their company and are interviewed in their business, not their personal, capacity. This contrasts with B2C research, which involves end consumers. Are there any differences between the two? The answer is yes.

Those in business are often a more rare species. The right people to speak with may be harder to identify, and sometimes there are gate-keepers such as personal assistants or secretaries intervening between them and the researcher. The demands of their work, and indeed requests from other research companies, mean they can be difficult to get hold of and are less tolerant of long interviews (or are already over-surveyed). In all, as a general rule, getting hold of someone in business and completing an interview can be more of a challenge than finding a quota of nationally representative people to undertake B2C research.

Respondents can be quite geographically dispersed, and while this is no longer quite as much of a problem as it used to be now that the internet and online research have opened up, the fact remains that access to 'difficult to get hold of' business respondents is still an issue.

Sample and sample size differences

In many markets such as countries in Europe the 'universe' in B2B research is restricted – samples tend to be smaller and more specialized. Where this occurs it has implications, in that the normal sampling rules do not necessarily apply, as even a small sample can have important results. (More of this later.) If we wish to talk to people in business who are interested in virtual private networks, or to companies wishing to invest in satellite phones, then finding them may be a real issue. In these cases, even a small sample can provide meaningful strategic informa-tion for the client.

By contrast, in other markets like the United States, the size of the country and the business base mean we are sometimes less restricted in terms of the universe. There is a considerable amount of B2B research conducted in sectors where there is a relatively large universe (for example, the business market for telecommunications, paper, printers, personal computers and the like). Here, the limiting factor on project size is more often cost. Of course, all business universes are small when compared with general population figures.

Another key difference from consumer research is that in B2B work, a researcher might need to speak to more than one person in an organization in order to meet the research objectives. Commonly, there are several different people (often at different layers in the organization) from whom views need to be sought. For example, the purchase of a piece of equipment may involve the product design department, manufacturing, quality control, possibly even sales and marketing and the purchasing department – a long chain, and people in all of these areas can materially affect the outcome for any new product being introduced. So a mix may be needed in the research process, and this may involve the purchasing director and the quality assurance manager or the HR manager in addition to the CEO. In practical and sampling terms, this means multiple contacts rather than just one.

Both 'who' we need to speak to and 'how many' can be different in B2B research from B2C. Where smaller samples and often restricted budgets are an issue, large-scale (large N) quantitative research using complex research models (as is commonly used in consumer work) is not practicable. Unless (for example) they can tap into syndicated, industry-wide studies, some clients in some markets do not have the luxury (or nowadays the time, even if they had the budget) to repeat studies very frequently. However, as noted earlier, in markets like the United States where there is a larger business universe in so many market sectors (due to the size of the country and depth of the business base), large-scale studies, complex models and repeat (and tracking) studies can be conducted successfully.

Even so, much of the work that a B2B researcher undertakes has considerable variety, with different markets and new subjects – new concepts, new products, new services, new frontiers, new applications and new market conditions.

Frequently, B2B research needs to employ 'one to one' personal interviewing techniques, as getting hold of the individuals who are relevant for samples is not easy, and such interviews recognize the contribution they can make. Findings from just one interview can be hugely important. Or a few key interviews can materially add to the data – noting the

Pareto principle that 20 per cent of a client's customers can make up 80 per cent of the business and if the views of those 20 per cent are included, then these results are key to the overall resultant strategy.

Content differences

Often the 'what' of the research is also different in the B2B context. Sector knowledge and familiarity with technical terms are particularly important, as B2B research enquires into complex aspects of (for example) technology, markets, and the design and features of products. Hence, both the researcher and those contacting respondents must be fluent in the specialized language required to undertake the research. On the other hand, in consumer research, while many complexities may be covered in the research, it is often unnecessary and even undesirable for the talk to be at a specialist level. Often B2B research requires as much awareness of the intricacies of the business (or industry) itself as it does of research processes and techniques, owing to the complexity of the sector and the product area, plus sometimes complex decision-making and purchasing procedures.

In many ways, more demands are made of the B2B researcher. B2B market research tends to rely a great deal on spontaneity and creativity – there is less of a straitjacket in terms of acceptable or unacceptable research techniques, and there are fewer 'off the shelf' solutions. So, the drudgery of repeating monadic consumer market research tests and undertaking frequently repeated continuous research studies is not for us. Oddly, B2B research can appeal to the 'dilettante' in the researcher: the variety and sheer scope of much of what is researched in the most esoteric sorts of business can favour the researcher who likes a bit of change in life. I started my career looking at anthelmintics (wormers, for the uninitiated) in cats and dogs, and at coccidiosis (a form of disease) in chickens. This is not what I felt I had done a degree in French and Spanish for – but my, was I happy to be out in the open, rattling along country lanes, to interview farmers in far-flung locations! I had to get used to the overpowering smell of chicken houses, but for sheer variety, yes, every time.

In summary, some major differences between B2B and B2C research include:

- restricted samples (fewer and more specialized 'business' respondents);
- the need to speak to several in a company, not just one, due to complex decision-making processes;
- sector and product knowledge an important backdrop to any research;

- very varied research often involving innovative new developments at an early stage.

HOW B2B RESEARCH COMPLEMENTS OTHER RESEARCH

Sometimes B2B research is conducted on its own. This is the norm when a business or industrial market is being assessed or a new product innovation with uniquely business applications is being tested.

CASE STUDY: TELECOMS COMPANY

Main message

These results from key customers helped address a brewing discontent and possible deterioration in customer perceptions.

Respondent definition

Major IT and non-IT customers of a telephone operator.

Details

The company was launching a new IT-enabled knowledge management system for customers' use that was intended to be web-based. It was important to gather the views of customers on the proposed system.

A study was undertaken with N = 15 respondents in companies, all of whom were major customers of a large telephone operator with multiple lines and multiple telephony applications. Some worked in the IT area and some were non-IT staff , so there was a selection of types of respondent. A mixture of personal and telephone interviews was undertaken.

Findings showed that many found the website difficult to navigate and did not agree with the articles posted up by business gurus. Immediately, these cast doubt on the usefulness of the service being offered. Most importantly, many had lost their password for entry to the site, so its use was curtailed.

The company addressed these issues by reconfirming passwords to all relevant customers and ensured that what was posted up as new or leading opinion pieces was well-regarded articles by experts rather than from more dubious sources.

Nowadays, in some sectors such as IT and telecoms, it is more usual to undertake research involving both business customers and 'normal' consumers – for example research involving mobile (cell) phones, printers and printer supplies that span the consumer and SOHO (small office home office sectors), or personal organizers (PDAs) like a Palm Pilot or BlackBerry.

Other key reasons for simultaneous B2B and B2C research include:

- The need for speedy product or service testing and launch. This also has the advantage of quick feedback, essential in today's world of rapid innovation and change. Speedy feedback is increasingly advantageous where being first in the market place brings a huge financial advantage and being second, the 'me too' syndrome, can bring financial penalty.
- When large changes in the market place are having an impact on both business and consumer groups (deregulation in the utilities, pharmaceutical or other markets; 'new generation' product innovation such as the telecoms sector is experiencing).
- When branding is being looked at and it is important to ensure consistency of image and message across a business and consumer audience at the same time.
- When push and pull marketing strategies are needed (wooing customers away from old habits and 'pulling' them to new ones) with several parties involved, such as when prescription drugs move to being sold over the counter (OTC).
- In order to ensure that the design of the research reflects a true representation of the market place. Depending on the balance in the market place, a smaller (sometimes qualitative) study might be done with the business community (B2B) and a larger study with the consumer community (B2C).

So the B2B researcher is often involved in both the B2B and B2C research. Many researchers do not think of themselves solely in one 'box' as opposed to the other, but as business researchers, with the main link being that the product or service being examined has a business rather than solely consumer application. B2B and B2C research are complementary. They sit happily side by side and flourish together. Sometimes, to use a gardening analogy, the research process is more of a 'mixed bed' than a single bed, but the results are all the better for this, as good research is all about making connections. Too much isolation in research can lead to poor decisions – often, it is better to be able to see the whole picture in one go.

Research is frequently conducted at multiple levels with different audiences in order to obtain a full overview speedily without putting too much emphasis on one of the constituencies and too little on another.

THE TYPES OF BUSINESS PROBLEMS B2B RESEARCH ADDRESSES

Later discussion covers in greater depth the different sorts of B2B market research undertaken. It can be noted that, in general, the issues and questions that B2B research can address are not different fundamentally from those with which B2C research can deal. The problems or opportunities clients face may be the same, but the respondent base whose knowledge and opinions are tapped is different.

Traditionally, there has been a tendency for much of B2B research to be of a strategic rather than tactical nature. Tiny facets of a wire-pro connector or changes planned for it tend not to be subjected to rigorous market research; instead the technical department might test it out itself or ask some close clients. Rarely will it require market research to be undertaken on smaller issues. Of course, there is a lot of product-oriented and tactical work carried out, but strategic work is just as common. This is one of the reasons that B2B research is so interesting: more often than not the subject is strategic in nature and the findings may have a significant impact for the client.

Research using external respondents

Most research is done with respondents who are external to the client company and covers the following issues:

- **Decision making.** What are the key criteria used by customers or potential customers for decisions? How are decisions made? Who influences the process? Who ultimately decides? What are the trends in the market?
- **Market sizing and assessment.** How big is the potential for a product? What share could the firm aim for? Which markets or regions are ready (offer the most potential) for a product or service? Who are the competitors and what are their strategies, market positions, strengths and weaknesses? How easy would it/they be to penetrate?
- **Products and services.** Where are there gaps (if any)? Are there any opportunities for innovation, new products or service ideas, or new applications? Can the potential be assessed using an early prototype via concept or real-life models (to gauge the likely acceptability, or refinements needed)? What is the likely volume uptake and forecasting? What are the optimum packaging or pricing regimes (basic pricing platforms, tariffs, discounting strategies)?
- **Performance assessment and tracking.** How well are the products or services performing (compared with last year, or compared with others in the field)?

15

■ **Marketing and communications.** What are the key messages that underpin a company or a company's products? How best can these be advertised and communicated to the business audience? What are the advertising and brand 'platforms'? What aids understanding of the key sales criteria and sales force? What are the best distribution networks or channels? What unique selling propositions would be needed to provide 'cut through'?

■ **Branding and corporate reputation.** How is the company perceived? How does this differ across groups in the customer base, across stakeholders, or with opinion formers?

And for more sophisticated clients and/or those with larger customer bases and appropriate research budgets:

■ **Segmentation.** How can the customer base be segmented into different types? What are the needs of the different segments? To what degree are different customer categories driven by need or by attitude? Can the organization gain by tailoring its products/services to different customer groups?

Research using internal respondents

Some companies conduct research with their staff as 'internal' respondents. This normally focuses on subjects that relate to their employment and the conduct of the business itself:

■ **Quality assurance/productivity studies.** How do staff perceive the operations/the problems/opportunities for improvement? What improvements can they suggest? How can internal systems be improved to give a better experience for the customer?

■ **Employee research/climate studies.** This gauges employees' satisfaction with the company, their division or their jobs. It looks at staff morale, suggestions, or readiness to embrace change. It may ask about reactions to new ideas/plans, or where employees feel resources should be spent. (Employee research is not always seen to fit into B2B but it is mentioned here as it has a role, albeit a tangential one.)

THE USERS OF B2B MARKET RESEARCH

Those using B2B market research to help their business decisions can broadly be defined as:

■ Organizations that provide products or services **solely to the business market.**

- Organizations that provide products or services **to a business and to a consumer market**, including those that use professional intermediaries or a distribution channel in marketing: for example, the pharmaceutical industry with Rx (prescription) drugs, and providers of unit trusts or managed funds using financial planners in product marketing.
- Organizations that provide products or services to a **consumer market** but that, in the course of their business, also need to research their **suppliers or business clients** (outside their main customer base).

The first two user categories will frequently research their products and/or services via B2B research as well as undertaking other forms of research such as market sizing and customer satisfaction research. The third category will be as interested as the previous categories in issues such as market sizing and customer satisfaction with relevant business constituencies, but will put more emphasis generally on their consumer work, given that the ultimate consumer is their main customer.

The bulk of the companies engaging in B2B research are those operating in business markets, in particular representing IT and information provision, telecoms, transport, finance, manufacturing, energy (oil, gas), pharmaceuticals, agrochemicals/veterinary products and chemicals. Those in construction, and professional services (accountants, management consultants, law firms) also engage in it, though to a lesser extent. Traditionally, other sectors like engineering undertake relatively little market research – and for reasons of history have not been major research buyers.

Examples of companies that typically undertake lots of B2B research are Microsoft, Dell, Intel, IBM, Sun Microsystems, Apple and HP in the IT sector; Motorola, Nokia, Vodafone, Ericsson, SBC (telecoms) and AT&T in the telecoms sector; Dow, DuPont and ICI in the industrial sector, Merck and the other pharmaceutical giants; Exxon, Shell, BP, BASF, Chevron, Texaco, British Gas and PG&E (a US utilities company) in the energy and chemicals sectors; Novo Nordisk and Monsanto in the agricultural sector; American Express and Reuters in the financial sector; FedEx, DHL, Ford, Hertz and Caterpillar in transport; and General Electric across many diverse business bases. Global conglomerates tend to be 'business savvy' and some, if not all, are good at transferring information across sectors. There are always new companies coming up – nowadays, with innovation being the name of the game, those with ground-breaking new products or services can soon become big players.

Why were some sectors mentioned as undertaking less B2B research than others? Partly, this reflects where the bulk of their business lies. There are some, such as finance, for which most business is with the ultimate consumer (B2C), and most research work tends to be with this 'retail' interface. However, banks and insurance companies do a lot of work with business clients on issues such as leasing, services for small business (such as credit), work with Intermediary Financial Advisers (IFAs) or financial planners and brokers, mergers and acquisition work, research with financial trading counterparties – anything relating to the running of businesses that does not involve consumers in the equation. Hence, they spend research money in both categories.

There are also some sectors that are on the borderline of our definitions of B2B. These include the pharmaceutical sector, the professional services sector, not for profit organizations and quasi governmental organizations. These last, such as Business Link in the UK and the New York City (NYC) Department of Small Business Services, offer business support services but are not themselves corporations as we know them. They, as well as others such as the US Chamber of Commerce and the ASBA (American Small Businesses Association), undertake research but at a broader level than the single corporate.

Let us look at one of those 'on the borderline': the pharmaceutical sector. Pharmaceutical companies undertake a huge amount of research with those in medicine including doctors, pharmacists, nurses, practice managers, sales representatives and health care providers (HMOs). In some countries, such as the United States, where medicine is more of a 'business', classically this sort of work is termed B2B; but in other countries it has not traditionally been included in the B2B definition. Rather, it is termed pharmaceutical research and kept as a separate category.

Ideally, our definitions should not be too exclusive but should be as inclusive as possible. With so much diversification and cross-fertilization of fields, the term B2B is now much wider than it was 20 or even 10 years ago. The professional services sector, again, is one where more research is being done now. Few law firms or accounting companies had specialist market researchers 15 years ago. Even now, many smaller ones have only a partner who is responsible for marketing and research, without specialist knowledge. However, increasingly professional services companies are investing in such expertise. Consequently, they are undertaking more research on their own behalf with their business clientele, especially in the area of customer satisfaction and image tracking. This professional services sector is also an area that is now more and more thought of as coming within the umbrella of B2B research, even if some see it as a 'niche' area.

Finally, as mentioned in the third category above, there are the companies that undertake B2B research even though they are themselves businesses that deal primarily with consumers. These are often FMCG manufacturers that produce everyday goods such as foods and detergents. On occasion they need to have recourse to B2B research, such as when they need to know how well they satisfy their business partners, or to assess their corporate reputation. An example is supply chain research assessing customer satisfaction with purchasing directors in the major retail chains such as Wal-Mart, Target, Tesco, Netto and Lidl, and with opinion leaders in the markets where they operate around the world. Here, the research is quite different from their typical work with consumers in new product development (NPD), for example, and they commission B2B researchers who know how to approach key business clients and discuss topics at a level and depth commensurate with the seniority of the respondent.

SUMMARY

In summary, B2B research appeals to those who like detail because of the minutiae of the subjects covered, and at the same time to those who like seeing the broad view and can grasp the strategic implications of much of the research that is done. This combination of detail and broad-brush is one that attracts a certain form of researcher. Many researchers prefer researching everyday items with consumers, but for those who are attracted by rather more wide-ranging areas and who like talking business, B2B research can have equal fascination.

2 Sampling for B2B research

SAMPLING CHARACTERISTICS OF BUSINESS MARKETS

Defining the business universe, or population, to be covered

As was outlined in Chapter 1, one of the most important questions a B2B researcher must ask is who should be interviewed. The next important job is to identify those people in a way that works easily in the research process. In conjunction with the client, we must first identify the 'population' of appropriate respondents. As Phyllis Macfarlane states in her excellent chapter 'Sample design in selection and estimating' in *Researching Business Markets* (1991), 'A universe, or population (sic), is a statistical term used to cover all the potential (sic) units which make up the market to be covered by a market research study.'

Sometimes the population will be pre-set and well described by the client (in a brief or request for proposal (RFP)). Other times, some clarification is necessary either pre-proposal or afterwards. None of this is unique to B2B research, but often it is more complicated than in traditional consumer research. From a practical point of view, a set of critical questions to ask is:

- What criteria must be met for the person within the companies (who will be interviewed) to qualify for an interview? For example:
  - Current customers? Lapsed customers? Non-customers?
  - Decision makers only? Influencers? Authorizers? Purchasers? Users? (And so on.)

- Where are these individuals to be found? (That is, in what types of organizations do they live? How high up do we need to go? Where will they be physically located?)
- Are there particular subgroups we need to include (possibly in particular numeric ratios) to ensure that the resulting sample has the 'right' characteristics and/or so that we can look at their opinions separately? For example, splits by:
  - Company volume? Revenue?
  - Type of industry (eg SIC code – UK, ASIC code – Australia, new NAIS code – United States)?
  - Loyalty or commitment to the brand? Use of competing brand?
  - Distribution channel? And so on.
- Will they be able to answer all the questions, or will others need to be approached to answer the remainder? (For example, brand share figures for a retail chain may need to come from head office as the store managers may only have their local picture.)
- How many layers are involved in organizations or in the process under investigation (so increasing the number that may need to be interviewed)? (For example, when undertaking the research we may realize that the logistics director can take our learning so far, but that it is those running the supply depots and warehouses who know the detail that we are seeking.) On occasion, in B2B, sampling may need to be more evolutionary rather than totally set in stone right from the start.
- Do some individuals play a number of disparate roles (wear a number of 'hats') – especially the case in smaller organizations?
- Finally (of course), can we fit the work as specified in the budget allocated for the research (the pragmatic approach)?

While many of us do not know intimately the nature of the market for semiconductors or for equipment used in drilling oil such as oil bores, the business issues at hand should guide the definition of the population and the subsequent research design. We rely on the client commissioning the research to tell us as much as it knows about how these markets work or how decisions are made. Table 2.1 shows how we might define our population and begin to establish our sample frame.

Sizing the available respondent group

The universe or population may differ in size according to the nature of what is being researched. We may be limited in terms of the population of respondents from which we can draw when working in some

Table 2.1 *Population and specifics*

Initial definitions of the universe (or population)	Relevant refinements in the specification
Surveyors	Those with the formal industry qualifications only? Those working full time only? Those who specialize in private property as opposed to commercial? Those who specialize in public sector included or excluded? Does the surveyor also need to personally conduct the valuations?
Food service companies with 100 or more employees	Is it companies or establishments (a company has a number of establishments/ sites/divisions with over 100 employees)? Should food service companies also operating retail (direct to consumer) outlets be included? Part-time or full-time-equivalent to be included in the count?
Companies planning to acquire videoconferencing facilities in the next 12 months	How is videoconferencing defined (one particular technology)? Hire and/or purchase qualifies? Conglomerate, company or business unit (eg NewsCorp versus Fox Channel versus Fox Sport)? Is the decision taken at head office or at individual sites/divisions? Should influencers be included or only those making the final decision?

markets – for example, those buying or supplying military software or high-end medical imaging equipment like MRI scanners. Even if the items to be researched are expensive, and hence the market has a large monetary value, in these cases the numbers of people who could theoretically be interviewed is small. It is not uncommon for B2B research to be undertaken where the population is small. By contrast, other B2B research may involve categories where there is a large number of potential respondents from which to draw – for example, purchasers of semiconductors, office photocopiers, photocopying paper in photo-processing shops, or establishments accepting American Express cards.

PUTTING THE STUDY INTO ACTION

Deciding on the sample frame

The sample frame will be determined in conjunction with the client by the researcher so that the resulting market research meets the brief and addresses the client's business issues. It contains five key elements (illustrated in Table 2.2).

In order to get our final sample of completed interviews of those who qualify – and possibly in the right proportions – we must first make up a larger list (as mentioned earlier in Chapter 1) that the interviewing team uses to contact respondents. We work on developing a list of the names of potential companies and their address(es) and/or company (switchboard) telephone number(s) and any other relevant information for our sample. As discussed earlier, the ideal situation is for named respondents to be known, but very often this is not the case, and all we have to go on is type of company where the sorts of respondent/s may be found.

How to count the customer/respondent is a perennial problem in B2B. A key difficulty is determining whether the 'customer unit' is to be the conglomerate (such as NewsCorp) or the division (such as the Fox television channel) or the unit (such as Fox Sport) or the three to four people who are involved in the decision making. At other times, the issue is whether we should be working with the 'enterprise' (often listed in the government census and other useful statistics) or the 'establishment' (location). A major energy utility may supply power (and send monthly billing accounts) to a steel manufacturing company that has 20 locations nationally. Deciding whether the research should count this as 20 customers or as one customer means taking into consideration:

- Does our client count this as 20 customers or one?
- Do the 20 locations have independent decision-making capability (for example, they can switch suppliers)?
- Are we doing the kind of research that needs to include these individual relationships and views (for example, a customer satisfaction survey – after all, head office accounts is unlikely to have known that there was a power outage three weeks ago)?

How we 'count customers' has huge implications for surveying, for creating the sample frame, and for establishing market share figures, for instance, if this is one of the desired outputs.

In summary, sometimes drawing a business sample for interviewing is a real challenge, particularly if it is to be representative of the population as a whole. Frequently there is a lack of published data on particular business markets, a lack of reliable (or at least accessible) information

Table 2.2 *Specifying the sample frame*

	Example 1	Example 2	Example 3
Population definition	Decision makers about material supply in clothing businesses that both design and manufacture in the United States	Buyers of risk management software in financial markets	Shipping clerks who have sent 25 or more air freight shipments (national + international combined) in the last month using DHL
Total sample size*	N = 200	N = 200	N = 200
Subgroups of interest	Companies with annual revenues of US $50 million or more Smaller firms grossing under US $50 million	Buyers in: United States UK Germany Japan	
Quotas*	N = 66 large N = 134 smaller	N = 50 each country	Nationally representative of the customer base as defined above
Sample points (locations and subquotas)*	New York Chicago San Francisco Atlanta	New York Chicago London Frankfurt Hamburg Tokyo	Chosen to reflect regional distribution of customer base

* More on these issues later.

on market sizes and market shares, and a lack of known sources from which to develop a robust sampling frame.

Sourcing the sample: lists

Client lists, if they are provided at all, can be provided on paper or, more commonly now, in other formats such as Excel spreadsheets or other 'exportable' formats. A client-provided sample may not be perfect: often the information is not current; it is difficult and time-consuming to update for a research project; it may be difficult to extract from company records and processes; computer departments are not familiar with the way data need to be provided in a market research context; it is often transactional in nature (based on purchasing or invoicing data) rather than relationship-oriented; it can contain multiple records and be difficult to 'de-dupe'; it might be slow to arrive; it could arrive on paper only or in a computer format that is not easily incorporated into market research field systems; or it counts rather than describes (no qualitative information). Typically clients have information on their existing customers but little or none on prospects or potential customers. (One exception here is with advanced business information systems that provide data on lead generation, sales performance and so on.)

However, on the positive side, client lists are very useful. Among the benefits is that when it is useful to speak to 'known' individuals rather than to have to find relevant individuals in a certain organization, being able to source contact information for known eligible individuals can considerably reduce costs. Often, the list is used as the start for the search for the right respondents (for example, tracking down who is doing Mr Jones's job now if he has left the firm).

As mentioned, obtaining information in such an organized way is most unlikely unless the company commissioning the research has good databases from which it is able to extract information easily. More frequently, in B2B research, no such databases are available, and we have to do one or more of the following:

- ask the commissioning client to compile such a database for us (maybe asking its sales force for clients or lapsed clients' records, or asking its accounts department for contact details that can be utilized);
- set about developing a list for sampling from scratch by buying in lists (from, for example, list brokers or compilers);
- set about looking for companies to approach (for interviews) by using various published sources or directories.

Bought-in lists can have their own problems: duplicate names that need to be weeded out; classifications may not equate with standard industry classifications (SIC codes) or the way the client breaks down its market place; incomplete or out of date data, omissions, and inclusions of companies that have changed names or are no longer in business. That being said, it is often easier to start with a list than to totally 'free find' company names. (Free finding is where no names or sample is provided and researchers must use their common sense and knowledge of starting points to start to find suitable respondents.) Comprehensive lists of company names or business respondents generally cost a few thousand in whatever currency, so other options should be explored first.

What are the outside sources (aside from lists) that can be utilized in order to acquire a sample? Online directories and company websites are revolutionizing our ability to develop samples in many areas of B2B research. Online business directories from Yellow Pages and other competing commercial organizations provide virtually instant information on a host of different companies supplying business services. Company names appear by just typing in the sector of interest (plumbers, surveyors, air conditioning installers, perfume stockists, general practitioners or primary care physicians) and the postcode (zip code), or place name. Similarly, some companies (such as British Gas in the UK) offer a search facility on their website to find relevant companies or affiliated groups by profession, topic and postcode.

Government statistics remain a useful source. Again, an example from the UK is illustrative. The Inter-Departmental Business Register, IDBR, combines data about business operating in the UK from diverse agencies such as Customs and Excise (VAT returns), the Inland Revenue (tax) department on PAYE, and various surveys – for example, the Labour Force Survey conducted by the Office of National Statistics on behalf of the British government (Department of Trade and Industry).

Where the public sector forms part or all of the sample, good sources (in the UK) are Year Books, now also via internet sites such as the Municipal Year Book (MYB) (www.municipalyearbook.co.uk), MYB Emergency Services and Health, Pearson Education Year Book, Civil Service Year Book, the Social Services Year Book and many other directories that provide names of those working in the public sector. In the private sector, equivalent directories include Crawford's Directory of City Connections, www.crawfordsonline.co.uk, excellent for sourcing financial companies quoted on the London Stock Exchange or on the Alternative Investment Market (AIM). It includes the following details on major UK companies:

- Head office address, telephone, fax, website, e-mail addresses;
- directors (including chairman, chief executive, MD, finance director, company secretary, investor relations, executive board members and non-executive directors where appropriate);
- substantial shareholders;
- turnover;
- number of employees;
- pension fund name;

- professional advisers;
- techMARK companies highlighted.

However, the most usual business directories used when sourcing larger companies are business directories and database search facilities offered by consulting companies like Dun & Bradstreet (D&B) (a major supplier to the research industry worldwide) and Thomson. In the UK, directories include Kompass, Thomson Directories, and D&B's Key British Enterprises (KBE). Another resource is WOW (Who Owns Whom) from D&B if you need to know a company's pedigree. In any country there should be a comparable company offering these types of services, and The Market Research Society should be able to assist you in locating these, as will a search engine on the web (such as Google or Yahoo!). Other useful list brokers include the following (while none covers all countries, their websites show what is available and in which markets):

- International B2B, computer related (that is, if you need to find organizations with a certain number of PCs or using a particular operating system or who have over a certain number of servers etc): Harte Hanks www.hartehanks.com or compuBase www.compubaseonline.com.
- International B2B and consumer (lifestyle and RDD style) sample: Dudley Jenkins www.djlb.com or Survey Sampling www.surveysampling.com.
- International consumer (lifestyle sort of stuff: people who drive a certain make of car, have an interest in photography or whatever, which is of less interest to B2B than in B2C but may be occasionally useful): Schober www.schober-international.com.

In the United States, a branch of the internet service of D&B's sales and marketing arm, Zapdata (zapdata.com), provides lists, reports and market information with a B2B orientation. Many other sites are available by paying a subscription fee.

Research agencies tend to either buy the directories themselves or, more usually, buy in a specified sample as they need it for individual projects. The different lists or directories have varying amounts of detail about the companies listed and also vary in terms of their coverage: to what extent are small businesses included, or sole traders, or those running businesses from home? A drawback can be that only larger companies tend to be represented, and often we need to check whether head offices are listed as well as the multiplicity of company locations (offices, manufacturing locations and so on). We need to be careful not to introduce a bias to the sample so derived. The lists also vary in terms of the information they contain about each of the listings:

whether turnover is included, industry code, named decision makers (by function) and so on. Sometimes purchased databases do not have sufficient splits in their business classifications – for example, in the D&B database it is possible to drill down 'Manufacturing' quite considerably, but there is much less split than is desirable (and useful) for financial or technological companies.

Obviously, the more specialized the criteria are for inclusion in the research, the more difficult it will be to generate a sample list in the absence of good client information. For example, one interesting case that requires considerable care in developing a sample frame is research into the SOHO community (small businesses and home businesses, or single-unit companies with no employees other than the business owner). It's possible to either screen a small business database to see whether the business address matches the residential address, or use 'lifestyle' databases as the source of the lists (or to complement a small business database).

When interviewing business people internationally, using the domestic databases, public sector listings or lists of membership associations or industry bodies, and information on the internet is a first start, and telephone directories are an obvious source. Frequently, international B2B telephone fieldwork agencies such as Kudos and Facts International in the UK use telephone directories as the main sample source.

It is important that requirements are specified as precisely as possible when sourcing lists, and specifying specific fields in databases that can be used in a search process can reduce the workload. For example, undertaking a study of the hotels and motels in the London area required a specification of SIC codes 55111 and 4412 from the list provider; while researching small businesses that had terminated a business loan in the last six months required the financial institution to screen its database on three criteria (business size, type of credit lines held, and time frame for the loan) then called for de-duping records to eliminate businesses that had merely refinanced an existing loan.

In summary, aside from client lists, the main sources for samples include:

- specialist direct mail lists (list providers or brokers);
- telephone directories/Yellow Pages or their websites;
- published business directories;
- government-sponsored publications and websites;
- public sector Year Books and listings;
- trade association and industry body listings;
- private directories.

Generating the sample

While we may want $N = 200$ *final* fully completed interviews in our sample, we will need many more names to start with. However we source our lists – whether client-provided or from external sources – we need to take into consideration the likely rate of respondent refusal, allow for inaccuracies and the like in the lists, and to provide for some contingency.

Typically, as a rule of thumb, it is sensible to request between three and ten times as many names as we want to interview. So if we want to interview $N = 200$ people, we should be asking for between 600 and 2000 names to start from. The 'right' multiple to request is a judgement call based on experience in the category, knowledge about the population with which one is dealing – in particular, its diversity (where there is less homogeneity, it is better to have a larger base from which to start), geographical spread, and information on the quality of the origin of the lists.

CASE STUDY: MULTINATIONAL QUANTITATIVE CORPORATE REPUTATION PROJECT

Main message

Specifications (specs) to clients need to be clear so that the researcher gets what is needed and in the right form and format. Some explanation and justification of requests is common.

Detail

This is how the lists required by the market research agency from the client were described to the in-house client team that was to assist the research process:

Sample names required

This study will cover three countries: UK, France and Germany. We are looking for $N = 40$ total completed interviews per market (making $N = 120$ in total), split across the agreed different sample types of opinion former (detail not relevant to the case study).

We would like from you a sample list (from your records, contacts etc as agreed) to be compiled for each country separately using either Microsoft Word documents or three Excel files. Ideally, we require 400 names for each country (a ratio of 10:1 of sample list to completed interviews). This will be required in order to be able to achieve the requisite number of completed interviews.

While we will also source some individuals for the interviews ('free-found' by us), we need these lists as the basis for proceeding. As you can imagine, free-finding these people will not be a simple job.

Evaluation of the sample frame

Once you have agreed what the ideal sample frame is, the question arises of how likely you are to be able to achieve it. It is useful to evaluate the sample frame before launching into the fieldwork to determine where are the likely pitfalls and what could be done to improve it before commencing. Importantly, upfront we should be aware of issues related to the sample frame such as:

- How complete is the list from which we are working?
- How up to date is the information?
- Are there duplications?
- Are there inherent biases we should be aware of (for example, in many countries, compiled lists of e-mail addresses are biased toward tech and internet-savvy companies)?
- Is it easy to use for sampling?
- Is it consistent over time (especially for tracking studies)?
- What information is recorded for listings? For example, elements that it may be useful to have, or indeed will be required, in order to provide a representative sample of the market place include:
  - type of company or sector;
  - industry classification code (designated by the Statistics Bureau in the relevant country, for instance SIC Code – UK; ASIC Code – Australia; new NAICS code – United States);
  - size of company (we would have to determine relevance/appropriateness for our project of this dimension and the category breakdowns listed);
  - number of employees;
  - other data (member of trade association, member of larger conglomerate or group, accredited Six Sigma/Investors in People or whatever);
  - fax numbers;
  - direct telephone number of the individual (switchboard or mobile/cell phone);
  - e-mail addresses;
  - designated decision makers (by category, for example head of marketing).

Companies can often have more than one SIC code. SIC codes from most database lists *need to be checked in the survey itself*. Traditionally, SIC codes have been rather manufacturing-biased and less detailed for service industries. However, in the United States the SIC codes are being replaced by the North American Industrial Classification System (NAICS). One of the main motivations for the amendments is the need to accommodate the 'new economy', and in particular, the growth of the services sector. As Dawn Iacobucci points out in a chapter entitled 'Services marketing and customer service' (2001), new industry categories in the NAICS system include those for information processing (publishing, software, broadcasting, motion pictures, telecommunications), arts, entertainment, and recreation (performing arts, spectator sports, producers and agents, museums, casinos, amusement parks), professional, scientific and technical (MR, advertising, legal, accounting, management consulting, computer design), health care and social assistance (nursing homes, healthcare, child care and so on). Many of these are B2B services.

Normally, lists will only give you so much. Sometimes the information can be adjusted so they provide much of the basic data you need (company names, contact details and so on) and be in a format that is easily usable by the field team.

Sampling can be single stage, where the sample is selected directly from the sample lists – often the best solution for B2B research – or multi-stage, where the sample frame provides an initial selection of sample points such as geographic areas that then need to be further selected according to particular parameters such as where 'clusters' of eligible businesses appear.

A pilot is often a good idea – particularly to test out the interviewing script for identifying the correct respondents and for estimating (or double-checking client figures on) 'incidence' or 'hit rate'. For example, we might be searching for retail merchants that accept a particular type of credit card. The client might tell us that only one in every 20 establishments does not accept that card: hence, assuming for now that everyone is happy to be interviewed, we would only need to approach 21 companies to get 20 interviews. However, we may find that actually one in five rejects the card, so we would need to approach (on average) 25 companies to get our required interviews. Again, none of this is different from consumer research, but commonly things like incidence figures are harder to estimate, often because of the lack of published data.

Quotas or stratification of the sample

Random or quota sampling is a big decision in market research, but in B2B almost all samples are quota samples. (Random sampling is now more the norm for large consumer, government or social research studies, and is very rare in B2B research.) Stratification of a sample, or 'quota sampling', is useful and may indeed be required in order to meet the research objectives (as mentioned earlier). This applies where there are different categories of respondents within the overall population that must be interviewed.

Stratification plays a particularly useful role where the universe, or population, is known, and subsamples can be chosen from it. Quotas can be specified in order to ensure that the resultant sample largely represents the population, or can ultimately reflect the distribution of those groups in the population, by using post data collection weighting procedures (discussed later). In these cases, we would need to ensure that there are 'enough' of a group's views expressed in the initial sample that its contribution to the findings is appropriate.

An example is a study of brand image and supplier reputation of home appliances (among other issues) among appliance retailers. The market is made up of department stores and several chains that own multiple store locations, and a host of smaller independent players. By knowing the relative volume of sales through these types of stores from external statistics, we can select the number of stores of each type we need to interview (for example, N = 20 Department store X; 15 Department store Y; 40 Chain A; 30 Chain B; 50 independent) in order to ensure that our sample adequately reflects the appliance retailer market place.

It is also useful to impose quotas where it is deemed necessary to 'over-sample' a subgroup (that is, to sample more of a particular subgroup than would be normally present in a representative sample), if for some reason there are relatively few of them, but they are very important or influential – for example, the client's top 15 customers or customers in a key, growing market. Other groups may be populous, but of lesser strategic importance, so their sample numbers may need to be fewer. Often, in B2B interviewing, this is a judgement call made by the researcher in conjunction with the client as to how many in each category should be represented. This takes into consideration the survey objectives, how important each group is (or is not), the integrity of the research design, and budget issues.

With modern CATI or CAPI (computer assisted telephone/personal interviewing) systems, sample management systems, handling quotas, and sample stratification in fieldwork have become much easier.

Selection of sample size

Fundamentally, many factors will influence the decision of how large a sample should be, including:

- How many are readily available in the universe. For example, if there are only 10 major suppliers of the type of microchip in question, it is useless to expect to undertake a large-scale 'bells and whistles' quantitative survey, but interviewing these 10 respondents is what will be required.

- How important are the decisions being made as a result of the research.
- The type of research being conducted. It might be qualitative, which implies a small sample, and in-depth, intensive, one-on-one interviews requiring a longer length interview, or involve business issues that may need a semi-structured interview and interviewer probing. Or it could be quantitative, which could mean a larger sample with lots of issues addressed numerically. Possibly it involves easier to access respondents or a shorter interview, which again would suggest a larger sample.
- How accurate (or predictive) the final data must be. (Table 2.3 gives the magnitude of the error in the data that can normally be expected for various sample sizes.)
- Whether we need a strictly fully *representative* sample (in which each subgroup is represented in the sample in the same proportions as it exists in the population as a whole).
- The need for the data to be analysed by subgroup or stratum. For example, if a usage and attitude study is being undertaken with hospital procurement officers and nurses on hospital beds, and at least 50 of the nurses need to be from intensive care units (ICU), this will dictate the minimum size of this particular sample cell and, to some extent, the size of the overall study.
- Budgetary limitations. For example, are those to be interviewed expensive to recruit and interview? Are there subgroups that are harder to get hold of?

We must keep in mind that, typically, we do not undertake a census: that is, we do not interview all businesses in the universe with which we are dealing and collect (say) brand share statistics. If we did this, there would be no estimates taken and no error in our measurements! Rather, we undertake a survey of a particular sample size and our brand share statistics are actually estimates of what the 'true' number might be.

In Table 2.3, standard errors are listed for sample sizes typically used in projects. These are calculated based on a two-tailed test of significance at the 95 per cent confidence level. The formula for calculating this can be found in any basic statistics book (see for example Ferguson 1976 or Poynter 2004).

If the client needed a more accurate brand share statistic, we would need to do more interviews (if this were possible – see the note later on small population sizes). Hence, we can use tables such as this in an a priori fashion to guide our research design (and the client's expectations). Additionally (and using the same example as in Table 2.3), if we are monitoring (and hoping for improvements) in brand share over time, a 57 per cent brand share in Wave 1 for Quarter 1 2004 and a 52 per cent brand share figure in Wave 2 for Quarter 2 2004 would not necessarily mean poor sales in Quarter 2. Sales could indeed be down, but these two figures are within the sampling error and could just reflect random variation.

Where we have a small population from which to draw, the normal assumptions related to calculating sampling error effectively go out of the window. The 2004 BIG Conference article by Ray Poynter of Virtual Surveys provides some guidelines on how to sample from small populations (and calculate error). '*At the end of the day, the sample size decision is a trade-off between cost, time, accuracy, and confidence.*' (Definitions of common terms that may be encountered when reading reference material, research reports or papers can be found in the Glossary on page 294.)

Small can sometimes be great; big can sometimes be greater

A study with which I was involved recently involved surveying 12 experts in language e-learning across the world via in-depth qualitative interviews. In this rather esoteric field, the universe of acknowledged experts is small – they live in language schools, universities and institutes, and in organizations such as the British Council. For this project, a 'reading' from even as few as 12 interviews gave the client quality information about the current situation and expectations of future trends. Getting the research design right, choosing carefully who to sample, finding out where they are, successfully recruiting them, asking the right questions, and getting the most out of each interview are the challenges that must be met in projects such as these.

In B2B research, it is not unusual to undertake research with a total sample of only 100 or 200. For example, a corporate image study for a food manufacturer consisted of a sample of N = 100 because of the nature of the population, even though four different countries were represented in the study. Although this entailed translation of the questionnaire into three additional languages as well as briefing of interviewers in four separate locations, the importance of the individuals in the sample frame chosen (and their 'market place significance') was such that undertaking such a small sample was still deemed critical to making the business decisions that were required. Computer tables were produced analysing the data category by category and country by country despite very small numbers in each sample cell.

Where we have a small sample overall and responses from an even smaller number of respondents in a subgroup are to be examined, both researchers and clients need to tread with some caution. Depending on the size of the subgroup, of course, results should usually be treated as 'indicative'. (See the discussion on weighted and unweighted data on page 37.)

However, much B2B research is conducted with the kind of large sample sizes typically seen in consumer studies. This is especially true of customer satisfaction studies and research programmes designed to monitor and track brand share, the impact of advertising, and the effectiveness of marketing programmes. Needless to say, 'big brands' – particularly those with an international footprint – will often conduct larger studies than companies with fewer resources. Also, companies that have a clear segmentation philosophy in their marketing programmes (and especially those where there are several key segments) tend to undertake larger-scale studies as a matter of necessity. There has to be sufficient depth of numbers in each key subgroup to make it possible to analyse the results separately (and with numerical confidence). Samples can be as large as several thousand, though rarely much above that number.

RESEARCH PRACTICES RELATED TO SAMPLING

Screening

Screening for eligibility plays an important role in B2B market research. 'First find your man/woman' should be our catchphrase, and writing very careful introductions is needed in recruiting. There are two issues. The first is the right 'manner' – and this is part of the interviewer training that we would expect from a good fieldwork house or an in-house training programme for market researchers. The second is developing a set of questions and 'decision tree' that allows an interviewer to determine the eligibility of a respondent.

If there is no named individual in the sample provided, then the interviewer will have to be skilful in negotiating the rapids of either the switchboard (where often operators do not know much about who looks after what or where to find them) and/or if they are very high up the scale, the individual's PA or secretary. Many an interviewer has fallen at the final fence here. Like doctors' receptionists, personal assistants sometimes seem to have a personal goal to ensure that those unknown to the precious boss cannot get close to him (or her) and speak to him (or her) directly. The ability to persuade and to be able to explain authoritatively the rationale for the interviewer's speaking to him (or her) direct is a skill not to be underestimated in the B2B world.

If the screening criteria are complex, ensure that the screening questions regarding eligibility are asked about upfront in order to avoid wasting anyone's time. While the order of questions has to have some logic, it is useful to ask first the questions that are most likely to eliminate a respondent. This will reduce the time spent to find respondents who are eligible. Also ensure that accurate contact sheets are kept when

Table 2.3 *Error related to sample size*

Sample size N =	Standard error of measurement
50	13.9
100	9.8
150	8.0
200	**6.9**
250	6.2
300	5.7
350	5.2
400	4.9
450	4.6
500	4.4
600	4.0
700	3.7
750	3.6
800	3.5
900	3.3
1000	3.1

The second column gives typical 95% confidence limits. That is, if there is a sample size of N = 200 (see highlighted row), and a brand share figure of (say) 52% for Brand X resulting from the interviews, we can be sure 95% of the time that the 'real' brand share will be within 6.9% of this figure. That is, 52 – 6.9 = 45.1% and 52 + 6.9 = 58.9%, so it will be a minimum of 45.1% and a maximum of 58.9%.

respondents are being approached. Sometimes, response and contact records are as important as research results in themselves – in particular when incidence, market size and eligibility for future marketing are being measured.

More specific examples of screening questionnaires are given later in the book. It is standard practice to ask questions in a logical sequence so that first, inappropriate interviews are closed down quickly, and, second, specific quotas can be fulfilled according to the research design and sampling frame.

In B2B, samples are not always based on the characteristics of the respondent individuals, but the key criteria are in fact details about the company or establishment. For example, if a study is specifying 'companies with over 200 cars in their company fleet', the upfront screening questions should first determine whether the company meets this definition, then whether the individual being approached is responsible for the fleet.

As a general rule, where a number of individuals in an organization are eligible for interview, selecting the actual interviewee should be as random as possible in order to reduce bias.

Weighting and grossing up

These two processes are conducted after the data are collected but prior to full data analysis. Arguably, in quantitative B2B research weighting and grossing up are not used as frequently as in consumer research. Nevertheless, there are occasions when they are useful.

Weighting

Weighting can be used to:

- Correct slight imbalances in the sample (for example, fewer interviews were obtained than desired with companies with low volume sales, as specified in the sampling frame). Here the word 'slight' is important. If the weighting appears to do too much readjustment, questions should be asked on the legitimacy of the sample in the first place.
- Ensure that the final sample most closely matches the distribution of the population from which it is drawn (for example, in industry categories). That is, the weighting achieves a representative sample for the final set of data following completion of the interviewing.
- Apportion the relative importance of subgroups and their contribution to the final results (for example, if appropriate significance is to be given to the high importance of the top 20 customers). Up-weighting may be used where a category of respondents has been under-represented and yet their contribution needs to be more accurately reflected in the data. Weighting can also be used to down-weight 'boost' (or 'booster' samples) – where additional interviews in a category have been included so as to be able to analyse their results separately – in the 'Total' data.

Weighting involves assigning weights to each respondent in a sample, thus making some people more important than others. Figure 2.1 explains this more fully.

In practice, computer techniques are now available that use 'target weighting' techniques. These techniques use as input the original research design and sample frame numbers, and 'automatically' adjust the data and sample numbers to reflect the initial desired design in the weighted data results.

Remember to show unweighted bases on tables or presentations as well as weighted bases, to indicate the reliability of the data. It is important to be able to check back what actual sample sizes were, so that if the unweighted sample base was small, ridiculous conclusions are not being drawn on the basis of a very tiny number of responses.

As a general rule, if the original number of a subgroup in the sample was not large, and hence its numbers were 'uplifted' by post-data collection weighting procedures, the research results for the unweighted sample should be the key reference point if analysis for the particular subgroups is required. This may require two sets of data analysis to be undertaken (and two printouts). It also necessitates extra attention in analysis and reporting by researchers, and additional care to annotate the report carefully and accurately.

Grossing up

Grossing up (also called 'estimation'):

- uses data from a representative sample;
- extrapolates it to represent the total market;
- is commonly used when undertaking government business surveys, for instance when a full market view is needed.

Grossing up is scaling-up, or extrapolation, of the results of a survey to the whole population or market. Consider the case where there are 20,000 small to medium-sized enterprises in Sao Paulo. We have sampled $N = 700$ businesses and have data from them on the likelihood of taking up a new internet service (say, 35 per cent Extremely likely or Very likely). In order to determine how many actual businesses might be in the market for the new service, each enterprise in our sample is grossed up by a factor of 28.57 ($20,000/700 = 28.57$). The client can now be told that there are 7,000 businesses to which it has a good chance of selling the service.

Extrapolations of this sort are only really valid if a substantial sample size is selected in the first place. It is valid to gross up to 20,000 from a sample of 700 if those 700 have been chosen representatively. It would be less valid if the sample was only 100, for example, or if there was some skew in the sample.

Profiling

For some types of data analysis, it may be useful to count (or profile) by the characteristics of the 'companies' and the characteristics of the

To calculate a weight:

Weight = $\dfrac{\text{Number of people you want to have}}{\text{Number of people you have in the sample}}$

A simple example

Sample of 100: 60 male owners, 40 women owners
Requirement is 50% men and 50% women
Weights to be applied
Men = 0.833 (= 50 / 60)
Women = 1.25 (= 50 / 40)

To weight the data:
Men: 60 × 0.833 = 50
Women: 40 × 1.25 = 50

NB   A weight of more than 1 'up-weights' a respondent or makes him/her more important.
A weight of less than 1 'down-weights' a respondent or makes him/her less important.

Figure 2.1 *Weighting procedures*

'individuals'. Hence, in data collection, we would need to include relevant questions related to the respondent as well as the company. An example is a study undertaken in the mid-1990s for a large computer manufacturer, which examined its reputation and decision making among IT managers. It was found that younger IT managers tended to have different opinions about the reputation and relative merits of the top three brands of high-end data servers than the more experienced managers. As a result, the client modified its communication strategies in order to reduce some of the negativity identified among older decision makers. This resulting strategy would not have been possible if some demographics/psychographics on respondents had not been included.

SUMMARY

Getting the sample right is the foundation to good research. The process looks complicated, but the key elements and principles are relatively straightforward. If in doubt, consult experienced colleagues, look up reference books, and draw on the hard-won knowledge of the field force management.

3 Trends in B2B research

DRIVERS

While many trends that relate to the world at large, to what is happening in businesses, to technical innovation, and to market research generally could be discussed, here the focus is on those we feel have the most important impact on B2B research. Three drivers emerge: whether the changes are driven by market, research or technology.

Market-driven trends

Market-driven trends include:

- fashion: 'flavour of the month' research;
- the move to research on services rather than products;
- the effects of market place deregulation, including diversification of companies into new areas and, simultaneously, company consolidation;
- new decision-making structures;
- more channels to market and intermediaries/brokers in the process;
- market sector growth/decline (IT, biotechnology: spend up; agriculture: spend down);
- emerging markets and growth in new areas (China, Asia–Pacific, Russia, India);

- merging of B2B and B2C in product development, applications and marketing (not just research), especially in technological fields such as mobile telephony, software and IT;
- client demand for independent quantification and tracking of business performance, including making the 'business case': linking research to return on investment/capital (ROI/ROC) calculations, especially when evaluating product launches or product/service extensions;
- more need-based and targeted product development with the concomitant early product/service research phase to test out demand and applicability;
- advertising, brand tracking, holistic tracking tools applied to measuring the effectiveness of above the line (advertising) and below the line (direct marketing) activity as well as other elements such as public relations (PR) with B2B audiences;
- more prominent B2B branding;
- increasing sophistication of B2B marketing and requisite research tools;
- broader B2B research constituency, for example non-MR traditional groups and consultancies;
- business respondents who are ever more time-pressed;
- procurement procedures applied to market research buying.

Research-driven trends

Of course, some of these issues link with the above. Research-driven trends include:

- a broader base of B2B clients conducting research, and hence more diverse categories of respondents;
- telephone and internet research growing; face to face declining; postal almost non-existent;
- a move to transfer some B2B research activities offshore;
- closer partnerships and interrelationships between research supplier and client (sharing of databases, secondments);
- an increasing role for incentives (which are common for medical research; IT, for example, is becoming more 'incentive aware');
- B2B marketers adopting:
  - research methods that are more efficient than the old form of desk research – for example, internet trawls, chat rooms or focus groups on the net and quick e-mail surveys;
  - more specific research requirements – for example, respondent bases are becoming more specific and it is more demanding to

find the right respondents, but many clients have yet to recognize the research and budgetary implications (many are unwilling to pay the cost of screening);

- brainstorming and more innovative qualitative enabling techniques, observation and some of the newer forms of neurolinguistic programming approaches (NLP), ethnography (examining the respondent's cultural frame of reference) and semiotics (understanding symbols and icons).

Technology-driven trends

Technology-driven trends include:

- growth of the internet and e-commerce;
- increased speed of change and innovation in technology means more emphasis on early stage, future-looking business issues rather than on historic data gathering;
- reduced need for business travel due to technology (BlackBerries, cameras in phones, videoconferencing, data transfer);
- increased usability of reports – move away from 'just numbers' to insight and recommendations, more reports being web driven, greater interactivity and 'real time' reporting;
- more integration of business research results with other internal company input, documents and strategy;
- the internet itself:
  - access to those in business we want to speak to who are increasingly computer-enabled and can be reached via their laptops or mobile phones even if they are always travelling and on the go;
  - an easy way of obtaining answers;
  - growth in B2B e-commerce is driving research for products and services using the net (in 2004 in the United States alone, the estimated market for B2B e-commerce was several trillion dollars).

Conflicting demands

In the above, there are some conflicting demands. For example, the pressure to be 'first in market' or to quickly introduce innovation indicates early-stage research with industry experts, possibly some competitor intelligence (normally undertaken by those outside the market research community), and qualitative work with a sample of potential business users. However, the need for greater business accountability dictates research that is more substantial and quantitative (possibly using tracking in order to quantify performance and prove success and linkage with

ROI). Some of this can be resolved by higher budgets but sometimes there are other factors (such as small universes) that militate against too much performance tracking and promote rather smaller-scale research.

Some of the trends we saw in the 1980s such as the move to customer satisfaction research still influence the B2B marketplace but in a different form. Today, customer relationship marketing (CRM) is an important element in monitoring business health but (in some countries) has encouraged the growth of non-traditional research providers who link research data with other inputs (relational activity, complaints, re-purchase). Some companies' services straddle telemarketing, lead generation, database building and market research while not being bound by the professional codes of conduct of the Market Research Society or ESOMAR. Many believe that a confusion of the disciplines ('selling' and 'market research') does not sit comfortably with the objectivity of the market research profession.

Similarly, the 1970s and 1990s saw a move to basing businesses on quality models and the growth of quality assurance tracking and organizations providing quality accreditation, leading to the need for research on similar issues – the best processes for quality tracking, quality protocols, and service level agreements. These all presented businesses with a need to evaluate and track across all their audiences, whether consumer or business.

As James Lenskold (2003) points out, the current focus of many businesses on ROI has led to the need for formal business metrics to evaluate the success of marketing, PR and advertising initiatives. He gives a case study of Dendrite International (a supplier of CRM software), where the effectiveness of a 2001 marketing and advertising campaign was measured by implementing an intensive, quick report tracking programme to measure key performance metrics using inbound calls, faxes, website visits and registrations, and a measurement of customer perceptions pre- and post-campaign. Following this review, commitment to marketing spend was confirmed with the continuation of the marketing programme. Lenskold highlights the growing influence of technology here also, in the potential for the 'automation' of some of these measurement processes. Quoting a Forrester Research report by analyst Jim Nail, Mastering Marketing Management, he argues that in the future, more use will be made of tech-based application tools to measure and subsequently enhance the success of marketing spend.

Technology continues to drive changes in the client's business environment and that of the research community. As Kate Pitts, 'futurist' of Royal Mail, UK, said in a recent keynote speech, 'The impact of technology is always overestimated in the short term and underestimated in the long term.'

SPECIFIC TRENDS AND ISSUES

Technological advance and its effect on B2B research

Technological advance is affecting all those in the market research world– clients commissioning research, agencies and individuals conducting research, those responding to research, and users of research. Researchers are affected in particular ways:

- Desk research (now very heavily, if not exclusively, internet-related).
- Competitive analysis (increasingly web-based and possibly automated).
- Process management (new automated project management tools, database set-up and management).
- Survey design and analysis (which can be conducted using new software).
- Interviewing software (touch-screen technology, using the newer forms of interviewing device such as O2's XDA technology for CAPI ((used, for example, by ORC), online panels, and real-time quota controls).
- Analysis tools (the ability to tag and analyse questions by mode of answering, data mining tools).
- Reporting mechanisms such as delivering data by portal – where users can access their own data – or as a link to a PDF containing tables; web-based reporting– 'back end' reporting mechanisms that make for more interactive and real-time data for clients. Portals can allow data to be merged more easily, good news for those who see research as just part of the jigsaw, not the whole of it.

All these technological advances are particularly apposite for those in business research. Those we interview and work with often work in technologically enabled companies and favour new methods of approach.

CASE STUDY: QUESTIONS ON CLIENTS' INTERNAL USE OF TECHNOLOGY

Main message

While aiming for 'best practice' is admirable and not all achieve it, knowing where one stands can help to identify where improvements can be made and when progress has been achieved.

Respondent definition

Members of AURA (the Association of Users of Research Agencies) who undertake research in the UK and internationally.

Details

In 2002, AURA undertook a survey with members on the key research technology issues for clients. It revealed that many clients were not using technology as fully as they might:

- 80% had no means to cross-reference customer data against transaction data.
- 54% had a data management or data protection policy.
- 44% had multi-disciplinary knowledge management or information forums.
- 33% did not publish research findings internally or externally (despite most firms surveyed having both websites and corporate intranets).
- 31% could only use their web browsers to view their corporate intranet or local pages and were denied access to the internet.
- 23% of firms' customer attitude data remained with their external research suppliers and was not accessible internally.
- 20% used specialist data mining and data visualization tools.The facts and figures provided gave useful benchmarking information and a practical starting point for researchers waging the arguments for wider access to available technologies in their own organization.

Technology and research

This book outlines a number of case studies showing how technology is being used for research purposes (the BusinessWeek panel (page 133), the Virgin.net case study (page 130) and others). Technology is putting results much more in the hands of those who will use them, and take actions on the basis of them. The time when researchers come and 'present' the data may be passing, and given our audience (business people or those who know how to 'read' information quickly), it is likely that the staged set of periodic reporting back by agencies face to face may be replaced by much more occasional compilations of results that present a more holistic rather than 'one off' picture. This has already happened in the world of ad tracking in consumer research.

The following case study illustrates the use of technology to enhance survey capability.

CASE STUDY: TOUCH-SCREEN TECHNOLOGY
FOR BUSINESS SURVEYS

Main message

By using the right technology, the research process can be improved as can outcomes for the client and their customers.

Respondent definition

Attendees at a conference.

Detail

Every year, ExCel runs a major conference in London with thousands of business delegates passing through. In the past, only 600–700 per conference show could be surveyed using pen and paper methods. So the company decided to use touch-screen terminals, set up by market research firm Vivid Interface. Sample sizes have increased to several thousand per show with a higher response, faster interviews and lower costs. By using the touch screen surveys, ExCel was able to have larger samples for decision making. Based on the results, it addressed two particular issues that had been causing visitors aggravation: the conference catering facilities and the lack of a single point of contact for account handling relating to the conference.

These speedy and immediate surveys are perfect for clients wishing to survey the business visitor in venues such as exhibitions and conferences, where a lot of, often inaccessible, people pass through in a short space of time and are in a frame of mind that is conducive to undertaking a quick and unobtrusive but relevant survey.

Source: Research in business supplement, *Research* magazine, March 2004.

One recent description of sophisticated data capture methods is presented here that allows data to be sifted through, interesting findings to be captured, and evidence to be accessed quickly. This may be less relevant for B2B research work with smaller samples, but it is important to know what is available and that in the future quicker, more effective data capture across all audiences may become the norm rather than the exception.

CASE STUDY: NEW AND EFFICIENT METHODS OF DATA CAPTURE

Main messages

Technologies currently being developed by software suppliers are available to the B2B researcher to aid them in the research process.

A cost–benefit analysis should be done in order to ensure that the system, package or proprietary methodology delivers what it promises and meets the needs of both the MR provider and the client.

Detail

New data capture methods using the latest character-recognition technologies provide user and workflow administration tools, and can alter the speed with which useful data can be aggregated and produced. High volumes of data can be scanned, although a large hardware infrastructure involving storage units, high gigabyte network bandwidths and servers with multi-processors may be needed if a project is large. Some users report significant decreases in the time needed for data delivery.

Source: Research in business supplement, *Research* magazine, March 2004 (referring to Pulse Train's Bellview Scan package).

Although sifting through vast quantities of data is still not the norm in B2B research, it is useful to be aware of the new technologies such as this and others such as E-Tabs Lite Reader facilitating such data capture and delivery. Such a product can be installed on a company's intranet to deliver table reports, with indexes and keyword search facilities. For business users, individual pages can be printed out or a split-screen option is available to view wide tables of data. Such technology comes, of course, at a price. Agencies or others using it must have a licence for it and be trained in publishing their technology-enabled reports. However, providing access to data for staff in client companies that relates to their part of the business encourages use of research results. Software innovations are making operations vastly more efficient and are providing additional access to research findings.

As mentioned above, some of the new software or hardware do require licences to be bought, keeping some of the more expensive tools in the hands of larger research agencies. However, technology-dependent research does not only need to be for the larger players. There will always be a place, especially in qualitative B2B, for the research specialist who is not highly dependent on technology but on his or her market knowledge, research expertise and brain. But the role of technology is growing in B2B, so we are wise to take account (and advantage) of it.

Many of the larger agencies with sizeable divisions specializing in B2B such as NOP World, Research International, Synovate and TNS offer much of this specialist technical know-how, but so do some other, more specialist smaller agencies. Even in markets the size of the United States and Canada, however, there are few exclusively B2B agencies; most agencies undertake a mix of work, and for those specializing in the business arena, a mix of B2C and B2B is the norm.

CHALLENGES FACED BY B2B RESEARCH

Negatives

Factors that discourage rather than encourage B2B research include:

- **Research overload:** the over-intrusiveness of much research today. Business people are subject to stresses and strains in their business role as well as personal life. Often, it is difficult to distinguish legitimate market research from telephone selling or 'sugging' (selling under the guise of market research). Without good interviewing technique and proper explanation and clarification, response rates will decline and business research will be swept up in today's maelstrom of both real and bogus 'research'.
- **Genuine lack of time:** in particular, the business respondent's lack of time for any research that is (too) lengthy or poorly constructed or does not use the right market language.
- **Data protection legislation and 'licence to operate':** if legislative restrictions are imposed, mainly directed at consumer research but this is also likely to affect B2C and B2B research.
- **Consolidation of companies** can mean that less research is undertaken because there are fewer buying points – for example, in the pharmaceutical industry.
- **Business competition** from management consultancies, advertising agencies and so on. While sometimes they can genuinely offer market knowledge, expertise and 'added value' to strategic decision making, at other times the research is ham-handed without the strong expertise needed for quality work.

Other issues

Some challenges worth notice include the following:

- While not necessarily driving the volume of business research down, there is a trend (for example, in the automotive sector and increasing now in many others) for the research buying process to involve procurement officers in procurement departments, or sanctioned by them. This can have the advantage for the client company of helping in the negotiation of prices or maintaining a clear-sighted and non ambiguous process. Depending on the experience of the people involved, real differences in the niceties of what the B2B researcher is offering are not always understood.

- Some clients are now using internet auctions to obtain bids. For example, GE Capital is only accepting web bids. In this sort of scenario, we believe that good judgement calls are more difficult and it is more difficult to add value.
- Budget pressures and cost cutting – business research is often an expensive business, as samples are small and business people are difficult to get hold of and recruit. Time is money. Have your arguments ready to justify cost – why the research approach is legitimate and how the deliverables will contribute to the client's business.
- Market sector fortunes – see the growth and decline (and recent resurgence) of telecoms research. Some MR agencies become trapped in a time warp of a sector's success and decline. For example, some companies flourished in the mid-1980s and beyond with major undertakings for the agriculture and agro-chemical sectors but experienced difficult years in the 1990s. Without diversification and ability to adapt to growing fields, we can be left stranded by the (lack of) market need. We must watch sector growth as well as individual client fortunes to understand the dynamics of the market, and make suggestions as to what sort of research might help clients keep ahead.
- The time to research products and services 'properly' (especially technology) and the need to get to market quickly present conflicting needs. This can make B2B research 'elective' and can militate against it being done at all.
- In brief, world economics, sector prosperity, the introduction of new technology that can make old technologies and approaches quickly out of date, the need for ever speedier research, and the fact that much research in B2B is elective, can all threaten (or promote) the use of B2B research.

IMPLICATIONS OF CURRENT TRENDS

Research market place changes

Some changes appear to be here to stay:

- **Out:** 'industrial research'; old-fashioned 'desk research'; and single-minded attention to market sizing and share.

- **Status quo:** Demand for thorough and deep qualitative interviewing – because of the depth of knowledge of those we interview – will continue to be used by both small companies with small budgets and major companies with larger budgets for large trackers with specialist publics (top opinion formers), research modelling (customer relationships, loyalty, market forecasting) and segmentation.
- **In:** Internet 'trawl'; NPD (new product development) and innovation research in order to be early to market; quick e-mail questionnaires; an interesting combination of in depth 'qual' and short, sharp 'quant'; and in general, a readiness to use research and to see it as a useful ally in overall business intelligence. Good!

Our knowledge base and how we conduct business

As the B2B market becomes more sophisticated, so will the research tools used to interpret it. All this means that the B2B researcher must, even more than ever, be in tune with what is happening in the world in general, with trends and drivers in business processes and disciplines (haunt the Business section in local bookshops and make sure you know what is hot). There is a need to have a broad perspective, and be able to apply knowledge and insight to the wide range of business problems that clients bring to market research.

Being fast on our feet and flexible in what we do must be two of the main messages. It is likely that the internet will continue to radically affect the way we do research in the future. Are we looking at a time when the face-to-face business interview will be a thing of the past, and when interviewing via mobile phone will be the more usual mode, or will there always be a place for more detailed investigation when the respondent is someone with real expertise, a lot to impart, and where the cost of the contract is high?

In order to maintain or improve response rates, it is likely that the provision of incentives will become more widespread, or at least it will be necessary to show a more obvious link between respondent participation and the benefit to their company. This might foreshadow an increase in costs. Counter-influences to increased costs are more multinational research being possible in English – or Business English at least – reducing translation expenses, and interviewing with verbal and visual technology rather than actual travel to different locations.

The overall picture is one of increasing:

- competition;
- need to link our offering to the client's business and key performance indicators;

■ desire to use technology to stay ahead in research, to automate what it is possible to automate and to provide 'real time' data.

Ensuring a strong B2B market research offering

Positioning B2B research

Some argue that B2B research is a dying duck. That is far from my view: it will always have a place, and it is likely to grow. However, to protect our business and for it to flourish and be seen as a discipline that marketers and strategists immediately turn to when thinking of doing something new, we need to look at the ways in which we market our services and promote our contribution to our client's enterprises. Somehow, because the research we do is often 'behind the scenes' and undertaken prior to other research such as consumer research that may receive greater publicity, all the precepts of good marketing are often not put into play. Selling ourselves is not something that the B2B market research industry has traditionally been good at.

What we *can* do is, effectively, to get fully *'into'* B2B research:

■ Show *interest* in, and knowledge about, the sector and product field or service area under research.

■ Understand the mindset of the client and its business imperatives.

■ Develop research that translates business need into research objectives, and undertake quality research that uses appropriate samples and research tools.

■ Draw on our learning from, connections with, or experience with similar issues across from other sectors' research while not breaking confidentiality. For example, when conducting corporate branding work for a commercial vehicle manufacturer, bring in other references to how branding works in general in the automotive and transport sectors.

■ Bring independence of thought, objectivity and suggestions about research possibilities so that the client knows that results are free of bias.

■ Deliver easily understood results with recommendations for strategy that link in with the client's original needs/objectives, its business organization and modus operandi.

■ Frame the findings to be accessible to as wide an audience as possible.

■ Tap into the B2B community. Go to conferences or other meeting places attended by others interested in business so that we can learn and share. In the UK, the annual BIG conference or regular BIG meetings are a good place to start. Details of useful associations in other countries are given on page 240.

We must show clients that it is worth the investment to use dedicated B2B researchers, or at least people who understand business research.

Selling tips

Here are some tips on selling and conducting B2B research effectively. While they are particularly relevant to the agency researcher, they are also useful for the client-side researcher selling B2B 'internally' in order to secure the undertaking of research prior to any risky decisions:

- Before approaching a client, do your homework in order to understand the client company, its competitors, and the business context: go on the website, look at the pages on recent press releases or for news of recent innovation, read about the company's goals and mission.
- Speak the language of the business: get to know the jargon (visit sites such as www.whatis.com that provides an explanation of technology/telecoms and IT terminology).
- Ban long proposals – short is best, and where possible, discuss the issues and proposed design with the client prior to putting pen to paper.
- Where appropriate, provide cost options – often there is relatively little money available for B2B research, so providing alternatives is a good idea. For example, suggest using a business omnibus if it is a possibility, or a mix of telephone and face-to-face interviewing in a qualitative project to focus resources on key targets and reduce cost.
- Demonstrate experience in recruiting business respondents who are in short supply or difficult to get hold of.
- Highlight knowledge of how business customers 'tick' so which techniques work and do not work well with them.
- Use technology wherever possible to conduct projects quickly with the least intrusion and to allow interactive reporting.

CASE STUDY: USING TECHNICAL TERMS

Main message

Prepare and brief well when faced with a research area that is highly technical or uses significant jargon in order to ensure the quality of the data collected and enhance the interview experience for respondents.

Respondent definition

Business customers of mobile telephony (current and lapsed) among other categories.

Details

A mobile telephony provider was examining the potential for advanced technical add-ons such as GPRS and MMS and others in development. GPRS, or General Packet Radio Service, is a new way of sending and receiving information using a mobile phone. With a GPRS phone you can be connected to internet services, whereas with non-GPRS phones you have to log in every time you want to access information. Accessing services like the internet, WAP or one's company's intranet can be quicker and easier. The company wished to know awareness of the technology, the need for it, current usage, assess the preparedness to purchase, and identify desired applications and functionality that had appeal. It also wanted to segment the market by business and non-business customers.

A series of in-depth face-to-face qualitative interviews was conducted with current business customers – in large companies investing millions annually in mobile telephony for their staff, as well as those in smaller companies with only 10 handsets or more – and with a few lapsed customers. However, for all, it was important for the researchers to 'speak the language' and know the principles of mobile phones and their applications. Use of jargon and talking about things such as WAP, Bluetooth, connect cards, mobile office cards and BlackBerry was important. Of course, some abbreviations such as Push WAP* had to be explained to some respondents. Best practice is to know something of the issues, use jargon as appropriate, but to explain jargon and technical terms if there is any chance the person being interviewed will not know what the terms mean.

* NB: Push WAP – a WAP URL for a 'useful' site is sent to the mobile. The user selects the URL address and is taken to the information on the site.

SUMMARY

Evaluate technology wisely with a careful eye towards investing in things that will produce tangible benefits, not just for the technology itself. Seek ways to add value as B2B researchers to preserve the business case for using us and to prevent our market from being eroded. We should not be afraid of actively spelling out and selling our expertise.

4 What works and does not work in B2B research

POSSIBLE RESEARCH APPROACHES OR METHODOLOGIES

All those who have done any market research will know that there is no perfectly 'right' way or 'wrong' way to do it. The way one agency or team designs a project may differ hugely from the way another agency would do it. We all have our idiosyncrasies, approaches that have worked well for us in the past, and preferred ways of doing things. It is often easier to say what is wrong with an approach than to be certain about what is the 'right' approach. For example, in B2B research it is more common to conduct in-depth individual interviews than focus groups. This is not because focus groups are 'wrong', but because experience has shown that business people with busy diaries and who are, more often than not, geographically dispersed, are unlikely to travel to attend a focus group. Also, it is hard to get enough respondents together at the same time. Commercial sensitivity, particularly if any competitors are present, means that they may be guarded in what they say. For these reasons, a business researcher may be more likely to suggest interviewing business respondents individually: not a question of what is right or wrong, but what is a pragmatic solution.

Primary versus secondary and qualitative versus quantitative research

Whether we are talking about B2B or consumer research, broadly there are two key dimensions that describe the different types of research that may be undertaken: secondary/primary and qualitative/quantitative. See Table 4.1.

Useful descriptions of types of research

Before we go much further in discussing methods, some other definitions may be useful.

Ad hoc versus tracking/monitoring studies

- Ad hoc: 'one off', or custom-designed, research projects that may not be repeated.
- Tracking: measurements are taken on several occasions (waves) and data are reported comparing performance on key variables (such as advertising effectiveness, brand share, image) over time. Tracking studies may be:
  - 'point in time' – say, 300 interviews are done each quarter but in a fieldwork period or 'batch' of (say) two weeks;
  - continuous – while 300 interviews are done each quarter (and the report is, say, each quarter), the interviews are fully spread (usually as evenly as possible) over the 12 weeks.

Interviewing methodologies

Many different ways of interviewing are used in B2B as in other research:

- internet – web or e-mail;
- telephone – frequently via a telephone centre, using CATI (computer-aided telephone interviewing);
- face to face – individual interviews lasting from 15 to 40 minutes on average;
- one on one – in-depth interviews normally conducted by research executives;
- paired interviews;
- focus groups.

Field interviewers are usually engaged for the quantitative interviews, and executives or those close to the survey with any qualitative interviews. (See Chapters 6, 7 and 11.)

Table 4.1 *Key categories of research*

Secondary	Primary
Often called 'desk research' or 'searching around for data'.	Direct collection of information from respondents using whatever methodology is appropriate.
Uses published, accessible sources (public, private, government, corporate).	Commissioned direct by client or agent.
No direct collection of information from respondents in the market place in question.	Can be: ■ **customized:** tailored to individual client needs;
Different methods can be used, including the more modern 'internet trawl'.	■ **syndicated:** several clients jointly undertake research using an independent researcher and share results (or different elements);
	■ **omnibus:** a survey covering several (unrelated) topics for different clients conducted on a regular basis (quarterly, monthly) by a research agency.
	Unless specifically released by clients, the data are owned only by research sponsors rather than being available for public review.
Qualitative	Quantitative
Typically, small samples of respondents.	Numerically based data. Large samples.
Focus is not numeric/measurement.	Use of statistics to show differences and significance.
Depth aimed for in information gathered.	Questions specified in advance.
Semi-structured interviewing with questions specified but allowing for probing, clarification, and richer data.	
Use of topic guides that cover the issues but with a more flexible approach than in a quant survey; lots of 'open' questions.	

Panel research

A panel is a sample of people (often who have previously agreed – and are paid incentives – to participate in research that takes place over time), from which information is obtained on more than one occasion. Repeat research on the same or different issues can be undertaken with panel members. Sometimes, panels can comprise 'experts' in a field. They are often used in specialized research such as the pharmaceutical/medical area. They can be 'in house' – privately compiled and researched by a corporation – or run by a research agency, and therefore available to different clients. Online panels of business respondents are suddenly appearing, and business publications are beginning to supply panels for B2B research.

Omnibus

Effectively, an omnibus is a subscription quantitative survey to which client questions can be added. Typically it has a large sample size, the respondents of which have been recruited to be representative of a given population (for example, the US population, or small and medium-sized businesses in the UK). Usually quotas are established based on national census data or other published sources so that appropriate subgroups are represented (but random sampling procedures within the pool of people who qualify do apply), and then weighting procedures are applied to match the population distribution on key characteristics (for example, in a standard consumer omnibus, distribution of gender, age, geographical location, and urban/rural).

The survey is conducted on a regular basis (weekly, every other week, monthly or quarterly) by a research agency or field force. Generally, it will cover several (unrelated) topics for several different clients – hence, the most common uses of an omnibus methodology are when a client has a small number of questions, wishes to establish incidence of a behaviour (for example, usage of a digital camera in the last month), or wants to verify findings from a more specialized study with a broader population. Agencies have set fees based on the number and complexity of questions. Unless specifically released by clients, the data are owned only by the research sponsors rather than being available to public review.

An example of the use of an omnibus to address the issues of a major media group is shown in the next case study.

CASE STUDY: USING THE MEDIA TO CANVASS BUSINESS OPINION VIA THE CNN TIME OPINION POLL

Main message

We can utilize many different routes to find businessmen and businesswomen whose views and behaviour are of interest to our clients.

Respondent definition

Time Warner business people based in the United States and internationally.

Details

Time and CNN, part of the Time Warner portfolio, are two of the world's most recognized media brands. Having enjoyed most success in the United States, they wanted to position themselves at the heart of the European debate and provide relevant content for editorial in the region.

The CNN Time poll is the biggest editorial opinion poll of its kind. Carried out in two parts (a quick poll series of questions and a separate tracker programme), the research was reported back to the firms' editors and revealed attitudes towards topical issues. The success of the project in 2003 led Time, CNN and the research firm TNS to agree to renew and expand their partnership deal for 2004, covering more European countries and extra topic questions. Negotiations have begun to extend into the Asia–Pacific and the Middle East, with a view to creating a global poll in the near future. It is an example of how strong the media and an international research agency working together can be in finding out business opinion speedily and playing back what is most on people's minds in news coverage and editorial comment.

The presentation of this research programme won a Commendation at the 2004 *Marketing* magazine research awards for the media partnership, Time and CNN in the Best International Research Project category. It also highlights how the media can be an increasingly effective conduit to difficult-to-find business people at an international level.

Source: *Marketing*, Research Awards, July 2004.

RELATIVE USE OF THESE APPROACHES IN B2B RESEARCH

While in B2B all these forms of research are undertaken, some are less prominent. Even in B2B research, primary research is conducted somewhat more frequently than secondary research, although this greatly depends on the research category, the extent of published (for example public) data, and the difficulty of conducting primary research. Secondary research may be a good precursor to any business interviewing but frequently there just is not that much that is published to provide sufficient background, so interviewing some experts on a particular topic, for example, may be a quicker route to enlightenment. For many business issues, qualitative research is the preferred method – and sometimes it is the only possible method, where the population is small or the budget does not allow a quantitative solution. Quantitative surveys are often used in follow-up projects where quantification is required, where the available sample is large enough to accommodate it, and the client needs 'hard numbers' to justify a business case. Typically, in quantitative surveys, internet and telephone methodologies are replacing face-to-face interviewing.

Semi-structured interviewing has the benefit of obtaining depth through the use of unstructured, open-ended questions and the ability to follow through or explore a line of questioning with an individual respondent that may vary across those interviewed. In a semi-structured questionnaire as many as 20 issues may be included. At the same time, numbers of pre-coded or 'closed' questions can be asked so that some quantified data can be supplied.

Frequently, this approach is selected for business samples where the population (or universe) is not huge and where each interview must provide as much richness as practicable in terms of both insight and 'numbers'. It may be more satisfactory for the busy business respondent to express some views in full via open-ended responses and in detail in a quantified manner. In many ways, the semi-structured interview is an ideal vehicle for many B2B research surveys.

Fewer tracking studies are conducted in B2B than in consumer markets, although this may change over time. Today, most projects are ad hoc. First, the nature of the issue or problem is very specific and the business audience can be unusual or niche, and second, it is usual for companies in B2B to not want to reveal information about their plans. For very good reasons, it is often a rather secretive commercial environment and this is why research ethics are particularly critical in B2B research practice.

Some research providers do run business syndicates, and others run business omnibuses. In Scotland, for example, George Street Research conducts a 100 monthly telephone omnibus with CEOs/financial directors in a quota sample of Scottish businesses. In the UK, NOP World conducts omnibuses with GPs and hospital specialists and a Small Business Omnibus (every other month) by telephone among businesses with turnover of up to £1 million, spread by region and sector, across England and Wales with a Scotland boost available. NOP also conducts a Small/Medium Enterprises Omnibus among businesses with up to 250 employees, spread by region and sector. An example of a B2B omnibus in the United States is Research Strategies' Executive Omnibus – interviews with senior executives across a spread of functions from the top US manufacturing and service companies, fieldwork being conducted by telephone once a year.

In terms of tracking, larger research providers undertake some very large tracking B2B surveys. Most tracking work in B2B is too expensive to be very regular (that is, more than quarterly). If tracking research is done with business samples, this will often be on a six-month or annual cycle rather than the weekly/quarterly repetition of a consumer goods study. Syndication in B2B is not that common, but in Australia, BIS (formerly BIS Shrapnel) regularly conducts syndicated studies in a number of B2B markets, including home appliances, food services, and studies of the building and property market.

To date, relatively few business panels are in operation, although these are more common in the United States than in other countries – for example, US-based Survey Sampling International (SSI) has expanded its B2B Online sample to include new selections for IT professionals, reflecting increased demand for research in the sector. Bloomerce provides an internet panel with business as well as consumer panels for European coverage.

An important issue is, would business respondents want to be on a panel, and what would they get in exchange that might make it worthwhile? Their enthusiasm to join such a venture may be less than in the consumer context. Growth in business panels and their management is an area to watch in the future. Of course, the key question to ask with respect to panels (B2B or consumer) is to what extent the panel is representative of the group in question: has the method of recruiting, interviewing (for instance, posted questionnaires on internet sites), incentives (such as money or 'bonus points' to spend on select goods or services), or replacing respondents who drop out, or a combination of the above, biased the composition of the panel in any way? These should be key questions asked of a research provider prior to considering this approach.

DECIDING ON THE APPROACH

The principles

Each project's objectives, issues, respondent population and budget will guide the research design and methodology. It is not uncommon for a combination of qualitative and quantitative research to be undertaken, and for qualitative and quantitative work to be done at different stages of the research process (as reflected by the demands of the business issue at hand). Table 4.2 shows some typical patterns in B2B research.

Table 4.2 *Typical B2B research projects*

Small project or low budget	Larger project
Desk research (when little is known of the market; some basic facts or a 'feel' only is required for size, players, potential)	Exploratory qualitative (determine key issues, language, range of possible responses, likely appeal) followed by quantitative (quantify and detail)
Stand-alone semi-structured interview	Qualitative followed by semi-structured (if some quantification is needed)
Stand-alone qualitative	Qualitative followed by quantitative followed by further qualitative (second qualitative to 'disaster check' execution of concept etc identified as best choice in quantitative) Several quantitative stages (numeric tracking of performance over time on key measures; monitoring change in the marketing mix/product or service delivery, etc)

CASE STUDY: DESK RESEARCH ASSISTS NPD IN AN UNKNOWN MARKET

Main messages

Initially, by gathering as much published information as possible on the market, the idea was not chopped down before a full NPD plan could be designed and executed to more fully evaluate potential.

A phased approach to research (more costly detailed and targeted research conducted later) ensured that the idea was progressed only as far as the flags at each stage remained green, not red.

Details

A small team of engineers developed an all-in-one piece of equipment that enabled a number of grooming activities to be done using just the one device. Likely users were, in particular, hotel chains for hotel rooms and householders. Nothing was known about the competitors (small appliance makers, makers of irons) in this area, and as this was an entirely new concept (NPD), the development team had no idea where to start to see if there was a potential market or what potential customer reactions might be.

In the end, desk research drawing on published data such as Mintel and an internet review was undertaken looking at the market, and simultaneously non-market researchers conducted competitor analysis using business intelligence methods. This stage was followed by in-depth interviews with experts around Europe, and later by semi-structured interviewing with hotel equipment buyers to gauge price level and possible uptake.

Choice of qualitative versus quantitative

As indicated previously, very often both qualitative and quantitative research needs to be undertaken, and at other times, for reasons of time or budget, the choice has to be made of one over the other. In the business research context, what are the benefits and drawbacks of each? Table 4.3 suggests some of them.

Let's now focus on the circumstances when qualitative and quantitative research is particularly useful.

Qualitative

Needless to say, qualitative research plays a vital role in B2B research. It is the preferred approach when:

- finding out views on broader issues such as market trends, customer service provision, likely future needs and so on;
- undertaking early-stage exploratory research to determine key issues, language, range of possible responses, and likely appeal;
- gaining insight into market dynamics and perceptions, decision criteria, perceptions, competitive context – in sum, the 'grit' needed to understand a market;
- refining a product or service near to launch or planning the key marketing messages, tone and language;
- depth and detail are needed.

Qualitative research allows us to observe interaction between individuals in a paired depth interview, mini group or focus group. It can give clues to non-verbal as well as verbal reaction, and this can be especially useful when business respondents tend to the rational in their verbal response. It is valuable where research needs to be done when a small or discrete sample only is available, and provides an excellent backdrop for quantitative research, fleshing out and explaining some

Table 4.3 *Benefits and drawbacks of research types*

Qualitative research	
Benefits	Drawbacks
Quick.	Executive intensive.
Useful where universe is small or people difficult to get hold of.	No measurements or statistics.
Stimulus material (mock-ups, prototypes, concept boards can be used in face-to-face interview).	Can be expensive if lots of travelling is involved or extensive translation if international.
Provides insight into motivations.	Samples can be too small to be deemed fully representative.
Provides anecdotal richness and lots of verbatim quotes.	
Direct experience of respondents, own words and expertise.	
Sets the scene, finding out broadly about trends, concepts, ideas, aspirations, needs, barriers.	
When decision making etc is more idiosyncratic/personal.	
Gives non-verbal as well as verbal clues.	
Good at exploratory *and/or* refinement stage.	
If focus groups, useful interchanges between respondents to show dynamics.	

Quantitative research	
Benefits	Drawbacks
Can give reassurance that more people are canvassed.	Less strong on insights and less depth.
Delivers statistics for measurement.	Project time can be longer.
	Restricted time available for interview (shorter surveys preferred by business respondent).

quantitative findings. Its many uses provide a central plank of much current B2B research.

One challenge is not allowing others (especially those who are not highly experienced in research practices) to want quantification from a qualitative study – to try to squeeze figures from it even if only 20 people were interviewed. Some numbers may be produced (for example, a short questionnaire pre- or post-interview), and a show of hands in a business mini focus group helps shorten a long-winded discussion or forces individuals to give a view. However, obviously, this is not equivalent to being able to tell the company board that, from a sample of 400, and with an accuracy of plus or minus 4.9, 72 per cent of customers prefer wording A as the corporate slogan or tag line. Neither is it comparable to use in strategy planning a 4.9 rating of concept B versus 3.5 for concept C from four groups of eight financial planners each (N = 32) against the same mean ratings obtained from an N = 200 sample. Beware of qualitative researchers bearing numeric gifts!

Quantitative

By contrast, quantitative research is most often required when:

- validating qualitative results and authenticating suggested actions;
- a degree of accuracy rather than judgement is needed in terms of numbers and statistics on key dimensions, for example, in customer satisfaction measurement, performance tracking, market sizing, volume forecasting;
- selecting among alternatives the product/service that seems to offer the best potential for launch or market/portfolio augmentation;
- benchmarking and making comparisons – comparing performance or trends over time or comparing one organization or unit with another;
- segmentation forms the basis of the company's marketing strategy.

Of course, some companies and disciplines will have an inherent preference or bias towards qualitative or quantitative work. Many will always opt for a quantitative approach if this is available (for example, those that are numbers-driven, where disciplines other than marketing have the main positions in the boardroom and where engineering, design, exploration, chemical knowledge or some other rational scientific-centred activity is the main driver). Here, presenting qualitative research as a 'stand alone' can be a challenge as it often will not provide the hard-based evidence that such organizations require. Similarly, government organizations may steer away from qualitative work as it will not provide enough of the sorts of data on which to base the reports they write to contribute to policy making.

Using qualitative and quantitative research together

The combination of both qualitative and quantitative research can offer the best of both worlds. As Tables 4.2 and 4.3 showed, qualitative research can be used as an exploratory, preliminary stage where hypotheses can be tested, lists of common occasions, product features, characteristics wanted or not wanted, perceived benefits or drawbacks, perceptions, attitudes, brand or corporate imagery can be derived, and an early understanding of the broader context is understood. Post-quantitative qualitative work is useful to further refine a concept in action, an execution strategy, a communication platform, a market entry strategy, or function as a 'disaster check', for example, when a new product or service is being introduced and when there are a lot of unknowns. Quantitative research can provide the statistical validation that is necessary in some circumstances where sample size allows it.

While many B2B researchers (and clients alike) might want to do a fully comprehensive, staged research programme, often this cannot be accommodated in the available budget. However, compromises can be made (using guidelines such as the above) so that the research design can address the majority of the client's business objectives.

CASE STUDY: BENEFITS OF, AND DRAWBACKS TO, ITERATIVE RESEARCH IN NPD

Main messages

A qual–quant–qual research design can be a useful and thorough approach.

A great deal of time spent on research and other development can mean however that valuable time is lost in coming to market.

Respondent definition

Decision makers in retail establishments regarding which payment methods would be deemed acceptable in store, and consumers (not discussed here).

Details

Some years ago, a company developed a concept (let's call it WorldChip) using new technology to provide a smart card (like a debit card) that could be used anywhere in the world as an alternative to cash. The idea then was that soon carrying local currency would be outdated because everyone would want to be able to use this 'cash card' for small or medium-sized purchases.

Research was conducted via focus group and questionnaire with retailers (the B2B element) and consumers. A series of staged focus group research projects was conducted with retailers who were the decision makers in their shops/chains regarding whether to replace current cash tills or add to them so that smart cards might be used in payment for goods. First, the concepts, reactions, pricing, barriers, likely uptake, and what might encourage acceptance were the kernel research issues of the focus groups. Second, the same questions were examined in a quantitative context with a larger sample in several countries to verify the earlier findings to provide quantification. Finally, more qualitative work was undertaken to test out further how barriers to uptake could be avoided and what strategies needed to be adopted so that the smart card would gain acceptance among retailers as well as consumers.

Events took over, with other products coming to market that made this product less viable. Nonetheless, it has been successfully introduced in the Far East, and elsewhere WorldChip has taken its place amongst technologically enabled payment methods in the world today.

Addressing the business issue using a qualitative or quantitative approach

Often, valid answers to a client's business issue or problem can be addressed using either a qualitative or quantitative methodology. However, the questions need to be framed rather differently.

Qualitative questions will tend to:

- be more wide-ranging in content;
- vary a little in the exact way of framing the question between interviewers and respondents in order to secure their understanding and particular point of view;
- allow more openness in responses (possibly allowing fully verbatim responses).

Quantitative questions are more structured in both:

- the question (a specific wording will be given to interviewers that is strictly adhered to in order to maintain consistency and quality);
- the possible responses recorded from the respondent (for example, pre-coded/listed set of answers in the questionnaire plus 'open' – to be recategorized later at the data analysis stage).

Figure 4.1 illustrates questions asked of SMEs relating to mobile telephony, using first exploratory qualitative work followed by a quantitative phase. The question framed first in the qualitative context illustrates the 'broad brush' and open-ended approach, not pigeonholing answers too quickly but looking for responses that later on, for the quantitative stage, could be written up into lists for pre-coded questions. The quantitative style demonstrates such a pre-coded list, with

Qualitative question: 'Thinking of when you get your mobile phone service provider involved if you have a query or a problem, what would be a typical scenario? What sort of queries or problems did you have? Can you "walk me through" your last call that related to a technical query (rather than billing or promotional offer):

> ➤ Who did you first call?
> ➤ If Company X, did you go via 145?
> ➤ Who did you speak to? Or who (ie service provider or network provider) did you THINK you spoke to? What was the issue you wanted to discuss with them?'

The rather open qualitative questioning above was replaced at the quantitative phase by:

Quantitative question: 'Please can you now think about the **last** time you phoned Company X with regard to a technical issue–that is, an issue that **didn't** involve either billing or a promotional offer. Please can you say why you phoned?'

DO NOT READ OUT. PROBE. MAY BE MULTI CODE

Coverage issues	1
Problems roaming	2
Handset damaged/problems	3
E-mail problems	4
Setting up a data service (such as e-mail)	5
Setting up an MMS service (such as taking/sending pictures)	6
Setting up a PDA or laptop to work with a mobile phone	7
Setting up a connect/network card to go into a laptop	8
Enabling a service	9
Problems with a data service (such as e-mail)	x
Problems with an MMS service (such as taking/sending pictures)	v
Problems/queries with Bluetooth devices	1
Other (write in)	–
Can't remember	X!

Figure 4.1 *Qualitative and quantitative ways of addressing an issue*

the queries that had emerged during the qualitative exploration now being written up so that the relative importance of each response option could be evaluated quantitatively.

Another methodological note

When interviewing is undertaken by telephone, this reduces the stimulus material that can be shown, although often this is not too much of an issue in B2B research. The advantage of being able to telephone respondents at a time that is mutually convenient at their office or indeed elsewhere, and the less intrusive aspect of a telephone rather than individual face-to-face appointment, can often mean the benefits of telephone interviewing outweigh any drawbacks such as lack of stimulus. Internet access – or fax – can be used to send or view documents such as outlines of what the interview is about, or written concepts or visuals.

SUMMARY

Careful reflection on the client's objectives and ways market research can address their business issues and opportunities will produce a workable research design. While there is no single right way to design a study, generally being mindful of what methods cannot be used to deliver the specific information or data point required (or are less successful in producing a good result) aids the design process. It also tends to produce fewer headaches and 'Please explains' from the client when expectations are not met.

There are very many different approaches and ways available to researchers – and many yet to be discovered. Let us be creative in our approach.

5 The B2B research process: I Desk research

Some of the issues affecting sampling and methodological approach have already been discussed. This and the next chapters aim to cover in more detail the process of each of the sorts of research discussed, in particular, for B2B:

- desk research;
- qualitative research;
- quantitative research.

Desk research, also called secondary research and touched on in Chapters 1 and 4, can be quick to do and relatively inexpensive. Invariably in B2B it is a less costly option than interviewing respondents (primary research). The only limitation is that the very specialist nature of much B2B work means that the specific information we are seeking is frequently not covered by published sources. However, it is almost always worth looking to see what is available. Often, desk research is seen as a 'backdrop' to qualitative research or quantification. It is especially useful when little is known about a market or the players within it. The case study of the new small appliance (page 61) illustrated how it could be used as a precursor to more traditional forms of research. However, in some circumstances, it can stand on its own rather than being complementary.

Desk research can be painstaking. Most secondary research (apart from accessing traditionally published government statistics) is a process of discovery and evolution, more like stepping stones over a river than a bridge. Hopping from one source of data to another and letting one lead you to the next can be the most productive way of approaching it. It can be gratifying to start knowing little and at the end of a few hours – by looking up information, giving people a ring, asking around, leaping from one source of data to another – to have a reasonably good, first-start picture of the subject. Few researchers start with an expertise in facilities management, cross-border acquisitions, or the Japanese market for machine tools, but after a few hours of searching around, it is amazing what you can discover. Perseverance, a desire to get on top of the subject, and an ability to get the most out of colleagues and people such as information librarians tend to pay off.

THE DESK RESEARCH PROCESS

Though not necessarily linear, the process is as follows:

- First have a clear idea of what you need to find out about. (It is easy to be distracted when on the internet so setting yourself a clear brief is helpful.)
- Make yourself a cup of coffee and free up some time (a 'clear run' is better than doing it all piecemeal).
- Start by a general overview of what is available.
- Write down all the possible sources that come to mind.
- Make some telephone calls to others who may be able to help or suggest other useful sources of information – or start looking, and then make calls as you go.
- Go on the internet and see what is available.
- Start writing down useful sites/contacts or information.
- Go to one of the major libraries if the project is a large one with esoteric data needs, for example, business libraries such as the City Business Library or British Library (UK), the Library of Congress or the New York Public Library (United States), or business schools' and universities' libraries.
- Order any publications or reports that you think might be useful (watch costs).
- Write and chart up the findings as you go, sorting found information logically.
- Review what you have found, and check that your major information needs are being met by the data to hand. Try not to get distracted down rich, but secondary, paths!

■ If comparable data are needed (for example across countries where typically data are sorted and stored in different ways), check that there is sufficient depth for comparing data sets or deciding on 'equivalences' where data are organized differently.

RESOURCES FOR DESK RESEARCH

There are some reference books that may be useful such as the annual *Marketing Pocket Book* in the UK or *Americas Marketing Pocket Book* (available from the WARC bookstore site), the CIA's *World Fact Book* or industrial yearbooks. Business-oriented newspapers and magazines are also useful starting points, often doing well-researched supplements on market sectors or companies. US publications especially tend to publish annual overviews of their markets. A business site like that of Reed Business Information will show all the business magazines the company publishes, listed by sector. This can be useful if, for instance, you want to look up recent articles or find out who is advertising in the computer sector.

Trade associations are useful, although they sometimes give only restricted access to those who are not association members. If a reason can be given for your interest and it can be shown to be of legitimate help to their sector, they may be helpful and can provide inside information and knowledge that can be difficult to find elsewhere. Trade or professional magazines can be bought (not all are subscription only).

Other sources include publications such as the Economist series, which contains reference material, market data, commentaries and useful case studies (see Bloomberg.com/economist books for a full listing): for example, *Guide to European Union, Directory of Business, Directory of Economics, China's Stockmarket, Globalization, E-trends, E-commerce, Guide to Analysing Companies, Guide to Economic Indicators, Guide to Financial Markets*. Similarly, the Harvard Business Review series of publications are reputable sources covering numerous aspects of business environments and business experience.

Relevant academic and more general journals that may be useful include *Harvard Business Review, Brandweek, Advertising Age, Journal of Business to Business Marketing, Journal of Advertising Research, Journal of Marketing, Communication Research, Journal of Marketing Research, Marketing News* and *Marketing Science*.

Much of what had to be done in the past by looking up reference tomes has now been overtaken by internet browsing, which can provide a richness of data sources and data in double-quick time. The internet does not rule out the use of traditional published sources.

Specialists are available to do desk research for you. In the UK, they may be contacted via the Independent Consultants Group (ICG) website www.indepconsultants.org. Founded in 1993, the ICG provides names of researchers who undertake almost any research task you could wish. Similarly, in Australia the Market Research Society website, www.mrsa.com.au, gives a list of independent consultants (Independent Researchers Group), and this may help identify someone suitable.

Often government statistics are the basis of much contextual research; information on useful government statistical websites that are normally the first start point for such investigation is given in a list of useful websites in Table A1.1 on page 248.

Some UK organizations

Some organizations have their own excellent libraries and reference sources. A good example in the UK is the Royal Mail Information Centre, Infobank, which houses all past research reports and a mass of published data concerning postal and allied services. The e-mail for this is Infobank_Content_Update@royalmail.com.

Also in the UK, the Institute of Directors can provide useful information at its headquarters in Pall Mall, as can the British Library, but for specialist knowledge, the City Business Library (www.cityoflon don.gov.uk\citybusinesslibrary), based at 1 Brewers Hall Garden, London EC2, telephone (00 44) 20 7332 1812, is a particularly useful venue for those seeking business information.

Research reports available

Apart from its own books, maybe more important is the access the City Business Library offers to three of the most useful sources of market research data for the UK and Europe:

- Data Monitor;
- Key Note;
- Euromonitor.

These data sources are available in hard copy or online and are free. The one drawback is that the only way to access them via the City Business Library is by going there and booking in at one of its terminals. It does not have Mintel, one of the other major sources of data and written reports. It costs several thousands of pounds annually to subscribe to Mintel; the larger research agencies tend to subscribe to supplement their market knowledge, but for a small company it can be expensive to obtain access to it in totality. However, it may be worth buying the odd one-off report.

Euromonitor is another of these report data banks. Snapshots of four sources of these specialized reports that are particularly well known are given at the end of the chapter. Reports are not inexpensive. As at July 2004, a report on *Telecommunications Retailing in the UK* for example cost £995, US $1,795 or €1,495; the *Energy Supplements* US report cost £1,664, US $2,995 or €2,495.

There are other market research reports available for purchase such as via www.marketsearch-dir.com.

The British Library, as mentioned, provides a mass of information for the business researcher as well as for the casual visitor or specialist. The Library operates an online newspaper archive and a Business Intellectual Property Centre as well as offering a research service for those who are interested. (See page 252 for details.)

Identifying syndicated studies is another source of information about a market, its brands, and dynamics. Typically, these also require a financial investment so they tend to be used more once a project is commissioned than at the proposal stage. Identifying what is available is yet another process of search. In addition to general web searches, the websites of industry organizations, marketing bodies and market research societies are a useful source – for example, the AMSRS (Australia) gives a list of syndicated studies and information on them in different categories, many of which are B2B topics rather than strictly consumer research (including, interestingly, 'Industrial research').

Online sources

It is not always possible to disaggregate hard-copy sources of business information from online sources. Very often information is available simultaneously online (though sometimes in reduced format) and in longer written (and paid for) versions. If a report is available on a subject of interest, it can provide much of the background but rarely all the subsidiary information, which then needs to be sought from additional sources. Desk research and online sources rarely provide a 'one stop shop' but the beauty of online is that it is so easy to move from one source of data to another. The sources mentioned earlier refer largely to large databanks of specialized sector-specific and sometimes country-specific reports. There is also day-to-day news that can be useful if recent information is required. Online plays a particularly useful role here for topical updates.

Two major sources of online information are Reuters and Bloomberg, www.reuters.com and www.bloomberg.com. Both are credible and topical information sources regarding business and the world at large. Reuters provides topical news, information on the financial markets, and some research reports (including an e-news bulletin). Bloomberg also provides world market news and financial information (and, as with Reuters, is a credible provider of information to the financial markets generally). Other useful information banks for business are Reuters Business Insight www.reutersbusinessinsight.com (for energy, financial services, healthcare, technology, telecoms and e-commerce); World Markets Analysis (telecoms, automotive, healthcare, energy) and MarketResearch.com. If you are undertaking market reviews and want to find out who supplies or sells goods for B2B worldwide, look on www.MFGTrade.com (a free B2B trade portal).

For current information on markets, UK Trade Invest provides Business Monitor International giving daily industry news and five-year forecasts for 50 global markets – website www.uktradeinvest.gov.uk.

As researchers, we have several new up-to-date market research-specific news services, most of which concern broader research issues, but with some items relating to B2B. One of these news services in the UK is *MR Week's* free bulletin, edited by Philip Kleinman (www.mrnews.com), e-mail editor@mrnews.com, telephone 00 44 207 272 8826. Another is the website MrWeb, edited by Nick Thomas, which again gives useful weekly news of what is happening in the research industry and is particularly strong on business and B2B issues: e-mail DRNO@Mrweb.com.

ANOTHER TYPE OF DESK RESEARCH: DATA MINING

Data mining is a technique for bringing data from diverse sources together, and 'mining' it. Its objective is to facilitate decisions on corporate strategies; in particular, in refining corporate knowledge and intelligence, in identifying potential for business development, in crafting future strategic initiatives, in enabling process change work that aims to enhance the customer experience, and in the broader context of customer relationship management (CRM). The raw data are collected from a variety of sources: internal sources of information that companies typically already have about their customers and their behaviour stored in the company's computer files or with their data bureaux (for example, corporate transactions, customer histories and demographics) and external – published databases including industry data, credit bureau records and phone lists.

While more commonly used in B2C research, increasingly data mining is being used in B2B strategy development, partly because of the growth in enterprise data management and retrieval software but also because of marketers' growing awareness that they are sitting on vast amounts of valuable information (much of which is untapped) in their own databases. In the United States, the descriptive use of data mining is often labelled as 'customer discovery'. Many companies offer data mining software, including SAP, IBM, Oracle, DataMind, Information Builders and

Acxiom Corporation (where there are some case studies on the website axciom.com). In business prospecting and lead generation, software that is tailored to 'fish' for business listings by SIC code is particularly useful.

Data mining techniques consolidate and describe large amounts of data, uncover previously unidentified patterns, predict trends, and (when done in conjunction with a market research study using a smaller sample), cross-relate the market research results with the company's database to size and gross up these findings to a customer population or to estimate the lifetime value of a customer by extrapolating from current behaviour and characteristics.

Apart from basic profiling and classification, techniques can include a myriad of statistical tools such as regression, forecasting or predictive modelling, time series analysis, clustering (segmentation), association analysis (for example, joint purchase of product A and B is especially common), and sequence discovery (for example, Event A follows Event B 90 per cent of the time) as well as the use of decision trees and genetic algorithms, fuzzy logic and neural network modelling.

When research results are linked with database analysis, difficulties commonly arise; many of these are technical, related to formats and lack of easy compatibility between research data formats and company databases; dealing with incomplete or missing data; how to easily slice up the customer base in order to work with the data for the desired groups; working with IT staff in order to develop programmes and undertake data runs to achieve the desired outcomes; getting data processing and IT staff to talk the same language, and so on.

Developing strategy from data mining must overcome the transactional (purchase, order, withdrawal, or deposit was made at X time, cost Y, and the account was settled at Z time) rather than relational (knowing about contacts as businesses and business representatives, and their nature of their relationship with the company) nature of most companies' databases. We may want, for example, to use data mining to predict whether an individual (business) is likely to be 'ripe' for a credit line in the next year, so we would want to integrate transactional and relational information.

While there are companies that specialize in data mining, market research agencies are often asked to undertake an add-on task after the main research that involves some form of data mining, or at least working with the company's database in some way. This has the potential to significantly add value to the research findings. However, it can prove to be a time-consuming, expensive and frustrating exercise – especially if it was not included in the cost of the research or if the demands of the task mean that some renegotiation with the client on price and time is needed. Be careful of promises.

VALIDATING DATA FROM DESK RESEARCH

Of course, it is important to test out the credibility of online sources – or, for that matter, any secondary research source. A special watch is sometimes needed if the source emerges from a search-engine search as a sidebar (paid for) listing. Common-sense 'Does this make sense and match with what I already think/know to be the case?' questions and double-checking are invaluable. The number of websites and sheer volume of data available can be a challenge. The real expertise is sifting through it, being selective, and developing meaningful data from the desk research. As Kate Pitts, Futurist at the Royal Mail, said in her keynote speech at the 2004 BIG conference, 'Data are going to be so commonplace and there's going to be so much that collecting it is not the issue. The challenge will be between collecting data and finding relevant data and interpreting it.' Kate was talking too about data-gathering technology (which is improving rapidly), database design and data mining. Her view was that much of what we do now soon may become obsolete because of new technological possibilities such as a 'Google-type of interface interpreting data for companies'. An area to watch – if much can be done technologically in the future, the added value of distillation, extracting useful comparison and insight, is what will count.

SUMMARY

In summary, when conducting desk research consider:

- libraries (central, city, university, business school, organization and others);
- bought-in reports;
- publications, magazines, pocket and year books;
- government information for statistics;
- online websites, online data sources and company websites;
- trade associations/industry bodies;
- specialist directories.

A lot of the information may be rather dry, and much will not be easily comparable country by country, but it can be satisfying finding out as much as you can, and after a search you will certainly know a lot more about what is available. Then is the ideal time to decide and plan any primary research, speaking to people direct.

6 The B2B research process: II Qualitative research

Chapter 4 outlined the benefits and drawbacks of qualitative research and where qualitative research is indicated. Here, more detail is given about the qualitative research process.

MAIN TYPES OF QUALITATIVE RESEARCH

The main forms employed are in-depth interviews and focus groups, along with creative brainstorms.

In-depth interviews

Usually, in-depth interviews are individual (or 'one on one') interviews with respondents and can be conducted by telephone or in person. A variant is the 'paired interview' approach. This interview type is often used in consumer research with couples, where joint decision making is an issue or where the presence of the second person is deemed to aid the discussion. In B2B, paired interviews may be particularly useful where it is practicable to get two people together who may have somewhat different perspectives on a problem or issues covered. Where a senior person such as a director or company proprietor might have a broader view but one of his or her managers might have more detailed knowledge about an issue, having them both together for an interview can be more productive. For example, when interviewing Members of the European Parliament in Brussels, it was helpful to be able to speak to both the MEP and his or her assistant for a short period at the same time, allowing the chance to gain different information through their differing relationship with the client company.

A qualitative survey for a bank on outsourcing, where it was useful to understand the strategic and the tactical view, employed telephone interviews with finance directors and accountants as senior decision makers, and interviews (though not always at the same time) with finance operations managers and ledger clerks to hear the more day-to-day perspective. Here, although the interviews tended to be sequential rather than undertaken simultaneously, the aim is the same – to obtain a fuller overview and wider-ranging feedback than is available from just one person in an organization. Arranging diaries and the presence of the two people at one site at the same time can present logistical difficulties, so this does not happen as much as we might like, although as mentioned above, telephone depth interviewing can allow interviews with different people in a company to be undertaken either simultaneously or, more commonly, one after the other. Of course, psychological issues, politics, company hierarchies and competitive advantage need to be considered in case any of these is a barrier to gaining the 'true' picture in a paired interview where two people from the same organization are literally in the same room.

Focus groups

A typical focus group (also called 'group discussion') is a lightly (or less so, depending on the topic and the client demands) structured discussion among 8–10 respondents who jointly participate in the discussion led by a researcher (the moderator). A 'mini-group' includes three to five respondents. Respondents have been recruited ahead of time to attend a venue at a set time, and they are usually given an incentive for attending. Where facilities provide it, group sessions can be observed through a one-way mirror by the client (and others), but they are almost universally taped by audio, and a video can also be made. Respondents must be advised that they are being observed and recorded. Typically, focus groups last between an hour and a half and two hours, but can be extended sessions where products and concepts are being tested (up to three hours).

In B2B research, gathering respondents together at the same time and place presents a challenge. Mini-groups tend to be more common.

As business people are often used to having a reasonable 'share of voice', having fewer rather than more group members can be more, rather than less, productive. It also reduces the risk of respondents worrying about divulging information that gives their organization competitive advantage. Often, business focus groups are conducted at lunchtime or as breakfast sessions rather than during the evening. A good lunch at a quality venue can act as a good incentive to attend. For example, one project for a private bank ran early evening sessions with financial planners at five-star hotels and provided a top-notch buffet.

Generally, it is best to include business respondents who are of a similar seniority or have some mutually common interest in, or 'beef with', the issue at hand – too much respondent diversity can set up hierarchies in the group dynamics and tends to act as a barrier to expressing free-flowing views.

Creative brainstorming or strategy sessions

Creative brainstorming is another technique that can be included in a B2B qualitative researcher's arsenal. This most closely resembles a focus group. Sessions normally last a few hours and involve six to ten (at the very most) respondents. The mix of respondents depends on the project. Usually, it is employees within the client company closely involved with the business issue at hand, often from different groups (and therefore different perspectives), such as marketing, customer management, product design and distribution. Individuals from outside the company, including clients and/or suppliers (for example, the company's advertising agency, consultant, design team) may also be included.

The researcher is the moderator, but generally takes a much more active role in structuring the sessions than in a traditional focus group. Sessions are quite 'hot-house' – aiming (at the end of the time allotted) to come up with a range of suggestions for strategy. It is common for ideas and responses to be written up on flip charts. Often sessions are divided up, and various 'rules' apply:

- All are equal. No hierarchy.
- No war stories!
- Ideas only – no criticism allowed.
- Statements not questions (suspend judgement).
- Jot down your thoughts if 'in a queue' to speak.
- Assume positive intent.
- Do not self-censor. Absurd/wacky is good.
- Listen and build on others' ideas.

CASE STUDY: CREATIVE BRAINSTORMING

Main message

Brainstorming is a useful technique to include in the standard repertoire of strategy development.

Details

In the UK, the Royal Mail has undertaken many creative brainstorming sessions with Research International as part of its commitment to
look for innovative ways of reviewing, simplifying and streamlining its
processes in the business or in research into its business.

One creative problem-solving session examined new ways of
tracking the post (from pillarbox to doormat) to determine if there
might be easier ways of tracking letters than the traditional methods
of having people round the country literally sending each other
post and logging times to arrival. (Mail sorters had become accustomed to the special marks that were used by the research agency
that undertook this tracking and expedited any such letters they
found – thus partly invalidating the traditional tracking process.)

Since then, new technological tracking has been developed to
address the issue but brainstorming as well as keeping an eye on
what technical innovation is emerging is a good way to remain fleet
of foot and open to new thinking.

There are a number of approaches to creative brainstorming which
vary in terms of how structured (or regimented) the session is, what
techniques might be used, and whether researchers are trained in the
given approach. For example, the Synectics style is to encourage free
flow of ideas (the creative part), prompted by questions and facilitated
by 'mind games' as part of the first half of the session (to encourage
lateral thinking). Later, the idea evaluation stage encourages the writ-
ing-up of the best ideas that address the central problem at hand and
examines these in more detail – what are their advantages and what
are their drawbacks, and how can these be overcome?

Anyone who has a chance should try to attend such sessions. They
can be enormously productive and help free those in business from the
rational frame of mind that often can prevent creative thinking.

CASE STUDY: CREATIVE BRAINSTORMING IN PRACTICE IN B2B

Main message

There are a number of techniques and catalysts that, in experienced hands and with the right mindset of those participating, can
assist significantly in the development and refinement of concepts.

Details

The Major Business division of a telecoms company wanted to provide a 'state of the art' information service for senior executives and managers in client companies and for its own sales people. It launched an interactive business information platform that was user-driven (that is, the user could choose the communication channel, either web or web plus e-mail), interactive (provided two-way dialogue), and relevant to the user's business issues, function and sector.

Prior to undertaking more conventional quantitative and then qualitative research, two internal brainstorming workshops were held with the company's then creative agency, Proximity. The two key issues addressed in the creative brainstorming were:

- 'How to create the dialogue with customers.'
- 'How to make that dialogue sustainable and exciting.'

Various exercises were played including one where attendees imagined that they were from another 'world' (for example the circus, a church, the United Nations) and had to relate this to the two key issues.

A number of themes that the new information initiative should embrace were identified, including 'community involvement', 'intensity' and 'congenial atmosphere'. Words emerged to illustrate these themes: for example, 'total experience', 'frequent meetings', 'variety', 'dynamism' and 'colour'. From these, designating the 'essence' of what people felt the new service should embrace, action plans were developed both corporately and individually. Here, the creative problem solving became practical. Plans such as the following were developed:

- creating an internal archive of the site (so users could go back to things);
- more freedom of choice and ability to navigate the website;
- more specificity in 'hot buttons' so that the site elements were not too generic;
- engaging a top-level cartoonist to enliven the site and interchange.

THE QUALITATIVE PROCESS

Let us look at the process, or various stages, of qualitative research. The typical process is not very different from that used in consumer research, though more emphasis may be put on eligibility, sample source/s, pre-contact, confirmation (this is especially important and should not be overlooked as business diaries change) and follow-up. A typical process is as follows:

- Discuss the business and research objectives so there is a clear outline of what the research needs to achieve, why, and how it might be used.
- Design a research plan; what methodology is suggested, broad locations.
- Sampling – consider the optimum sample size and stratification, length of time to 'draw' a sample, sample format, and other sampling implications.
- Consider what, if any, incentives are to be given.
- Contact outside qualitative recruiters if you are not undertaking all recruitment yourself.
- Draw up recruitment guidelines/a screener questionnaire to allow suitable and eligible respondents to be recruited (this may be done by the qualitative recruiters if they are being employed).
- Start developing and refining the topic guide (series of question areas) and considering what, if any, projective techniques are to be included. Consult all those who might wish to contribute to the guide and review the questions to be asked.
- Contact those to be interviewed. Pre-contact is an essential part of qualitative research. Contact again the day before interview if face to face to ensure the time is booked in and no change in arrangements is needed.
- Undertake the fieldwork (interviews, focus groups).
- If recorded on tape, disk or (in the case of focus groups) by video, listen again, review notes taken during the interview or subsequently.
- Analyse the information (major themes emerging, what was most emphasized and with greatest frequency); draw up charts/diagrams/slides.
- Report on and communicate the findings.

A sample screener questionnaire is given in Appendix 2.

Recruiting

Finding and recruiting hard-to-find and hard-to-recruit respondents is an art in itself. Many of the larger research agencies use a small team of highly experienced individuals to recruit B2B respondents. An attractive voice, confidence, evident professionalism, plus charm and persuasiveness are key features that make for a successful B2B recruiter – and more women tend to be involved in this than men.

In B2B research it can be very helpful to encourage the commissioning client to alert those to be contacted (if it is supplying customer lists as sample), so that the initial contact from the recruiter or agency is not 'out of the blue'. Called 'warming', this can increase positive response greatly, although it can make the project's fieldwork phase a little longer. Respondents know to expect a call and can be more ready to agree to do an interview as they know the topic and the sponsor. Such pre-contact was undertaken, for example, by a large multinational for a study on customer service perceptions and corporate branding with purchasing directors of major retailers throughout Europe in order to increase response. It ensured a very high success rate, which would have been much lower without such an early pre-alert process. Telephone calls are made or a letter is sent as a formal request to potential respondents asking for their cooperation in the interview and explaining in brief why the research is being undertaken. Such letters are normally signed by a senior person in the organization sponsoring the research (the marketing director rather than brand manager for example) and on the firm's letterhead. See the boxed example.

CLIENT PRE-CONTACT RECRUITING LETTER (A WARM-UP LETTER)

Company X: Corporate image research

Company X is committed to high workplace standards, high quality products and to being a good corporate citizen by behaving responsibly towards the communities and societies of which we are an integral part.

We have appointed Agency Y, a market research company, to carry out a survey on our behalf. This survey involves a number of in-depth, structured interviews across Europe with leading opinion formers, such as you. The interviews will be carried out by an independent executive from the project team at Agency Y at a date and time that is convenient for you.

Agency Y is a member of ESOMAR (the European Society of Market Research) and abides by its code of conduct. May I assure you that any comments made during the interview will be treated in the strictest confidence. Your contributions will not be attributable to you (unless your permission has been given) and we encourage you to give your honest opinions on the subjects discussed. Sometimes issues are raised on which it may be useful to follow up – again, we are delighted to do so but leave this decision to you.

In appreciation of your participation we propose providing all those participating with an Executive Summary. The summary will be produced towards the end of the year and will detail the key results and information on the combined thoughts and views of other opinion leaders.

> I very much hope that you will be able to help. Your answers will provide invaluable information and will allow us to understand better how we can continue to serve our customers and the communities in which we operate.
>
> Yours faithfully,
>
> (Electronic signature here)

For B2B research, recruitment needs to be done well in advance: business people, professionals and tradespeople all lead busy lives and are frequently booked up weeks ahead. Do not expect to recruit anyone with less than a two-week time window at least, and, ideally give two to four weeks for recruitment – up to eight weeks for very senior individuals or special groups such as Members of the European Parliament or Congressmen. You may be surprised at how many clients do not want to allow sufficiently for these timing constraints. Also, take note of key yearly dates, normal holiday times, and times of seasonal pressure (such as pre-Christmas, Easter, Thanksgiving, lambing time for sheep farmers, annual conferences, fairs or exhibitions of professional bodies). Ask the client or visit the www.whatsonwhen.com website (or a similar website for your location) to check on some of these.

You can undertake the recruitment yourself or commission a recruitment agency. For very senior respondents, it might be advisable for the executive who is going to conduct the interview to recruit, although time and cost issues sometimes prohibit this. The recruiter needs to have:

- Information on why the research is being conducted.
- A convincing introduction and rationale for the research to engage the respondent (used by the recruiter and in the 'spiel' to any gate keepers and the respondent).
- Knowledge of what incentives are being offered, if any.
- A clear recruitment questionnaire that easily identifies eligible respondents and slots them into categories. Make this short, do not repeat questions, and make the language appropriate.
- Paper sheets or electronic spreadsheets to record:
  - who is to be interviewed, for example numbers in each category required/quotas;
  - contact details (first contact is usually by telephone);
  - availability of researcher/s – dates and times – to match availability with that of the respondent (and watch and monitor this over the course of the fieldwork as things change);
  - space to write in what is agreed – who is interviewing, at what date/time and location;

- specific instructions such as who to ask for, landmarks to look out for (if a face-to-face interview and difficult-to-get-to location).
- A well-established and routinely followed-through confirmation practice: by letter, fax, e-mail or follow-up call.

An example of a recruitment questionnaire used to recruit tradespeople for focus groups in the UK is provided in Appendix 3.

Incentives

It is relatively common to offer some form of incentive for B2B research (although this may vary from country to country). Clients are often surprised to discover that they need to offer some incentive – some very occasionally think that 'the privilege of being asked and to help develop a strategy or give feedback' should be reward in itself. But business respondents are human like anyone else (a client who had not thought it was necessary but then did offer a cash incentive asked for a rundown after the research – 55 per cent of the respondents took the cash!). Other approaches can be used, especially if the client feels or the culture dictates that money is too obvious, an insult, or 'crass', and one that works well is the offer to donate the incentive to a favourite charity. Good-quality wine or a breakfast/dinner in a well-recognized restaurant are also worth considering – but offer of alcohol is not appropriate in some cultures (often surprising ones, such as some parts of the United States). One business researcher once heard of an agency recruiting very hard-to-get respondents in a particular category by couriering one shoe of a pair of very trendy runners and offering a full pair in the right size if the respondent agreed to the interview.

Incentives can vary a great deal by type of respondent and what is being asked of them. Tradespeople such as fitters, roofers, electricians and joiners for instance will often be prepared to attend a focus group for the sake of £40 (US $70 or €56) cash in the incentive envelope. Hospital consultants may not attend unless there are hotel refreshments and £100–£200 (about US $262 or €210) for attendance. There are certain countries too where incentives can be inflammatory – do check with local agencies or others who may know local protocol before suggesting incentives in any 'blanket' way.

Some companies have a policy barring their staff from taking part in market research. This always infuriates me if, at the same time, they undertake market research on their own behalf, which they often do. In these cases though, apart from an appeal to higher authority, no amount of offering incentives is going to make any difference.

So, in summary:

- cash, cash and more cash if this is the local advice;

- donations to favourite charity;
- good-quality or hard-to-get wine – note that this is conditional on the country, culture, the context, practice in the sector, so use your judgement here;
- quality pen or office/desk accessories (but how many of these does the average respondent find attractive enough to do an interview for?);
- something 'nifty';
- if international, something that has international currency such as an internet voucher;
- very occasionally (though much less often than in consumer research), some form of prize draw or other sort of random selection prize.

Some guidelines on incentives for different types of research and when they are used are shown in Table 6.1.

B2B INTERVIEWING AND MODERATING

Practical aspects

Do not neglect the practical aspects. These are some that it is worth bearing in mind for B2B interviewing:

- Know where you are going if a face-to-face interview (plastics factories or chemical factories can often be in remote locations – give yourself enough time to get there). Take maps, ask for local landmarks. A colleague once had to interview on an oil rig with hard hat, helicoptered in. Allow enough time!
- Be early to be on time. Business respondents allocate you a 'slot'. Do not miss it.
- Be businesslike yourself in dress, demeanour, speech, briefcase.
- Have any stimulus material neatly in order – these are not interviews where you should look unprofessional by not being able to find things (check batteries, have spares of everything).
- Have your recording equipment all set up before you begin, but be extra careful to ask whether the respondent is happy for the interview to be recorded, and explain that anything can be said off the record with the tape 'on pause' if that would be preferred.
- If any incentive (gift in kind or cash) is being given, give it discreetly to the respondent. This is not an occasion to hand it to the secretary or PA. If incentives are to be sent afterwards, do not forget anyone. Mind you, if the PA has been especially helpful in securing an interview with a hard-to-reach respondent, a small thank-you gift here is worth the expense.

Table 6.1 *Incentive guidelines*

Type of interview	Type of respondent	Incentive
Telephone interview	All	Usually none. Sometimes a feedback report, or occasionally gift to charity or other such as Amazon voucher.
Face-to-face interview	Senior level/government	Very often some form of feedback or summary.
	Government or others who cannot receive gifts	Gift to charity or feedback summary.
	'Less exalted' such as farmers	Gift of cash, bottle of whisky, wine, other form of gift or feedback report.
	Senior/hard to get	Be creative!
Focus group attendance	All	Sizeable monetary gift or gift in kind (from £50 to £200 (US $87–$350 or €70–€280)). Very rarely any feedback provided to attendees to focus groups.

■ Send a follow-up thank you letter direct from the research agency, and signed by the senior project manager or the MD/CEO.

In fact, we could say that these niceties are critical for B2B research (and far more important to get right than in consumer research where individuals may be more forgiving). A pleasant interviewing experience may mean that respondents are more amenable to an approach to participate in research in the future: doing this well may be doing colleagues a favour.

Best practices

This is one of the most enjoyable research activities: you get to meet some amazing people with whom you may not have had a chance to converse otherwise (my collaborator on this book, Dr Kerrie Pinkerton, once interviewed Ken Done, one of Australia's leading artists, and many of us are put in contact with people we would not meet normally), and you also get to learn a lot about the intricacies of various sectors, products, functionalities and technology.

Good interviewing and moderating skill (whether telephone or face to face) is so important in B2B research because the respondent is important to the commissioning company, must be handled with care and feel that the interview was worthwhile. As time is short with much to cover, it is important to gain as much as possible from the time with respondents.

Here are some guidelines that can help effective B2B interviewing:

- Keep the topic guide 'short and sharp' – we have 20–40 minutes only for questions.
- Prioritize key questions to ask in advance (agreed with the client) maybe just by highlighting so that these questions are always asked no matter how brief the interview must be.
- To start, thank the individual for giving his/her time. Hand over a business card if you have one and accept the respondent's if he or she proffers it. Explain briefly the purpose of the research. Confirm the time the respondent has available and adhere to this unless the respondent wants to talk more. Ask at the beginning whether attribution is acceptable or not, and confirm this at the end.
- Be prepared to be flexible – if the discussion goes in a certain direction (and provided the material is part of the brief and does not jeopardize/bias later questions), go there when the respondent gets there – generally, this will save you time and irritation.
- Encourage the respondent/s by showing you are listening and interested. Add in the odd probing question. Generally business respondents are highly articulate and the skill is in keeping up with their thought processes and with the implications of what they are saying, rather than needing to prompt very much. Where relevant and time permits, allow the respondent freedom to expand on his or her specialist areas of expertise.
- Get started straight away. (My collaborator once had a CEO indicate that she had 'wasted six minutes on social pleasantries, so you have 39 minutes left' – his words – of the 45 minutes he could spare. He then ended up giving her 75 minutes because the material was personally interesting to him and they discovered a mutual interest in fine wine.)
- Explain, if projective or enabling techniques are to be used, what their purpose is – the rational business respondent sometimes needs to be given 'permission to play' and understand the reason for doing so.

■ Signal where you are in terms of time so that the business respondent knows you are getting through (respondents are normally aware of time) – for instance, 'We are halfway through the questions now' or 'Finishing up ...'.

■ Encourage respondents to suggest other people who might add to the debate (who you can follow up later). This extra source of names is useful especially if a sample is 'free found' rather than supplied.

■ Where time allows, at the end, sum up some of the major points the person interviewed has made and ask him or her to confirm your understanding. Summing up:

  – is helpful if the subject under discussion has been intense, technically detailed, or emotive rather than purely rational (customer service issues, for instance, can be inflammatory and you can end up thinking that the respondent is violently anti a company whereas in reality it is not too big an issue);

  – ensures that you as the researcher come away with the correct information rather than with a distorted picture;

  – reassures the respondent that you have listened carefully and will be responsible in accurately representing his or her viewpoint.

■ Thank the respondent. Let him or her know whether there is to be any feedback report and how the research might be used (respondents are often more interested in this at the end than at the beginning).

CASE STUDY: PERSONAL INTERVIEW WITH A MEMBER OF THE EUROPEAN PARLIAMENT

Main message

Time is often short: 'strut your stuff' and be prepared to be flexible on time.

Details

An interview was set up with an ebullient Italian MEP in Brussels. He chain-smoked and could speak no English. My Italian was non-existent, so we settled for communicating in French. He only had 10 minutes, as he was off to catch a plane back to his local constituency.

The interview concerned the corporate image and community involvement of a large firm with factories in his home country. His interest was in water cleanliness. Literally, we had a few minutes talking about what he knew of their current activities (little) and what he would like to see (lots). Much of the time was spent with him telling me about the fact that he is not allowed to smoke on factory visits.

We had a good laugh, and I came away with the basics of the information needed – not a long interview but it was supplemented by further conversation with his deputy who was happy to have a talk even if his whirlwind of a boss had to disappear. Satisfactory all round, though not the classic interview situation one might look for.

There are some 'Don'ts' in qualitative B2B interviewing also worth bearing in mind:

- Don't feel overawed by those with a big title: speak on a level with the respondent.
- Don't assume that the respondent knows a lot about research and the process. He or she might if he/she works in marketing, but many do not.
- Don't assume that respondents will indeed be able to answer all of your questions.
- Don't get flustered if your interview does not go the way you originally intended.
- Don't stop listening or immediately rush to the client's defence if the respondent is really riled about some issue with respect to your client. Remain independent, record the material faithfully, and communicate how you will use the information given.
- Don't worry about asking quite direct questions – there is no need to beat around the bush.
- Don't be afraid to ask the respondent to clarify terms or abbreviations with which you are not familiar or if the complexity of what is being discussed requires explanation.
- Don't hold back from asking for examples or 'How would that work in practice?' or 'What's the implication of that?' or 'Can you tell me when what you are talking about (in terms of application/functionality/technical failure or whatever is under discussion) had an impact on you or your business?'

Attribution or to reveal the respondent and transparency to reveal the client

Anonymity, confidentiality, attribution, and transparency need to be considered:

- **Anonymity:** not letting anyone, sponsoring client included, know that the respondent took part in the research is often offered in B2B research but very often is not an issue. Most respondents are happy to have their name known to those who commissioned the research and to 'stand up and be counted'. Usually, confidentiality is offered (that is, their views will not be shared with others and only the researcher will know what they said in detail) unless respondents say they are quite open about anything they say being known to others.

- **Attribution** is one of the ways B2B research most differs from other forms of research. Frequently, those being interviewed (who know their importance to the sponsoring client) will wish their views to be known and attributed so that their name accompanies any quote or anecdote given by them. They are less worried by the fact that the client may know the good and bad things they think about it than that the time they have invested in the interview might not be put to good effect. Attribution makes for rather more 'live' research results and gives the findings meaning, so wherever it is possible to ask for attribution, do so. Sometimes a respondent will be less happy for his or her opinions on close competitors to be made known (that is, the competitors of the client research sponsor rather than the respondent's own competitors), so this part of an interview might not be attributed whereas the remainder might be. What a respondent is and is not happy to have attributed must be respected.
- **Transparency:** More often than not, the name of the sponsoring client is disclosed upfront and has already been declared at the recruiting stage. Generally, the sponsoring client wants the respondent to know it is undertaking the research so that the research is part of an ongoing dialogue between the client and customer. As client names are often given to the researchers undertaking the interviews as a 'supplied' sample, it would be very odd to deny knowledge of where the sample came from and how the individual concerned was reached. Transparency and trust are important in the relationship. If research is undertaken without the sponsoring client 'showing its hand', then distrust may creep in. This is not the open relationship that most clients are seeking.

These caveats should always be respected, and the same applies equally to quantitative research. Never pass on anything that you have been asked to keep confidential except in aggregated and unidentifiable form. We need to safeguard the trust of the B2B respondent not just for now but for the long term.

Useful interviewing techniques

While a whole book could be devoted to this topic alone, two particularly effective techniques for the B2B interview are direct questioning and techniques that facilitate answers – so-called 'projective' or 'enabling' techniques.

Direct questioning

By far the most usual approach in B2B research is direct questioning: that is, asking a question straight out. As those being interviewed often are very expert and knowledgeable in their field, have a lot to say, and do not have much time – unless we are discussing more abstract subjects such as brand/company perceptions – generally the more straightforward the question, the better. Some typical direct questions from the beginning of a topic guide are shown here.

This was a study with clients of a corporate advisory company in the City of London undertaking an internal and external survey on its customer service performance and corporate image compared with others in the mid-market range. Those interviewed (via personal interview lasting between 30 and 60 minutes) were finance directors of large and medium-sized companies responsible for their organization's finance and capitalization. A very direct approach was taken, with very straightforward questions under different headings in particular for the first half of the interview:

Role/context
Please describe your organization and your role within it (responsibilities, length of time in role/organization etc).

Corporate finance
In terms of how the financial sector offers and manages corporate finance, to what extent is this meeting your current needs and expectations?

What are its strengths and weaknesses as you see them?

How is the corporate finance sector as a whole perceived by medium and smaller businesses?

Salience
In the corporate advisory sector, which companies do you think of first (are 'top of mind')?

And why is this one near the top of your list?

How have you come into contact with it?

In what ways do you have dealings with corporate finance advisory firms such as Company X? *(Explore whether the relationship is day to day/'hands on', or more remote/ infrequent, exposure only to their marketing/advertising not people, and so on.)*

Positioning
In terms of all the other advisory relationships that the client has – such as management consultant, lawyer, corporate communications consultant – where do you see the corporate adviser sitting?

To what degree has this changed over time? How?

Which would be your closest adviser would you say, and why?

Independent advice

How important to you is getting corporate finance/capital markets advice that is independent?

What are the benefits of independent advice to you? *(Probe for examples or anecdotes of where it is vital and how it makes a significant difference. Listen carefully to how those benefits are expressed.)*

And how is the need for advice that is independent changing?

Trends

What are the trends that you see currently with regard to the advisory relationship – what is changing, what is constant?

To what degree are you seeing companies change their range of products and services? To what extent are they altering their approach to doing business, for example their pitches, willingness to negotiate, ability to understand your business and take that into perspective?

How is this altering the nature of the relationship (between clients and the corporate advisors)?

And what changes would you like to see from companies as advisors?

Projective (and other) techniques

Projective techniques are methods used in qualitative research to overcome barriers to communication between the informant and the interviewer. They can also be called 'enabling' techniques because by using a concept or medium that is actually unrelated to the topic itself, they enable respondents to articulate thoughts or attitudes that they might not be able to do otherwise. These techniques are not as commonplace in B2B as in consumer research, but increasingly they are part of many B2B interviews. Indeed, they can be used to liven up what is sometimes quite technical and detailed discussion. By exploring what people have said and building on the projective answers, we can understand thought processes and unravel underlying meaning.

The sorts of projective (and other) approaches that can be easily incorporated into B2B qualitative research include personification, analogies/hypothetical situations, word association, shuffle cards and role play. The first two are often used in brand imagery, corporate reputation, and positioning research. Each is described briefly below:

- **Personification:** 'If FedEx were an animal/car/drink/restaurant/ city/type of holiday, what would it be?' Usually, for B2B work, some modification of the form of the personification that would ordinarily be used for consumer work is needed (cars may be more common than type of holiday, for instance).
- **Hypothetical situations:** 'If the New York Stock Exchange suddenly ceased to exist tomorrow, how would you feel/cope/how

would this affect your business? Why might it be missed if anything happened to it? Who would step into its place?' Alternatively, 'What would you say in eulogy at Microsoft's funeral?'

■ **Word association:** 'If I say "business regulators" what words or phrases come to mind? What else?'

■ **Shuffle cards:** Ask the respondent to sort names/products/services or whatever into piles on bases such as: 'Feel I know them very well', 'Know something about', 'Know little or nothing about', 'Would/would not try', 'Seem to compete in the same markets'. 'Put in as many piles as you need to show how they are similar or dissimilar in whatever way you are thinking.' This is particularly useful in a focus group.

■ **Role play:** 'If you were the head of a corporate advisory firm in the City today, what would be *your* main priority with regard to serving your clients?'

■ **Milestones for a company 'CV':** 'Imagine you are writing the CV (for Nestlé, Procter & Gamble, or any of their brands). What would you put as key milestones for the company? What might be their aspirations for the future?'

Least used in B2B market research are:

■ **Drawing or other non-verbal techniques** tend not to be used extensively but can be useful when asking business people to think about design: 'Draw how you would like your personal organizer to look'. This is not asking for a complete engineering design, but may be a helpful prompt and open up new avenues for discussion in terms of functionality and appearance that might not emerge through conventional questioning.

■ **Bubble diagrams:** Ask the respondent to write in what someone might be thinking in a bubble diagram format. This is rarely used, as most business respondents do not relate to this and can see them as silly.

If researchers do want to use some techniques, an explanation of how they work may be needed at the beginning or at the end.

When she worked at NOP Financial, Frances Hoskin often spoke at industry conferences of how she used enabling techniques with those in finance and business, and Martin Stoll of Ipsos Insight, the qualitative division within Ipsos, gave an interesting paper at the 2004 BIG conference entitled 'Advanced qualitative methods for researching the business consumer'. Some of the newer (or actually, reinvented in a different form) consumer qualitative approaches like observation (watching people in situ or by webcam – observing activities and recording them rather than asking questions) and ethnography (watching activities in the context of the 'tribe' or culture to which the respondent belongs) are rarely used in B2B work. Even so, there may be times when they are appropriate. Martin Stoll quotes the following example:

> A good example (of observation) is the case of trying to help pharmaceutical reps improve their performance when visiting general practitioners. We were asked by a pharmaceutical company to help them gain a better understanding of the context in which their reps were working and if possible to monitor the performance of the reps. We proposed that a researcher spend the day in a doctor's surgery, monitoring the pattern of work – number of patients seen, the phone calls, the letters written, the interruptions, the coffee breaks, the emergencies. Ideally the day researched would be the day the rep was scheduled to call so we would get a clear idea of the context of the call. Then we would sit in on the rep's visit and be able to identify more clearly what they were doing right and what they were doing wrong.

Ethnography can be useful on the rare occasion if access to someone's day/site/meetings is not too problematic, with the researcher taking photos or videos to record what is going on or even getting the respondent to take photos or videos. Throwaway cameras can be helpful here – researchers can then make video or picture diaries giving a vivid exposition of what the real situation is for those in the business environment, so that the context of their decision making can be better understood. In the above case, the doctor or the rep could have captured the exigencies of the typical day in the surgery on film. The final results to the pharmaceutical company could then be that much more lively and more easily communicated to those who will put learning into action (in this case, the pharmaceutical representatives and sales teams).

To quote Martin Stoll again:

> Looking to the future, there are trends in the consumer qualitative area that may well come into use in B2B. Not the online groups that were much feted but not much used, but the humbler e-mail and bulletin board. E-mail can be used with business people as a follow-up to groups or depths. And there is enormous potential too in the development of 3G telephony. With mobile phones and PDAs with voice recorders and in-built cameras and with systems that can track an individual's movements anywhere in the world, we have powerful tools for observation and for reporting.

As in all things, getting the balance right between direct questioning, probing and any interesting exercises within the interview is the key.

QUALITATIVE ANALYSIS AND REPORTING

Principles and practices

The precepts of good analysis apply equally to B2B and consumer research. There is no substitute for knowing your information thoroughly by listening very closely again to the recordings of interviews completed. Sometimes there is insufficient time for such a luxury, especially when a debrief (presentation) or report is required within a matter of days of the research fieldwork being completed. The trend is for speedy reporting, so occasionally taking brief notes while (or immediately after – 'brain dumping') conducting an interview or group is necessary. Above all else, organize the data, preferably while fieldwork is occurring.

What are the ways of analysing qualitative B2B findings? First, review the notes, audio tapes/disks, videotapes, photographs or respondent-generated outputs from any techniques used. Second, write down 'top-line' findings or implications (aspects and learning that have come into your head) before doing any other analysis – messages for the client drawn from the research. Consult with other interviewers or moderators – note what you have written down for top-line findings as opposed to what Elaine, Tony, Alison or any of the other executives involved thought to be important. This way, nothing major is missed, and one does not get into detail before recording the main points. Particularly in B2B research, because of the technical or specialist processes that are often recorded, it is easy to get lost in detail. Third, reread the brief and revisit the aims of the survey: what are the business and research objectives and key questions?

If you have not already done so, draw up the framework or template for the research report. What are the main areas that must be documented? What are the key themes or topics? How are they best arranged? (Note that it is often undesirable to present the results just according to the topic guide sequence.) What additional information has emerged that was not included as an issue in the client brief but which may have an impact on the recommendations? It may be worth considering drawing a 'mind map' – very quickly putting on paper/in the computer everything in your head into the logical groupings set out by the draft framework. Fifth, select your preferred way of analysing the data. You may prefer to choose from several methods rather than just one.

Analysis methods

Different analysis methods useful for B2B qualitative analysis include:

- **Electronic:** More useful for individual in-depth interviews than for focus groups. Take the headings from the (electronic) topic guide and, using a different colour or font for each respondent, use 'cut and paste' to write up the findings from each individual interview on screen. Excel spreadsheets can be used in the same way.
- **Pen and paper:** The tried and tested method of writing up the topic guide headings on large sheets of paper and, underneath each heading, adding the findings and quotes from each interview.
- **Transcripts:** Useful for analysing focus groups. Transcribers can be found who will type up all the interviews or focus group discussions word for word. They are sometimes hard work to unravel in B2B because of the complexity of the subject matter, but they can add useful detail and provide the executive undertaking the analysis with a quick refresher of topics covered. Go through transcripts with a highlighter to select interesting points.
- **Qualitative data analysis packages:** Import transcripts or written data into an analysis package and label text that relates to particular themes or topics with brief descriptions or 'codes'. Software can then be used to retrieve texts labelled similarly so that there is a logical grouping of data.

As mentioned above, nowadays there is new software appearing for qualitative analysis in addition to key word searches, which can allow more advanced forms of computer information sorting. In the future, this may become more frequently applied. At present, as the usual scale of B2B work is smaller than for many consumer studies, analysis by individuals who are close to the research is still the norm. But things may change. For computer-aided qualitative analysis, the main applications are reviewed at the CAQDAS website, http://caqdas.soc.surrey.ac.uk/index.htm.

Be careful when using electronic forms of analysis that no information from non-attributable interviews is sent on to the client: clients are often interested in seeing what individuals have said during B2B interviews, but their comments must only be passed on where we have express permission from the respondent to do so.

As Yvonne McGivern mentioned in her comprehensive book *The Practice of Market and Social Research* (2003):

> Qualitative data analysis packages are a good way of storing and handling data and making analysis accessible. They allow you to change how you think about the data, reworking coding schemes as new insights emerge, revisiting segments of the data quickly and easily. The search and retrieve functions allow you to interrogate the data more easily and so more thoroughly than you might with paper transcripts.

But she adds, 'Ultimately of course, any package is only as good as your own thinking and analysis skills.'

Reporting

Lastly, we draw up presentation charts or other forms of report:

- Key topics (as per the draft framework decided upon, but be prepared to be flexible as new points come up when preparing the charts) containing:
  - Main message or broad findings with key points on each issue to be dealt with.
  - Detail and supporting evidence plus illustrative verbatim quotes, anecdotes and so on. Find the right illustrative quote to demonstrate a particular point even if this is slightly longer and with more detail than would normally be in order for consumer work. Your rather knowledgeable audience is often rather critical, so 'the devil is in the detail' – you have to give that to them to back up your views.
- Implications, recommendations, and strategy: do not leave these charts till last.

Do review the presentation, double-check the validity of the points you are making – a 'reality check' – and watch whether you have:

- Correctly represented what was said, not over-interpreted what respondents were saying and not over-emphasized one person's or one set of opinions, but considered how frequently a response was given, and given all relevant weight.
- Taken into consideration how strongly views were held.
- Reported on what is relevant this time to the research objectives, or what is different this time round. This is important if the research is 'repeat research' or the subject has been touched on before (so the audience is familiar with the basic dynamics of decision making or customer satisfaction performance by others in the field, for example). If a study for an oil company has been undertaken, for example, with truck drivers across Europe to gauge their opinion of truck stops, and this has been done before, look for where the changes have been made, the improvements to the provisioning, food or sleeping facilities, or deterioration in service, differences according to region or country. Also, this is especially relevant the first time you research a market category – the learning is new for you but not the client.
- Looked for and reported on what is most significant – this is what an audience is looking for. Go for the jugular!

- Kept it short. Business audiences do not have the luxury to spend long accessing results, but if they do want to see anything in more detail, ensure you have on hand more than you were intending to show on the day. Write up 'hidden' slides or have some pages of quotes to hand out if the audience wants more detail on a particular topic. This is useful if the subject is highly technical or if findings might be surprising or contentious.

- Given enough attention and thought to the implications, recommendations, and suggested strategy/action plan. Remember the client who only has five minutes, or the internal audience that will only read the summary.

- Made links and relationships. In particular, where people are making similar or different points; look for the differences and similarities across those with different experience in terms of role, function, sector or country. Examine what are the key drivers of differences.

- Given sufficient evidence/back-up for your points. Verbatim quotes and anecdotes both provide evidence of the language that respondents use and are illustrative of their attitudes and reactions. They bring data to life in a way that cannot be achieved in other ways, either attributed or unattributed. If separate quotation lists are not provided, quotes should be liberally introduced to any debrief or other form of presentation to the client.

- Made the data pass 'the nose test': does something stand out as unexpected? Not fit with the other results (internal inconsistency)? Think of hypotheses for why such data are unusual. (Is it a segment? Special case?) Where possible, test out with the commissioning client (internal validity).

- Confirmed the validity of the research method and data collection. Look for bias, distortion, issues regarding small samples. For example, if an e-mail staff survey with lots of qualitative open-ended questions has been done, have all employees had equal access to computers to respond (theoretical validity)?

- Checked other known information or other sources: that the information acquired is not at odds with everything else you know or that the client knows (instrumental validity).

While preparing the framework and the presentation, try to think as visually and diagrammatically as possible. The audience is generally composed of people who are clever, short of time, and take in information quickly. Showing diagrams is quicker than lots of text slides, and can express difficult business processes such as decision making, operating processes, market configuration or logistics cycles much more

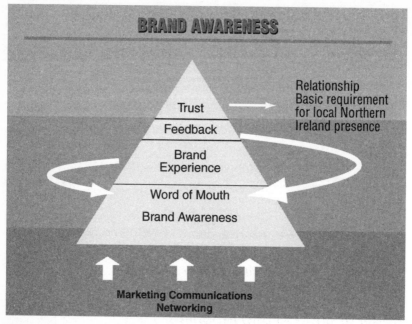

Figure 6.1 *Sample presentation chart: brand awareness*

effectively. Use presentation tricks (as long as they are not too 'cheesy')
– see the examples. Also, consider the best words and phrases to use,
keep in mind the client language, and work out how best to communicate results and/or recommendations.

Figure 6.1 shows the hierarchy for a brand and how the pyramid
was formed with trust as the highest point of the relationship between
brand and consumer; it collapses a great deal of informal spoken information into one graphic that encapsulates the key messages of the
research findings.

Figure 6.2 demonstrates how small business customers can be
divided into different segments or categories according to different
choice drivers (see also Figure 6.3).

The following charts depict some ways to present research results
and strategic recommendations that make use of graphics to illustrate
the points rather than plain text.

Figure 6.3 shows a segmentation result from a qualitative study in a
financial markets research project. Figure 6.4 illustrates how market
perceptions of a premium banking service for small businesses might
be described to clients. The third in the series from this study, Figure 6.5,
indicates to the client what the key ingredients of the service should be
as far as how the potential market sees it.

Choice/decision Making Process

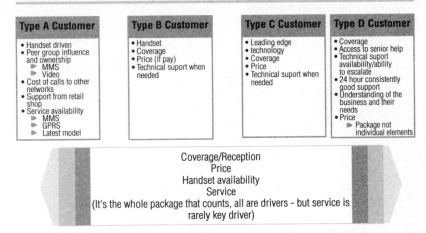

Type A Customer
- Handset driven
- Peer group influence and ownership
  ▶ MMS
  ▶ Video
- Cost of calls to other networks
- Support from retail shop
- Service availability
  ▶ MMS
  ▶ GPRS
  ▶ Latest model

Type B Customer
- Handset
- Coverage
- Price (if pay)
- Technical suport when needed

Type C Customer
- Leading edge
- technology
- Coverage
- Price
- Technical suport when needed

Type D Customer
- Coverage
- Access to senior help
- Technical suport availability/ability to escalate
- 24 hour consistently good support
- Understanding of the business and their needs
- Price
  ▶ Package not individual elements

Coverage/Reception
Price
Handset availability
Service
(It's the whole package that counts, all are drivers - but service is rarely key driver)

Figure 6.2 *Sample presentation chart: segmentation*

Insight in analysis and reporting

A key issue that is more intangible but perhaps more important than the above discussion of the 'nuts and bolts' of analysis and reporting is providing insight to the client. Insight is about spotting ideas, making connections, identifying the factors that make up the drivers of opinion and choices, and seeing implications that others may not have seen. It

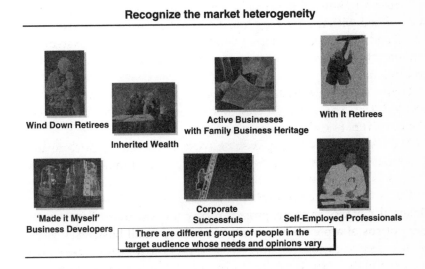

Recognize the market heterogeneity

Wind Down Retirees

Inherited Wealth

Active Businesses with Family Business Heritage

With It Retirees

'Made it Myself' Business Developers

Corporate Successfuls

Self-Employed Professionals

There are different groups of people in the target audience whose needs and opinions vary

Figure 6.3 *Segmentation result from a qualitative study in financial markets research*

Impression of 'premium' business banking

- Among those who have some idea about what this might be...

Knows me and my needs

Personalized

Expertise in services and product

Respects and recognizes my status

Expertise in people, special skills

Overall quality and competitiveness

Professional and responsive

Predictive towards goals and objectives

Best rates and conditions

Proactive not reactive

Service factors are highly valued in the mix

Figure 6.4 *Market perceptions of a premium small businesses banking service*

The ideal relationship with financial service provider

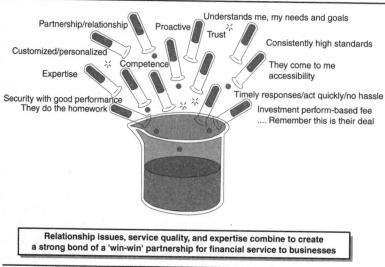

Partnership/relationship

Proactive

Understands me, my needs and goals

Trust

Consistently high standards

Customized/personalized

Competence

Expertise

They come to me accessibility

Security with good performance
They do the homework

Timely responses/act quickly/no hassle

Investment perform-based fee
.... Remember this is their deal

Relationship issues, service quality, and expertise combine to create a strong bond of a 'win-win' partnership for financial service to businesses

Figure 6.5 *Key ingredients of the premium banking service*

pinpoints the essence of the issue, creates the story behind the findings, and enables clients to look forward, predict and make use of research. Perhaps most importantly, it facilitates the processes necessary for the client to take action. Showing clear insight provides a better outcome for the overall research process – from both the client's perspective and the researcher's.

How do we provide companies operating in the B2B world with customer insight and the expertise to communicate it? First, we must be prepared to talk about the importance of customer insight and market research's role in providing the basis for hearing the customer voice. This is particularly important in areas such as the financial sector, utilities, construction and other industries, where customers may not have been as much the driving force as in more marketing-oriented consumer-led organizations. Second, we must become more involved in communicating findings and in broadening our work into the database area so that we too understand better how market research can link with other data and encompass all insight disciplines. Third, we must do more to really think ourselves about what research findings mean and what implications they have; this is the intellectually demanding part of what we do, but ultimately, unless we embrace this ourselves we could find ourselves squeezed out by others with wider database mining and integration skills who have taken a wider perspective.

Indeed, many companies are now considering the 'knowledge' gained by market research and other sources to be something requiring a management plan, and many consider it as a strategic business asset like any other business balance sheet asset (think of Nokia, Nike, Nabisco in the consumer field). To quote Steve Wills of Strategic Research:

> It is being recognized that differentiation will not come by being the cost leader, or developing the best technology. It will come by being the best at understanding the many and varied needs and characteristics of customers, and developing products and services that truly meet those needs. In other words – real, deep, embedded Customer Insight.

CASE STUDY: CUSTOMER INSIGHT

A best practice project on customer insight (both generating and communicating insight) has been sponsored by 12 companies. A number of these operate extensively in the B2B area: ICI Paints, British Gas, Nokia, Standard Life, Royal Bank of Scotland and Vodafone. One of the first early findings of conducting these sessions was that research skills are not enough – research findings can too easily be ignored or 'left on the shelf'. Those leading customer insight teams should also know how to communicate insight findings both via the explicit forms of transfer (reports, IT data transfer) that researchers typically are often good at, and via more tacit forms of transfer that they are sometimes less good at. These include engaging in active dialogue with decision makers and getting stored knowledge into people's heads such that it can be applied and shared.

Steve Wills believes the B2B sectors are lagging behind here, so researchers should make sure that customer insight is not drowned by 'too much data coming from the database, the finance systems, the sales force, and all sorts of other areas in addition to market research'. These all come from disparate parts of the company and research results, particularly in B2B companies, may take a back seat as they are not communicated well or forcibly enough internally.

Reporting requirements of clients

The preferences (and idiosyncrasies) of the client and any practices and principles of the research agency, plus time and resources available, will all influence the kind of reporting that is done. Some companies (for example, GlaxoSmithKline, Bayer, and to some extent American Express) have templates one must work with, as do research agencies (for example, Synovate). Reporting length and format will depend on the level of detail needed. In addition, frequently, qualitative results are not reported in a 'stand alone' manner but form part of a larger debrief that covers all stages of a research project.

Report style can range from an informal run-through of key findings soon after the research is completed – no charts but notes as you go put on a flip chart from what is in your head – to full-blown written reports as well as a PowerPoint presentation. We may even go so far as providing full transcripts with verbatim quotes or web-based reports or CD ROMs with video clips and excerpts illustrative of main themes or messages. However, watch 'PowerPoint-itis' – the tendency to think that nothing can be reported without recourse to charts. There are occasions when other methods may be preferable.

Of course, PowerPoint debriefs with charts and annotations are standard fare. Executive summaries (two pages or so of top-line findings) can be written as a result of a PowerPoint debrief or to summarize a written report. Full-blown written reports are less often now asked for than before, due to the immediacy of the reporting need and decision making, but can be useful especially for those who were not close to the research process, for future employees, and to record the detail needed in some technological B2B work that may be lost in a slide presentation.

One energy client I worked for was undertaking a great deal of research in many locations of the world and across a number of totally unrelated subject areas. It was difficult to keep up with the research output and to know what had been done. For this reason, the 'research snapshot' idea was developed (an idea originally taken from BT) to provide summaries or research snapshots of all research projects in a given format. A research snapshot had to be written up by each agency after every project, and stood as a record of aims, methodology, agency used and major findings. It is somewhat different from an executive summary in that it is written primarily for the market researcher audience rather than for those who will be using and implementing the results. It stands as an independent record of the process followed that can be useful when client teams are changing. An example of such a snapshot is given in Appendix 4.

Web-based reporting is on the increase – if more for quantitative and 'real time' data than qualitative research. It allows many more in a client organization to have access via their intranet to research results that may affect them. Any form of reporting that brings research to business users' computer screens and 'speaks' to them, increases their knowledge, and brings their customer voice to life, must be welcomed. As Leslie Sopp, recent Chairman of AURA (Association of Users of Research), wrote (2004):

> The advent of the internet has significantly shifted the balance of expectation within business to immediate delivery and use of research data. Clients are increasingly using the web as a resource for B2B and some specialist B2C research. Where web-based research is appropriate, results can be delivered much faster now. In the best cases, data feeds can be integrated seamlessly with in-house systems and refreshed on a continuous basis.

The creation of a CD ROM with live fieldwork excerpts is vivid, but feasible only where focus groups have been conducted or where respondents were happy to be videotaped (more questionable in B2B for reasons of confidentiality – more usual in focus groups with tradespeople or 'artisans' than other professional groups). Now, CD ROMs can be made fairly easily by editing software rather than requiring an editing suite.

SUMMARY

Like anything in business, research is a process that has some standard guidelines, and there are a number of practices and hints to draw on that make life significantly easier and more interesting. There are resources to help, but a clear head and some basic planning with a project, method and task timetable always provide a good start. Importantly, it is essential to remember that the research is not the end in itself, merely the vehicle that delivers the solutions that the client requires. This dictum is a good platform for thinking about many different aspects of the research from start to finish. Be prepared to tailor everything professionally in order to meet the client's needs. Qualitative research supplies huge quantities of rich and varied data. The key skill is to be able to both distil the key messages from it and at the same time retain the small details of interest.

7 The B2B research process: III Quantitative research

Many of the issues discussed in the previous section about qualitative research are equally applicable to quantitative research. Earlier discussions on quality of research design, implementation, interviewing and conduct; ethics and the fact that research represents the client; project management issues, and analysis and reporting are also relevant. Chapter 2 on sampling is a key reference. Additional and detailed aspects of quantitative research are dealt with in this section.

THE QUANTITATIVE PROCESS

As indicated earlier, the sequence and issues relevant to quantitative research have much in common with qualitative research. Key differences are, first, the design specification is often more complex (and exacting) than in qualitative research, and second, it is more likely that the researcher will contract out the conduct of the interviews to either an independent fieldwork company or an in-house fieldwork department rather than personally undertake the full number of interviews. Feedback from experienced field teams on design and layout of questionnaires can often be invaluable (and a life-saver to enable more efficient interviewing and to pick up errors). Third, there is an additional phase of preparing for and undertaking data processing (again either with an internal or external supplier) – including post-interviewing coding by the fieldwork group of responses that came from any open questions (more on this later), the researcher's writing of the data processing specifications, and running and checking the data tables themselves. Fourth, there may be additional analysis required (post-weighting of data, statistical techniques such as image mapping, regression and modelling). Fifth, we should note that in data processing, different systems, practices and programs are used in different countries. All these issues apply to B2B research as much as to other forms of quantitative research.

These additional stages hint at the additional time requirements that quantitative research tends to require. A typical process involving the four major stages of first, preparation into field and fieldwork; second, data specs, code frame and statistical analysis; third, data tables; and fourth, reporting, is as follows.

Preparation into field and fieldwork

- Following an initial briefing by the client (a request for proposal (RFP) and/or personal briefing and/or follow-up phone calls), determine the methodology and research design.
- Write a specification in order to request fieldwork quotations from relevant suppliers or the in-house field department. Review these and select a quote.
- Prepare and submit the proposal.
- Confirm suppliers or the field department project approval, likely timelines, booking of field dates, respondent definitions, final research design, quotas and any post-weighting techniques.
- Consult with a statistician on statistical techniques or modelling that may be required (this may affect the design and sample size).
- Draft the questionnaire, including initial screening questions to identify appropriate respondents, categorize into cells and count towards quotas.
- Submit the draft to the client and to suppliers or the field department to check. Review feedback on the draft. (Typically more than one set of changes is made, so keep strong 'version control'.)
- Deal with lists. Agree definitions. Check availability and make an internal request for lists or pursue external sourcing. Ensure format compatibility and usability for the field department, or send the list to the fieldwork supplier.
- Undertake any pre-notification of respondents by the client. Ensure the field team knows how this occurred and who signed any 'pre-warming' communication to possible respondents.

- Send the final questionnaire and any stimulus material, including *showcards*, to client, suppliers and/or the field department, and data processing. (Ensure they know which is *final*.)
- Write briefing notes and brief suppliers and/or the field department on eligibility, quotas, terminology, special issues, and (sometimes) likely responses so that interviewers can correctly code responses.
- Conduct fieldwork.
- Review progress. Where quotas are used, ask for updates. Communicate progress to the client where possible.

Data specs, code frame and statistical analysis

- Draft the data specifications (data specs): banner headings (banners are sample breakdowns for computer tables); tables (including filters and summary charts such as image map data in a summary form); checking of non-precoded numeric questions to determine ranges to be used for the left-hand side of the data table where responses are listed; abbreviations/summary words to be used. Submit to the data processing team and amend as needed.
- Draft the likely code frame for uncoded items (open questions with text responses) or those where 'others' and a written answer is given by the respondent. Check once a sample of responses is available from the fieldwork team.
- Specify in detail any additional modelling (such as correlation, regression, image/brand/perceptual mapping or positioning).
- Notify suppliers of requirements and timing. Deal with queries and any other issues.

Data tables

- Order a trial run of banners on dummy data and check everything including definitions and spelling. Get the brand names correct. Check the layout and order.
- Check the hole count printout (only in some systems).
- Check bases. Match expectations from quotas and field reports. Where filters are applied, check that bases in banners match corresponding bases in the tables (tab/stub).
- Apply weighting, recheck bases, and tables and resubmit to data processing (DP) department for a revised run with additional tables, additional/revised filters, and numeric or categorical re-codes (if any) as now identified.

Reporting

- Provide an interim debrief of key points, if required. Identify key results and themes.
- Draft charts, including selecting the type of graphical presentation and preparing any additional graphics or pictures required.
- Determine the key findings (overall and for key subgroups and so on as determined by the business issue at hand).
- Identify key strategies, action plans and recommendations. This may involve a team meeting. Draft the executive summary.
- Proofread the draft report, and make and check corrections.
- Confirm the personal presentation with the client and check equipment availability and room booking (client). Ensure all presentation materials and any equipment needed are ready: correct files loaded on your laptop, materials, guide, design and data tabulations.
- Amend the presentation and send out or e-mail the final presentation version to the client (and/or give the client a disc). Send the data tables if required.
- If personal debriefs are not required, workshops with the client or some other form of reporting may be discussed. This is not unusual in B2B research.

QUESTIONNAIRE DESIGN

General principles

Aside from sampling, one of the key skill sets when conducting a quantitative project for the B2B researcher is writing the questionnaire. It can be intellectually demanding because of the need to ask questions in as streamlined a way as possible and to cover the technical issues competently. Conversely, although modelling techniques such as conjoint or trade-off analysis are sometimes used in B2B, this is less common than in consumer research (where the larger sample size and longer interviewing time needed for such techniques make them easier).

The normal rules of good questionnaire design apply as always. There are four key things:

- Knowing what questions to ask (translating the research objectives into research questions that can be 'measured').
- Selecting the right language to use.

- Knowing the limitations of the respondents (where their knowledge starts and finishes, so as not to embarrass them, and get the information from the right sources).
- Knowing enough of the detail to compile pre-coded lists that will 'work' and have meaning for the respondent. This is where prior qualitative research comes into its own in revealing appropriate terminology, giving hints as to how questions *can* be asked, and yielding attribute batteries or other itemized lists, particularly when the topic is unfamiliar to the researcher or where the client is not very research savvy.

Tight, structured B2B questionnaires result from tapping into the researcher's knowledge and experience of the subject, client discussions, prior qualitative work (or other research projects the client has on hand), and (possibly) a small pilot conducted prior to the main fieldwork. There is hardly a research survey in B2B that would not benefit from a pilot (see later). Pilots are particularly useful in generating lists of features in NPD research or competitor companies/practices and problem areas for benchmarking research.

With B2B questionnaires it is particularly important to:

- Ensure questions are as clear, defined and simple as possible.
- Keep it short – 40 minutes is rarely exceeded, with 15–20 minutes being typical, only including the 'must have' rather than the 'nice to know' questions.
- Maintain the impetus of the questions by introducing variety (business respondents often have a short attention span) – but not just for its own sake.
- Make questions relevant to the respondent (include skips and re-routing as appropriate to avoid repetition or inappropriateness).
- Avoid overly long lists.
- Frame the questions in a way that assists rather than blocks obtaining respondents' knowledge (for instance, use of 'Approximately how many...?' rather than 'Exactly how many...?').
- Allow the respondent to impart his/her specialist knowledge and give fuller answers (via open-ended questions) where this is going to be helpful and recognizes their contribution.
- Clarify parameters with the respondent (the range he or she can answer about). Ensure that respondents are comfortable in knowing who they are speaking for (so they know if they are expected to be answering for the smaller, or wider, business unit), and clearly define what you want them to answer about. For example, you might need to state clearly that you want the respondent to be talking about *all*

the company's sites or the sites for just the South-East region, in order to reduce confusion and to be able to undertake extrapolation from the figures.

The majority of B2B questions will be pre-coded: that is, possible answers appear on the response list (the interviewer can see these listed). However, open-ended questions can also be asked, which require the interviewer or respondent to write or type in the full answer given. Additionally, it is often good practice to allow for the possibility of recording any additional answers (not already on the pre-coded list). These 'other specify' questions can be particularly useful (and good insurance) in allowing information on more unusual areas to be recorded. Most of us could write a good questionnaire relating to shampoo or fast food restaurants, but if the subject is sales channels for commercial hoses in Eastern Europe or likely uptake of complex share schemes for employees in chemical companies, getting the full range of possible responses right at the outset is more demanding. Answers for open and 'other specify' items are post-coded into categories after interviewing but prior to data analysis.

As will be noted in the examples given later, some questions require a single answer – *single response* – for example, what the respondent's job title is, a brand share figure, tonnage of steel shipped from Korea, or an evaluation on a rating scale. For other questions, as many answers as are relevant can be given – *multiple response* or *record all answers* – for example, listing benefits, drawbacks or reasons. It may be useful to record *first mention* before the other items mentioned, so the analyst knows which was the first benefit (or drawback) that the respondent mentioned – 'top of mind'. Allowing for multiple mentions overcomes any irritation that may occur if business respondents seem to be forced into a corner to give a 'black and white' response when they want to give a 'grey' one. Business respondents are often highly trained and highly analytical, and do not want to be boxed in if they feel possible answers available to them are not quite as they would like.

Diaries are more commonly used in consumer research. However, where it is important to know what people have done rather than ask them to imagine what they might do in a specific situation, it is useful to pre-contact them and ask them to keep track of their activities or responses during a set period. Typically, this is a week. For example, in a study by the Direct Mail Information Service, business respondents were recruited and asked for a week to keep a record of and store all the direct mail that came to the office (including that normally 'filtered' by a secretary), including all flyers, brochures, sales material and advertisements.

Occasionally you can use external sources for information (if individual respondent data from questionnaires can be linked) and combine this with the primary research data acquired (such as company turnover and profit figures), thus reducing the questions asked of each respondent. There is a good chapter with case studies on customer relationship management, data storage, data warehousing, data mining and data marts (department or subject-specific databases that allow information to be accessed more easily) and the relationships between data and research in the Chartered Institute of Marketing (CIM) book *Marketing Research and Information* (Ling and Stuart 2003).

Route map for a B2B questionnaire: design and content

In general, the following principles in questionnaire design apply, as they do in consumer research. Ask spontaneous questions before prompted questions, and deal with the more important issues earlier rather than later, in order to capture key information in case the interview has to be terminated or the respondent tires in any way. But we must ensure that the basic questionnaire logic is not jeopardized.

Usually, B2B questionnaires follow the normal route:

- First, an introduction and screening to check that the person undertaking the questionnaire is the correct one (this is especially important in the case of questionnaires where decision makers are required and in studies employing quotas). Refer to the section on recruiting in the discussion of qualitative research (page 82). Ensure the respondent knows why the research is being undertaken (it is important that B2B respondents understand the rationale and benefit).
- Second, ask some factual questions that will put respondents at ease. (Business respondents do not want to feel their time is being wasted and often like to start off with rational or technical questions where they feel on safe ground.) However, do not add trivial or unnecessary questions just for the sake of easing a respondent into the interview.
- Third, ask rationale, motivation, decision-making and attitude questions (lists/batteries) or 'feelings' questions.
- Fourth, ask any commercially sensitive questions such as views of competitors or other information. These are usually asked when the respondent is feeling more comfortable about the interview. Respondents should not be put under any pressure to answer, and must be given the right to refuse to disclose information if this is their preference.
- Fifth, ask any extensive classification questions (beyond any already asked upfront in the questionnaire or in any earlier screener questionnaire), possibly including some personal information about the respondents as individuals (their attitudes and so on) as well as company information.
- Thank the respondent and close.

113

Types of questions in B2B quantitative studies

In this section, some examples of key types of questions in B2B research are presented in the following order:

- screening and classification questions;
- factual questions;
- attitudinal questions;
- decision making;
- new product development;
- evaluation of quality, customer service, supplier reputation.

Screening and classification questions

As was discussed in the qualitative section, right at the beginning screening questions are vital to 'weed' out people and check eligibility. Only those questions needed for screening and quotas should be at the beginning; the majority will occur at the end of the questionnaire. Common classification questions relate to:

- use of specific services or goods (very broad);
- nature of business (type of business, SIC code);
- size of company (usually asked as number of employees, as approximate annual turnover or both);
- whether the individual is answering for the site, the division, the individual company or the wider group;
- the role of the respondent with respect to the business process/ issue under investigation (decision maker, influencer, authorizer, user or whatever), including his/her title (where this forms part of the required screening);
- location.

The classification questions shown below were asked of SMEs as part of a telephone survey commissioned by Business Link for London undertaken by the business fieldwork agency mruk. The study concerned the tourism needs of businesses – at this time relevant because of new initiatives within London and the bid to become the 2012 Olympic city. Confirmation of the SIC code determined that the business being interviewed was one of four SIC coded sub-sectors that qualified for interview. Note, the variable of Company Size (as measured by employee numbers) was not a screening variable and could have appeared later in the questionnaire.

S.1 Would you confirm that your business is a (**INSERT SIC DESCRIPTION FROM SAMPLE**)?

SIC CODE A	Yes	1	No	2	**CHECK QUOTAS**
SIC CODE B	Yes	1	No	2	**CHECK QUOTAS**
SIC CODE C	Yes	1	No	2	**CHECK QUOTAS**
SIC CODE D	Yes	1	No	2	**CHECK QUOTAS**

Q.X How many employees are at this site, that is (INSERT LOCATION NAME)? Please give an approximate number or range if you do not know exactly. **WRITE IN EXACT NUMBER (_____) AND CIRCLE CODE BELOW FOR APPROPRIATE RANGE OR USE CODES BELOW.**

0	1
1–4	2
5–9	3
10–19	4
20–49	5
50–99	6
100–249	7
250+	8
(DO NOT READ) Don't know / Refused	9

In the case of this interview further classification questions (see below) were asked at the end. It is usual to ask classification questions at the end that are not essential for screening. Also, by the end of a question-naire, trust has normally been established between interviewer and respondent and it is easier to ask some questions that the respondent would be uncomfortable answering earlier on.

In another interview:

Q.Y Finally, we would like to ask two questions to help us put your answers in context. Firstly, please can you tell us your job title? **SINGLE RESPONSE**

IT manager/director	1
Communications manager/director	2
Mobile communications manager/director	3
Technical help desk manager	4
Office manager	5
Sales/marketing director	6
Finance manager/director	7
Managing Director	8
Operations manager	9

Other (WRITE IN) X
Refused V

Q.Z And please could you tell us the annual turnover of your division? **SINGLE RESPONSE**

Range 1 1
Range 2 2
Range 3 3
Range 4 4
(DO NOT READ) Don't Know/Refused 5

Factual questions

These tend to be the crux of the B2B questionnaire. These are common questions in usage and attitude studies, decision making, positioning studies, competitor analysis and new product development. The bulk relates to facts and figures but they can also include evaluations and comparisons. (Remember, respondents are answering on behalf of their company and sometimes, their industry.)

- How big is the market/sector?
- What was the value of the XYZ widgets sent to Germany last financial year?
- When does XXX occur (occasions, time interval)?
- What are the various uses made of current products/services?
- How much of XXX is bought and in what quantity/parcel sizes/ volume?
- How much is spent on YYY? Is there a budget for this allocated at the beginning of your planning period? How are budgets set?
- What companies do you buy TTT from:
  - Currently?
  - Have in the past, but not now? Why have you switched?
  - Would never consider buying from (not on the 'consideration list')? Why not?
- What are the key criteria for purchase?
- What are the key features you want in terms of ZZZ products/ services? Nice to have but not essential?
- What is your experience (performance ratings) of ZZZ products/ services?

Numbers abound. How many, how much, what amount, are all questions that come up a great deal. Sometimes, where percentages are involved, we need to have the interviewer check that the answers add to 100 per cent. For example:

Q.7 Approximately, what percentage of your sales of hi-fi equipment would (**INSERT BRAND NAME**) account for? **WRITE IN AMOUNT (TWO DIGITS). INTERVIEWER PLEASE NOTE – SHOULD ADD UP TO 100%. IF DO NOT ADD TO 100, TELL RESPONDENT WE MAY NEED TO DO SOME ADJUSTING AND ASK RESPONDENT WHICH FIGURE IS MOST LIKELY TO BE OVERSTATED. RESPONDENT TO ADJUST UNTIL HE/SHE FEELS IS RIGHT. READ BACK ANSWERS AS NEEDED.**

NAD   ☐☐
Panasonic   ☐☐
Sanyo   ☐☐
Sony   ☐☐
Other   1 0 0

Behaviours (for example, purchasing habits)

When asking behavioural questions such as those relating to purchase habits, it is often a good idea to format these in a matrix or grid fashion. Typically, this is more logical, faster for interviewers, and saves

Table 7.1 *Purchasing habits*

	Q3a Primary Brands Used	Q3b Other Brands Used	Q3c ALL brands Ever Used	Q3d Last 12mth Purchase Unprompted	Q3e Last 12mth Purchase Prompted	Q3f First time last 12 mths YES NO
Acer	1	1	1	1	1	1 2
Compaq	2	2	2	2	2	1 2
Dell	3	3	3	3	3	1 2
HP/ Hewlett-Packard	4	4	4	4	4	1 2
IBM	5	5	5	5	5	1 2
Sony	6	6	6	6	6	1 2
Toshiba	7	7	7	7	7	1 2
Others (record)	X	X	X	X	X	1 2
....	X	X	X	X	X	1 2
....	X	X	X	X	X	1 2

Table 7.2 *Mobile phones and numeric pre-codes*

Q.R How many of these mobile phones or devices are GPRS-enabled (eg can send and receive e-mails or link to a laptop or PDA)? **READ CATEGORY. SINGLE RESPONSE ONLY**	
11–50	1
51–100	2
101–250	3
251–500	4
501–1,000	5
1001–2,000	6
Over 2,000	7
None	6
DO NOT READ Don't know/Refused	7
Q.T Approximately, how much is the average monthly bill for all mobile phones (including subscription and call charges) in your company?' **READ OUT**	
Under £100	1
£100–£250	2
£251–500	3
£501–1,000	4
£1,001–3,000	5
£3,001–£5,000	6
£5,001–£7,500	7
£7,501–£10,000	8
Over £10,000	9
DO NOT READ Don't know/Refused	x

respondent time also. The following is a series of questions asked of those buying portable PCs for their company see also Table 7.1.

Q.3 I am now going to as you a series of questions specifically about portable PCs.

Q.3a In your organization, which brands of portable PC are the main (or primary) ones currently in use? Any others? **DO NOT PROMPT. CIRCLE ALL MENTIONED.**

Q.3b Are there any other brands of portable PC in use? Any others? **DO NOT PROMPT. CIRCLE ALL MENTIONED.**

Q.3c I am going to read out a number of brands, and could you tell me if these have **ever been used** in your organization? **READ LIST AND CIRCLE ALL MENTIONED.**

Q.3d   Which brands of portable PC have you **purchased** in the last 12 months? **DO NOT PROMPT. CIRCLE ALL MENTIONED.**

Q.3e   Again, I'll read a list of brands, and could you tell me how many portables have you purchased of that brand in the last 12 months? If none or never purchased of that brand, just say 'None'.

Q.3f   **FOR EACH BRAND PURCHASED IN THE LAST 12 MONTHS, ASK** Was this the first time that you had purchased BRAND X portable PCs?

Very often, behavioural questions are pre-coded to make responses much easier. Equally often, ranges are given from which a respondent can choose an answer. This is often quicker for those responding: it puts them less 'on the spot' in terms of having to give exact information which first, they may not have to hand, and second, about which they may not be willing to be too specific. Do not ask too many open-ended questions involving numbers, in particular monetary sums. For example, while the question worded as 'How many of the mobile phones (your company uses) are GPRS enabled?' is somewhat challenging for the respondent, the following examples using numeric pre-codes are less difficult. (See Table 7.2.)

Attitudinal questions

Attitudinal questions are common, especially in studies dealing with corporate/brand image, supplier reputation, product evaluation, customer relationships and staff surveys. They give insight into what people are thinking about a company, its policies, its strategies, its product ranges and service provision. They are not about facts (for example, asking builders how many tiles they buy annually), but about opinions and judgements (their feel as to how well two different suppliers meet their needs). They are particularly useful when performance is being tracked. They are frequently used in tracking research, appearing as attribute batteries or lists with scales (see later discussion) with additional questions that qualify the numbers given – see those asterisked * below.

Typical questions include:

- What is the image of the various corporates/suppliers/products/ brands? (Often a list of image attributes, adjectives or descriptive phrases, is given here – modern, old-fashioned, technically ahead, technically lagging, at the forefront of supply chain management and so on.)
- * How are views arrived at? What is shaping them? Why are those views held?
- * Who is 'best in class', within the sector or even more widely?
- * Who does well and who does less well? Why is this?

Table 7.3   *Bi-polar*

Company A is:								
Innovative	1	2	3	4	5	6	7	Not innovative
Strong financial management	1	2	3	4	5	6	7	Weak financial management
In tune with customer needs	1	2	3	4	5	6	7	Not in tune with customer needs

- * How could improvements be made? (Here such a question is more often open ended or, if closed, with an 'other specify'.)
- * What effect is their experience of the supplier/new product/service having on their predisposition?
- Relative importance of different aspects?
- What is most/least important for the respondent with regards to customer service (or corporate image or whatever the main topic is)?
- * Why is that?

Measurement of these variables is normally using some form of scale:

- Numeric:
  - score out of 100.
- (Full) Ranking:
  - best to worst
  - most appealing to least appealing;
  - first consider, next consider and so on.
- Dichotomous:
  - yes or no;
  - applies or does not apply.
- Semantic scale (or categorical descriptors) on which we put numbers
  - typically a 1–5 (a Likert scale) or 1–10 or 1–7 scale, and we calculate percentage mentions, means, modes and so on:
  - 'strongly disagree' to strongly agree';
  - 'extremely unlikely' to 'extremely likely';
  - 'does not describe at all' to 'describes fully';
  - 'very poor' to 'excellent';
  - 'does not meet expectations'/'well below expectations' to 'exceeds expectations';
  - 'unsatisfactory' to 'excellent'.
- Osgood's semantic differential, where a 7- or 10-point bipolar scale is employed, is less common in B2B questionnaires. For example,

Table 7.4: *Association grids*

With which brands do you associate (**READ ATTRIBUTE A**)?

Attribute	Brand A	Brand B	Brand C	Brand D
A. Innovative thinking	1	2	3	4
B. Strong financial management	1	2	3	4
C. Being in tune with customer needs	1	2	3	4

Think now of the following brands – A, B, C, D and a scale where 1 is 'Does not describe at all' and 5 is 'Describes fully'. To what extent do you associate (**READ ATTRIBUTE A**) with each of the brands? **SEE RESPONSE GRID BELOW. CIRCLE NUMBER. SINGLE RESPONSE ONLY**

Attribute	Brand A	Brand B	Brand C	Brand D
A. Innovative thinking	1 2 3 4 5	1 2 3 4 5	1 2 3 4 5	1 2 3 4 5
B. Strong financial management	1 2 3 4 5	1 2 3 4 5	1 2 3 4 5	1 2 3 4 5
C. In tune with customer needs	1 2 3 4 5	1 2 3 4 5	1 2 3 4 5	1 2 3 4 5

'Please circle one box for each attribute mentioned. Do you consider Company A to be innovative or not innovative (**READ END-POINTS**):'

▪ A rating or association grid is more likely to be used than the above. In this, respondents can choose which statements they associate with different brands. As in consumer research, this is especially useful if a lot of information has to be collected speedily, or where there are lots of companies or brands to be compared. It can be done very simply, as in the first example (Table 7.3), or in a slightly more complex manner, as in the second example (Table 7.4):

When using rating scales, remember to:

▪ Include a midpoint – if possible, use an odd number of points on the scale.
▪ Label the end points so that the respondent has a frame of reference.
▪ Balance the end points so that they represent (as much as possible) the same degree of positive or negative viewpoint – just opposite.

Table 7.5   *Typical NPD Questions*

Q.Da I am now going to read you a description of a new service/
product that is being considered (may or may not name a
sponsoring company). **READ DESCRIPTION OF CONCEPT**.
On a scale of 1–5 where 1 represents 'not at all appealing' and
5 represents 'extremely appealing', how appealing is this new
product or service offering for your company?

Extremely unappealing (or – Not at all appealing)	1
Not appealing	2
Neither	3
Somewhat appealing	4
Extremely appealing	5
DO NOT READ Don't know/Refused	6

Q.Db In the next 12 months, how likely are you to begin using/
purchase the new service/product? **SINGLE RESPONSE**

Extremely likely	1
Somewhat likely	2
Neither	3
Not likely	4
Extremely unlikely	5
DO NOT READ Don't know/Refused	6

(Some follow-up questions)

Q.Dc If you were to use this product/service, would it replace an
existing xxx or would you be more likely to add this to the xxx
the company uses?

■ Being neutral (sitting in the midpoint of the scale) is *not the same as*
Don't know/Refused (so D/K/Ref should not score a 3).

■ Be consistent in use of high scores to represent a good or poor ver-
dict – do not mix (if needed, reverse the scale in data processing).

■ Include a positively skewed scale, however (more positive than
negative points) to increase the ability to discriminate where you
expect generally positive ratings will be given (for example, supplier performance).

■ Consider whether a scale will provide sufficient discrimination in
responses: that is, cluster too much round one point. This is often
either high, 'giving all suppliers a 5 out of 5' or mid-scores, 'employees meet expectations'. A longer or different scale or score out of 10 or
some higher number might be more discriminating. If the list is not
too long, ranking can be a good alternative, for example, 'Please
rank in order of appeal these six possible features of the new alkali
resisting primer paint.'

Decision making

Often, a suite of questions is needed in order to understand the company's decision-making process (relevant for a client in selling or servicing). Here is an example: respondents responsible for the purchase of portable PCs in their company (names supplied by the portable PC client company) from a study by NOP world:

Q.T I'd just like to ask a few questions about the purchase decision making:

i.   How often are portables replaced? How does that compare with the replacement of desktop PCs?
ii. How is the budget for equipment purchase made? Who is involved in this?
iii. Do you have a formal evaluation process of products/suppliers? Who is involved in this?
iv. How important is the role of re-sellers in this decision process? Why is that?
v.   Who (what job functions) is involved in the final decision process?
vi. What sources do you refer to in order to keep up to date with the portables market?

New product development

An example of a questions and scale commonly used in NPD is shown in Table 7.5.

Evaluation of quality, customer service, supplier reputation

In B2B research, many questions concern likelihood to remain loyal/buy again/recommend, as in this question using a simple rating scale: 'How likely are you to renew your contract or carry on using **(INSERT SUPPLIER)**'?

Other questions require evaluation of company or supplier performance along a number of dimensions. These are not dissimilar to the attitudinal questions discussed earlier. In these cases, give the respondent the framework/format for the evaluation, and then go through the items. As much as possible, keep questions together that use the same scale, and don't switch too often. And, again, be consistent in whether high or low scores are 'good'.

In summary, when writing any questionnaire, consider how the data will be analysed. Thinking about this in advance will save time and embarrassment later. Writing B2B questionnaires and administering them is not so very different from other types of questionnaire. Most of

Table 7.6 *Performance evaluation*

Q.E	On a similar scale to the above where '1 represents poor' and '5 represents excellent', how would you rate your supplier's performance on: **READ ITEM AND CIRCLE RATING. REPEAT FOR EACH ITEM ON LIST. ROTATE ITEMS**

i.   Product quality

ii.   Timeliness of invoicing

iii. Knowledge of sales staff etc

Poor	1
Fair	2
Good	3
Very Good	4
Excellent	5
DO NOT READ Don't know/Refused	6

the ground rules apply. But they sometimes do present particular challenges in relation to addressing complex and technical issues, in the need for brevity, and in engaging the busy business person's interest. Writing a good questionnaire on spare part distribution systems, on aviation fuel or on photo-imaging may not appeal to everyone, but it certainly is intellectually satisfying.

DESIGN ISSUES AND PROJECT MANAGEMENT RELEVANT TO PARTICULAR B2B METHODS

Typically, B2B quantitative research is via telephone – often conducted via CATI (computer aided telephone interviewing) – or online. Personal interviews of business respondents are becoming fairly rare events – usually done via CAPI (computer aided personal interviewing) so that results can be captured quickly, and more complex questioning such as conjoint exercises can be conducted more easily.

We now look at different ways to administer questionnaires: self-completion, online and multi-mode, and panels.

Self-completion questionnaires

Many of the guidelines outlined here for questionnaire design and project management when it is the respondent rather than an interviewer filling out all the answers also apply to postal or online surveys (next section). As noted earlier, postal surveys are becoming much less important in B2B research.

Surveys should be accompanied by either a letter or (in the case of the internet as a research vehicle) a good introduction which explains fully the importance of the questionnaire, what it is about, and the sponsor if revealed. It is preferable to address the questionnaire directly using a name (or if not, a title). Response rates will be much lower if there is little personalization: how much of your home mail addressed to 'Dear current occupier' gets looked at? So:

- Explain clearly the survey, how and why the respondent has been chosen, the benefits of the survey to the client sponsor/sector and how that will help the respondent's business.
- Reassure respondents that the questionnaire will not take too long and will be easy to complete. (Both these promises should be adhered to.)
- Give clear instructions as to procedure (beginning and all the way through).
- Give a contact name or number for queries or to check the genuineness of the survey.
- Ensure the respondent of confidentiality (if confidentiality is being promised).
- Give a date by which questionnaires must be filled in and returned that is not too distant in time; if people are given weeks or months for questionnaire return, they can easily get lost or be put to one side.
- Provide the option for respondents to get a feedback summary report of the survey results (if this is being offered). The respondent will need to provide his/her name and contact details in this case (but these details should be kept from the client if results are not attributed).
- Thank the respondent at the end.
- Make return of the questionnaire easy. Provide an internal postbox or stamped addressed envelope if it is a postal questionnaire, or another form of easy-return mechanism.

A self-completion questionnaire on organizational skills, sent to those who were in charge of training in their companies (SMEs in London), was undertaken recently in the UK on behalf of Business Link for London (BL4L) and is shown in Appendix 5. It illustrates how questionnaires with business people can be fairly simple, yet be effective and allow some flexibility in respondents' answers. Business advisers and others distributed the questionnaires to SMEs in order to assess their current training provision and training needs. An incentive of the chance to win up to £5,000 of training for staff or management was offered, and around 1,500 questionnaires were received back from around 5,000 distributed. Consequently, now much better information is available on current training provision in the workplace and where more investment is needed – a fairly simple design that achieved what it set out to do.

Online surveys and technological research solutions

As indicated earlier, B2B internet interviewing is growing, with more research being conducted among internet-savvy companies (such as computer companies, software developers, those providing computer hardware or peripherals, and those who conduct e-business), and especially where e-mail addresses for business respondents are becoming more available and up to date via lists or directories.

Writing online questionnaires that engage the business respondent will be a skill that is ever more in demand. Questionnaire design packages (ConfirmIt is an example) can be used, and this is likely to encourage growth for both surveys conducted by research firms and those managed in-house. For the latter, the researcher's main role may be to give advice (questionnaire design, analysis and data interpretation rather than project management).

Many of the guidelines discussed above apply here. (Note: any product names here are used as examples only, not endorsements.)

- Phase the invitations to take part, as too many invitations to participate at the same time can cause the server to crash.
- Keep questions snappy – no long preambles, though sometimes a more formal approach can pay off.
- Avoid big grid questions where possible, but sometimes this is still the quickest way for respondents to give their answers. Explore what software is available and how it can handle traditional ways of asking questions.
- Remember it is a self-completion questionnaire, so obey the rules for a self-completion: for instance, allow people to say 'Don't know' or to refuse to answer a question.
- Consider using a package like QcWeb that is interactive. It stops people missing questions and routes them based on answers to previous questions.
- If possible, provide a facility for respondents to resume a partly completed survey, particularly when the survey is complex. Respondents

get interrupted, and are often highly mobile. They have short bursts of time and may spare a few minutes finishing off a survey on trains or at airports, particularly where wireless connections are available.

- Check that the language is right, translations correct and unambiguous. Remember there is no one there to explain terms to the respondent.

- Take care in graphically displaying questions and response boxes. When using an online format, how can you allow a respondent to go back and add to an answer already given? (For some questions, maybe you don't want them to.) The response grid with pre-coded answers cannot appear at the same time on the screen for an unprompted (spontaneous) and prompted brand awareness question, for example.

- Show progress through the questionnaire so respondents know they are progressing and how near they are to the end.

- Add an e-mail address that respondents can use to get help if they run into technical problems.

- Generally, don't have more than two open-ended items. Otherwise respondents can feel it is taking too much time. There will always be exceptions to this, but it is a rule of thumb for large-scale online B2B surveys. Smaller more targeted surveys may rely more on open-ended responses. Recent research has shown that when respondents do answer open-ended questions online, they tend to do so more fully than by telephone, but it is a fine line to know how much to ask and when not to overburden.

- Consider offering incentives (especially if the subject is not very involving).

An example of an invitation to undertake an online survey is given in the box.

Dear Sir/Madam,

Please forgive the intrusion of this e-mail. We are currently undertaking an important project looking at the performance of mobile phone networks in the area of technical customer service. Our client wishes to improve its levels of technical customer service, and as a first step realizes that it must consult customers about the service they currently receive.

To ensure that we provide the best possible data to help these improvements to be made, we are asking that the questionnaire is only completed by people who are responsible for dealing with

---

user queries regarding technical aspects of mobile usage (that is, queries that are *not* related to billing or promotional offers or the more everyday aspects of contacting customer service) and able to answer detailed questions in regard to your mobile network provider's performance in this area.

If the above description is appropriate to you, please click on the link below and complete the questionnaire. The survey is in total confidence and lasts around 10 minutes, and is being carried out by an independent market research company, called Jigsaw Research, to ensure objectivity and confidentiality.

http://www.questionnaire-link

If the above description is not appropriate to you, we would be very grateful if you could forward this e-mail to the appropriate person.

Two case studies provide some guidance on best practice in this area.

CASE STUDY: ONLINE STAFF SURVEY

Main messages

1. Accessing the views of the staff can be an invaluable tool to engage them and re-engineer business processes, and using internal e-mail can be a cost-effective means of doing this.
2. Get respondent definitions right – even employees can be unsure as to who qualifies as an 'employee'.
3. Never assume that the quality of the database is good or is exactly what the client expects without double-checking.
4. If a sophisticated survey method is chosen, ensure that all those to be interviewed have appropriate access.

Respondent definition

Staff in the UK, Germany and France of a flight/hotel/other services operator.

Details

In late 2003, a project was undertaken to measure the morale and training needs within a multinational workforce. The client offers services, including flights, hotels and a range of similar offerings, via telephone and the internet. Although the client's workforce was based in several countries, this project focused on the UK, Germany and France (where there was a combined staff base of about 500).

The short story is that it was an amazing success, with a response rate of 47 per cent, all fieldwork conducted within two weeks, and the results delivered on time and to a tight (and modest) budget.

The detailed story exposes a number of potential issues that had to be dealt with and that show some of the limitations as well as the strengths of the online project:

- **Access to the staff:** Not all of the relevant staff were actually employed by the client. Technically, some were employed by third parties through outsourcing arrangements. Although the client could give us e-mail addresses for all its staff, it could not do this for its outsourced people. In order to reach the third-party staff, we provided the outsourcers' IT departments with a sequence of URLs to distribute to their people. We then had to liaise with them in cases where response rates seemed to be atypically low. (In one case the response rate was zero for the first week.) However, if the number of outsourced people had been large (more than 100), this approach could have presented real problems unless the third-party company had relatively sophisticated mail-merge facilities.

- **Quality of e-mail addresses:** You might think that companies have excellent e-mail lists of their own staff. We have found this is very rarely true. The list as supplied tends to have duplicates, errors, and misses some people. All these problems can be sorted out, but when the fieldwork is only supposed to last one or two weeks, the sorting-out process can become quite fraught!

- **Access to the internet:** Although all the relevant staff had access to the internet, not all of them had unlimited access. The agency needed to work with the client's IT department to make sure its screening process would allow the e-mails to reach the staff, and for the staff to reach the survey. In other projects where some staff did not have access to the internet, we had to decide whether to exclude them, provide internet access via a shared machine, or offer a paper version of the survey.

- **Languages:** The survey needed to be offered in three languages, a process that tends to be more expensive online than it does with a traditional modality. In particular, late changes are more expensive and time-consuming to implement. In three of the offices, there was no way of knowing in advance which language a particular member of staff might prefer to use – so flags and all three languages were used on the first page of the survey to allow the staff member to select the preferred option.

- **IT problems:** In a conventional B2C survey most IT problems go unnoticed, negatively contributing a small percentage to the response rate. In B2B, the need to deal with any problems is greater, if bias and dissatisfaction are to be avoided. Respondents with problems will normally contact either the agency or their IT department. This makes it important to have good lines of communication with the client's IT people.

The small number of people being surveyed made this survey relatively straightforward, with the following implications noted:

- Individual problems can be dealt with without creating resource problems.
- Tailored e-mail lists can be provided in awkward-to-reach cases.
- This client did not need to worry about the impact on its network of everybody going online at the same time, but in larger companies it is necessary to stagger the invitations to the survey.
- Problems with the e-mail addresses can be sorted out manually. If the population is large, problems need to be dealt with in a more automated way.

Source: Ray Poynter, Virtual Surveys.

CASE STUDY: WEB-BASED RESEARCH MANAGEMENT TOOL

Main message

Quick and efficient data collection methods can be used to provide ongoing feedback.

Respondent definition

A broad base of business and consumer customers.

Details

For Virgin.net, internet techniques have been vital in tailoring its broadband offering launched in 2002. First, a group of customers (business and consumer) was recruited for three months' broadband trial on condition that they provided back some structured feedback. Surveys were delivered and answers collated over the web using ConfirmIt developed by Future Information Research.

From these surveys, feedback on price points and usage compared with traditional dial-up modems was obtained. Now well after launch owing to that early experimentation, within 48 hours surveys can be designed, run, and results compiled. All Virgin.net's customers are invited to join the surveys (all designed and analysed in-house), which are delivered to those agreeing via pop-ups or via e-mail. Response has increased from 17 per cent with paper-based methods to 72 per cent using online.

The multi-mode approach

Increasingly, we are seeing more 'multi-mode' research, where data is achieved using several collection methods – that is, several response channels are offered to the busy respondent, or from the start, more than one method is put in place where it is obvious that different methods are suited to different respondent categories. While online research has a momentum of its own, it cannot always achieve everything that is wanted, and is not practicable in all locations and with all respondents, even in the business world. Historically, in qualitative work, B2B respondents have been offered telephone or face-to-face interview (with telephone increasingly being preferred), and for quantitative research, a mix of e-mail and telephone interview has operated, as respondents have been more 'e-mail accessible' in some countries than others. Ensuring we can write a survey that is common to all modes is one skill we need to learn, as well as to keep up to date with what technology exists.

John Allison and Chris O'Konis, researchers in Fidelity, a financial services provider, found that a staggering 88 per cent of their customers contacted by CATI agreed to participate in the US web survey they were running. When given a choice, most opted for the web survey option rather than for the telephone.

Some suggestions on how best to operate multi-mode research were given by Tim Macer in the "Research in business integrating MR and technology," supplement to *Research* magazine, March 2004:

> The central challenge of true mixed mode research is to minimise the operational complexity of combining both administered and self completion interviewing across a range of devices and methods and end up with data in the same place and in the same format, ready for analysis.

Tim Macer suggests suppliers (although this may reflect a European perspective) which include, at the time of writing, SPSS with their Dimensions range, Nebu, Askia, Pulse Train's Bellview Fusion, MI Pro and Sphinx.

Multi-mode approaches are likely to increase in B2B research where respondents are mobile, are technology-enabled and like to select their own form of communication channel.

Panels

The build-up of panels depends on good databases – those in business publishing such as Reed and EPSL (as we see in the *BusinessWeek* case study, page 133) are well placed to take advantage of their subscribers, to form panels and to provide research that is topical and up to date to business people. Such publishing-related business panels are likely to be the most usual form of building panel databases. However, panels of business people are beginning to be seen, and these are also found via recruiting for online consumer panels. For example, this is the case in the Ciao panel of business decision makers/IT decision makers who have been found by screener questions asking for details of organizational roles and job title, put to European consumers over 18 years. Although the primary aim was to recruit consumers to a panel, Ciao found that it could at the same time recruit sufficient business people to form a panel. So far, such panels are relatively untested.

Another large new panel of IT professionals is available in the US from Survey Sampling International (SSI), which has expanded its B2B online sample to include new selections for IT professionals, reflecting the increased demand for research in this sector. Its Business-to-Business eSample now includes almost a million IT professionals, and allows researchers to select individuals according to skill sets and hardware and software experience. For example, they can select:

- decision makers and purchasing decision influencers for telecommunications, internet services, computer technology/equipment, and other related fields;
- IT developers, software architects, NT and Oracle administrators, and those familiar with various other named products and systems;
- IT professionals by title.

SSI's website is at www.surveysampling.com. (Source: DRNO News, August 2004.)

The usual drawbacks of the possibility of over-research and respondent fatigue apply doubly to business decision makers and panels, so we should step here with caution. Is the base of respondents sufficiently representative of the population at large? Is there likely to be a bias in those who respond? Some guidelines could help reduce concern: creating a panel by random invitation; randomly selecting a subsample from the main panel to respond to the survey; carefully considering how incentives might affect response rates and who responds, and so on. Panels and online surveys might seem to be made for each other, but business panels present particular challenges, and the robustness of their results over time should be looked at closely before they are embraced with excessive enthusiasm.

CASE STUDY: *BUSINESSWEEK* AND ITS ONLINE READER PANEL

Main message

This is online research via panel methodology coming into its own, greatly facilitated by access to sound subscriber data and a willing public.

Respondent definition

Global subscribers of *BusinessWeek*.

Details

Following the successful launch of panels in the United States and Asia, the business magazine *BusinessWeek* set up a panel of subscribers in Europe called the 'European Advisory Board' with the assistance of the research agency, Skopos. *BusinessWeek* undertakes most of the actual surveying work, with Skopos maintaining the site. The aim in establishing the panels was twofold: to research subscribers and to provide tools for advertisers. The panel methodology provided speedy data collection and good sample sizes.

By combining with other panels, the addition of the European panel allows *BusinessWeek* to conduct global surveys, providing information on its panel members, their lifestyles, their interests and views. Given that all panel members have 'opted in', this enables business publishing to capitalize on its subscriber database and provide added value to both its business customers and those who advertise in *BusinessWeek*.

When this case study was originally reported, the European panel had conducted five surveys. Some of these investigated a particular market place while others were into 'coverage wanted' (where there was demand for more editorial coverage and comment in particular areas).

Source: Research in business, integrating MR and technology, supplement to *Research* magazine, March 2004.

ADMINISTERING QUESTIONNAIRES: FIELDWORK ISSUES

This next section looks at other issues related to making questionnaires 'work': piloting, briefing, different questionnaire formats, and technology-related issues.

Interviewing and project management quality

Getting it right first time is even more important for a business audience, so make sure that interviewers are adept at keeping up the pace and recording responses quickly and efficiently. It is not either easy or advisable to have to phone business respondents back if any mistakes have been made or anything is missed.

Piloting questionnaires

If possible, undertaking a short pilot is always preferable, particularly when a fieldwork agency is to conduct the interviews, or if the interview is to be by telephone or online – which is usually the case. If the 'kinks' can be taken out by the executive director or project manager spending an hour or two personally undertaking a few preliminary interviews, this can eliminate misunderstandings and ambiguity and save a lot of anxiety (and sometimes cost) later on. The main focus is on checking the flow of questions, the ambiguity and comprehensibility of questions, suitability of language, and questionnaire length. A secondary benefit is building on existing pre-coded lists and turning open-ended questions into pre-coded questions with an 'other specify' option – a cheaper alternative with reduced later 'back-coding'. Make sure the questionnaire 'works' for both the interviewer and for the respondent by undertaking between three and ten pilots.

Piloting an international B2B study in the different languages (and 'back translating' to the original language) is especially important. Translators can easily slip up on the more unusual technical terms. When relatively few interviews are being conducted in each language so that each one 'counts' a great deal, checking that terms have been translated properly is vital.

Briefing

A good briefing of the interviewing team achieves a great deal. Some suggestions:

- The researcher should prepare a set of 'interviewing guidelines' in advance that explain the background to the research, the key information outcomes desired, key eligibility requirements, quotas (if in operation), an explanation of technical terms, and any critical or complex skip/jumps.
- Consider adding a glossary (which the client can help to provide) for technical terms and their pronunciation – covering terms either in the questionnaire or likely to be used by the respondents when

answering (chemical reactions, business applications, production processes, discount systems, product classifications and so on).

▪ Where feasible encourage the client to attend the briefing. A good field company will be happy to have the added endorsement of client attendance. It is helpful for clients to give some of the background in detail and explain some of the more recondite technicalities to those who will be interviewing, and to be there to answer questions as they arise. Clients can talk with more knowledge than the researcher about the intricacies of their business – technical terms that are interchangeable, industry bodies or trade associations, competitor names and abbreviations and so forth.

▪ Give the field team access to resources such as product brochures, the client's internet site or competitor sites that may give context and clarification.

▪ Ideally, market research project executives should listen in to a first session of telephone interviewing to check that there are no problems with the interviews and questionnaire, and to be on hand if any early queries arise. This is particularly useful for more unusual or specialist question areas. Again, it is good practice to ask to see the first completed questionnaires coming through, especially in different languages, to check that the interviewers are conducting the interview correctly and are not misunderstanding any of the language or routing.

A sample briefing paper is shown in the box.

Sample field briefings: briefing notes

Telephone interviews were to be conducted across Europe for the Plasticizer Trade Association in Brussels. The study related to the plastics industry, and involved many complex terms and some jargon and abbreviations. The questionnaire was translated into several languages so interviewers who were native language speakers in French, German and Italian were present at the briefing at the Kudos East London Telephone Centre from where the calls would be made and the survey conducted.

To bring it to life, first several clients who were on the Trade Association Task Force came over from France and Germany to be present at the briefing, and show their interest in the process and results, and their own commitment to the study. Second, a screen was set up for the 15 interviewers at the telephone centre so that the internet could be used during the briefing. A glossary of terms was provided and discussed. This, alongside a browse through the sites of the trade association itself and a number of the major players in the

---

industry, gave the interviewers the confidence to know what phthalates were and to talk more knowledgeably about rather out-of-the-way topics such as polyvinyl chloride (PVC) and esters.

A combination of client attendance, pre-prepared interviewer instructions, glossary of technical terms and internet review provided the sort of thorough briefing that encourages interviewers to 'give their all' to the interviews.

SAMPLE FIELD BRIEFING PAPER: INTERVIEWER GUIDELINES

These guidelines were used for a telephone study across Europe with opinion formers on plasticizers, also mentioned in the briefing case study below. Very detailed instructions were given on the background and on the questionnaire itself to help the interviewers get to grips with the subject. Some of the notes used for these written guidelines used in the briefing are given here.

Objectives of the study

The focus of this project is to assess the views of the target audience towards the plasticizer industry, the European Trade Association and, most importantly, how its communications are perceived.

Plasticizers are esters (mainly phthalates) that are generally used in the production of flexible plastic products, predominantly polyvinyl chloride (PVC). They are typically used as 'softeners' and can be found in many everyday items ranging from toys and electrical cables to construction materials and life-saving medical devices.

Important note: Phthalates is pronounced with a silent 'ph' and thus is pronounced 'thalates'.

Sample

In order to conduct this assessment and to further understand future challenges this study is going to look at the opinions of four groupings:

- trade association members (companies producing plasticizers);
- customers (companies using plasticizers);
- legislators/regulators;
- media (trade press).

The questionnaire is broken into four sections:

- understanding of the plasticizers industry;
- understanding and knowledge of the trade association;
- perceptions of the plasticizers industry;
- assessment of the trade association communication portfolio.

Guidance on individual questions

(Note: just a selection of these are given in this case study.)

Q.1 Assessing knowledge of the European plasticizer industry. The question is in two parts and asks firstly about the industry and then products. The provided list should be read out to respondents. Please note that Don't Know should NOT be read out.

Q.5a/b This is the first question addressed to all respondents, so it will be the first question for Customers and Trade Association members. It is an important question, touching on the key issue of safety, as discussed above. Respondents are given a list of factors and this includes the Risk Assessment Report from the Rapporteur. The Rapporteur is responsible for reporting on the safety of phthalates.

Answers should be recorded as First Mention, Spontaneous and then for Q5b prompted for all those not mentioned in Q5a. Respondents should also be probed on anything else that is important to them.

Q.19 and Q.20 Focus on the openness and transparency of the industry. This is a very important issue for the client so attention should be paid to ensure that the respondent understands fully and is giving their most accurate answer. By openness and transparency, we mean that the industry aims to provide Customers and Legislators with relevant, accurate and comprehensive information about the products they produce.

Q.35 This question focuses on whether respondents believe phthalates can be used safely. If the answer is 'yes', but further spontaneous comments are given, these should be recorded at Q36. For example, someone might qualify their response – 'they're generally safe but not for such-and-such a purpose', otherwise respondents go to Q37. If the answer is 'no', reasons should be fully probed at Q36.

Pre-contact

It is relatively rare for business respondents to be at their desk ready and waiting for an interviewer to phone up, and to have half an hour free to undertake an interview immediately. Typically, a respondent will have been approached and checked for eligibility, with an agreement for a later phone call to answer the questionnaire. This means that completed screeners and main questionnaires need to be collected together. Information from all screening questionnaires – including all termination or elimination points (on what criterion do people drop out?) – can be used as vital information for incidence and market sizing.

Respondents may also have been sent in advance a broad list of question headings by e-mail, post or fax to provide them with an idea of what the interview will cover; they are also sometimes sent, in advance, lists of attributes or features, concept descriptions, or other stimulus material or visuals to help save interview time. This earlier despatch to the respondent of information, by whatever channel, must be included in any costing as it can add substantially to the overall fieldwork costs.

Stimulus materials

When interviewing is undertaken by telephone, this reduces the stimulus material that can be shown, although often this is not too much of an issue in B2B research. The advantage of being able to telephone respondents at a time that is mutually convenient at their office or indeed elsewhere, and the less intrusive aspect of a telephone rather than individual face-to-face appointment, can often mean the benefits of telephone interviewing outweigh any drawbacks such as lack of stimulus. The internet – or fax – can be used to send or view documents such as outlines of what the interview is about, or written concepts or visuals.

Requirement for more than one respondent

As mentioned in an earlier discussion, sometimes one individual cannot answer all the questions. If the individual respondent cannot answer, then that part of the questionnaire may need to be skipped over and someone else in the organization contacted who can supply the missing information. While this is somewhat messy, there are times when relying on answers from just one level or category of respondent does not suffice. If the questions are about drugs used in a hospital, for example, a consultant cardiologist might know which drugs he prefers to prescribe and approximately how often he prescribes one rather than another, but it would be the hospital pharmacist who would know the detail of the amounts prescribed and numbers of times. If we ask questions that are too difficult, impossible to answer, or that wander into too sensitive or intrusive areas, we can jeopardize the relationship and have respondents think ill of the sponsor and market research in general. Think of ways around this.

If you decide that you need to interview a number of people in an organization rather than one, you need to think about how you are going to analyse the questionnaires. Usually they are analysed separately, with the answers being grouped under the different respondent job titles (cardiologists versus pharmacists; HR directors versus finance directors and so on). On occasion, you may wish to combine the questions (if different ones were answered by different individuals) into just one questionnaire representing 'the organization'. How the analysis of the differing answers is to be approached must be considered early on in the research process:

- Sometimes, individuals from the same organization have different views on a question.
- An overall 'organization supplied' view may not be viable.
- The implications for data processing need to be identified and clarified.

Response rates

A response rate is the number of adequately completed interviews obtained from a survey, expressed as a percentage of the number of eligible individuals. There are no hard and fast rules for what are good or bad response rates. These will vary by respondent sector and function, by methodology and by all sorts of other factors such as the provision of sample, quality of interviewer approach, explanation for the rationale of the survey, whether the sponsoring client discloses its name, data collection method, length of survey, timeliness and relevance to the individual. If samples are small, maximizing quantitative response is vital. In B2B research anything over 50 per cent is regarded as very good and, nowadays, response rates of just 20–30 per cent may be more typical. If a company undertakes tracking research and finds the response rate is declining year on year, this can be a subject of concern.

Generally in B2B research, clients do reveal that they are the sponsor; this helps response greatly. A high response rate with customers can be interpreted as indicative of good customer relationships, and a poor response as reflecting poor customer relationships – just by itself, response may be a useful measure of 'brand health'. However, a low response from the total sample or from non-customers may also reflect the following:

- what is going on in the environment of the respondent population at the time of the survey (mergers, acquisitions, industry-critical dates);
- research being undertaken at too frequent intervals, with consequent attrition of interest;
- poor sampling or sample sources (the right people not targeted, or inadequate or out-of-date sample sources);
- the subject at hand being of little interest or relevance to respondents, or the survey requiring too much effort from them to make it worthwhile to agree to an interview;
- a lack of transparency in who is commissioning the survey and for what reasons; or suspicion, scepticism or cynicism in the market sector;
- insufficient time allocated to fieldwork, thus not allowing enough call-backs or diary reschedules to occur.

Table 7.7 *Differing response rates are evident by country*

	France	UK	Germany
	%	%	%
2001	17	32	41
2002	23	33	43
2003	26	34	41

Typical response rates also vary across countries, so results should be referenced against that country's norms. This is illustrated by the tracking study undertaken some years ago by Kudos involving N = 2,000 15-minute telephone interviews with business people after 3,000 had been contacted and screened, with similar base sizes in each country (see Table 7.7). Response rates were highest in Germany and lowest in France, with the UK being somewhere in between.

Cultural issues still influence what is likely to be the best methodology: for example, in Japan face-to-face business interviewing is still seen as the most courteous method, although this is weakening with increased time pressures. In Europe and still more so the United States, where personal interviewing entails so much cost, business respondents are more likely to prefer a telephone or e-mail questionnaire. Response rates may be higher using these more indirect interviewing methods. E-mail response is rising in some areas where surveys are kept short and where over-contact is avoided by flagging those who have been interviewed recently so that they are not subjected to too many research requests.

Fieldwork duration

Difficult-to-find samples can mean that samples need adjusting. I have often had to persuade companies (more often those generally new to research) against over-ambitious samples – that, for example, recruiting the CFOs of the top 30 companies in each country is not on the cards. If it is important to achieve 'ambitious' samples – those who are senior or difficult to find – and if the client is not open to negotiation on this, asking for sufficient time to undertake the research is the next gambit. Expecting B2B respondents to be free to undertake an interview when we want to do one is unreasonable. Therefore, we must allow them the courtesy of providing sufficient time for the fieldwork and letting them tell us when they can fit an interview in their diary. The implication of this is that fieldwork can often take longer. The rule of thumb is, the more difficult and senior the sample, the longer should be allowed for fieldwork. This applies more to telephone or face-to-face interviewing. E-mail surveys may be done more quickly, but even here, we must not presume that our interview is top priority and must provide a reasonable time window for participation. Most responses may come in during the first few days, but work commitments may mean that some respondents need to be given more time.

Incentives in quantitative B2B research

Even now in many countries most business respondents are not given incentives for large-scale quantitative research. That is the long and the short of it, and long may it continue. No incentive is better than a poor or inappropriate incentive. The best motivation is where the respondent feels he/she wants to take part because the survey is deemed to be worthwhile. This is a much sounder basis on which to build than the exchange of vouchers or cash gifts.

However, incentives are offered in some circumstances. A feedback report or summary as thanks for participation is the most usual and successful incentive (sent individually if respondents' details are known or re-contact has been allowed, or posted on a website). A successful incentive offer for example by Research Support & Marketing (RSM) dot-surveys following an online survey on current issues and conditions in the research market was unusual in that it offered three forms of incentive – feedback, a charity donation (a £3 donation to one of three charities – ChildLine, Oxfam or the British Red Cross), and a prize draw (all respondents were eligible for three prizes of £25, £50 or £100). RSM wrote a very good letter outlining all these and encouraged recipients (research professionals) to visit its website. In this case, incentives were used to good effect and left the respondents feeling good about RSM, the company sponsoring, and market research in general.

Incentives are not always well handled, however, as the case study below demonstrates.

CASE STUDY: HOW INCENTIVES CAN REBOUND – A PERSONAL STORY

Main message

Reward respondents appropriately and do not make it too hard to 'Pass Go... Collect the £200'.

Respondent definition

Doctors (hospital and primary care physicians) in the UK.

Details

As a thank you for participating in some recent e-mail research, a specialist healthcare research agency sent an electronic award of £10 redeemable against www.globalforce.com to doctors who had filled in the short questionnaire. However, there was a lengthy process to redeem. It went as follows:

- Redeem your reward by clicking on 'Redeem an award' or by contacting customer service by phone.
- Choose the country where you want to redeem your gift certificates.
- Check your balance by entering your award ID number (enter it exactly as it appears on the award: our number was WLYC-XRQ-TAQ-5ZWVCT).
- Choose where you want to shop and complete the order form.
- Click 'Place order' once you are happy with the information you have entered.
- The gift certificates from your selected merchant will be sent to you.

I completed all these processes for my doctor partner who had answered the questionnaire. By the end of it, I was infuriated as it took a long time to do – probably longer than the survey had taken in the first place. This is an example of how the benefit of providing an incentive can be destroyed by placing too lengthy a procedural requirement on the recipient.

Let us hope these electronic redeemable rewards do not become the new fashion. It may have our respondents up in arms (in particular, if they do not have broadband). They may be legitimate if the incentive is large and if the study has been reasonably long to do, but for short surveys or where the incentive is small, they can be counterproductive.

Pre-data entry

It can sometimes be useful to provide an edit spec with additional editing guidance to those in data processing, so that there are clearer instructions. A 'marked up' questionnaire is often used for this, although this was more usual where 'pen and paper' surveys were current rather than computer-enabled surveys where it is more difficult, for instance, for a respondent to be wrongly routed. Report edits can be requested for questionnaires ('records') that fail an edit check – here the business researcher may need to look at questionnaires individually and decide to 'correct' them or to exclude them from the data set. Such tasks are described better in general market research books such as those in the Market Research in Practice series. Here, the main message is that extra care needs to be taken when specifying and checking data of a specialist or technical nature, such as we find in much B2B quantitative research.

Coding

Coding is a process that occurs prior to data entry and data processing. All open-ended questions (and questions that allowed 'others' to be listed) require coding. A 'coding frame' denotes a set of categories into which similar answers are grouped or categorized under a single heading. These grouped responses appear on computer tables as a single entry (with percentage mentions or the like for each). For example, the same code (under the overall heading 'prices') might be given to the following responses: 'competitive prices', 'prices better than the opposition' and 'good relative price'.

Coding can be a lengthy process, but if the sample is small it is not too expensive, and an open-ended question may allow more lateral response than fully pre-coded questions. Open-ended questions coded up can add enormously to the richness of the output, especially when no prior qualitative work has been undertaken. Quotes can be given to the client from the actual questionnaires (with identities removed): then, respondents' opinions or processes can sometimes leap off the page. As a general rule, an open-ended question costs about twice as much as a pre-coded one to process (more if the questionnaire has been translated into many different languages). Nevertheless, in B2B where recruiting the respondent in the first place is the prize, including open-ended questions in the questionnaire can be well worth the extra coding effort. Online questionnaires too can include a certain number of 'other specify' possible responses at the end of the pre-coded lists to allow for more unusual or individual responses to be recorded.

Those coding the results of open-ended questions require particular expertise or guidance from the research team and client if the subject is highly detailed and technical, or if particular research hypotheses are being tested. Again, ideally use specialists.

Data analysis

The terminology for data analysis, practices regarding it, and specific programs (for example Surveycraft, SPSS, Excel, SNAP and Microtab) vary somewhat across countries, but some general principles apply. The two major forms of quantitative output to date are conventional computer tables (cross-tabulations) and multivariate analysis; this latter may involve correlations, regression modelling, cluster analysis, discriminant analysis and image/positioning algorithms.

For most B2B studies, straightforward computer tables are the most common output. Their usefulness and readability (particularly for clients) can be improved by:

- using short form or abbreviations for categories in the banner and responses given ('banner' means the headings on the computer tables – see the Glossary);
- ensuring each table specifies what 'unit' or filter is being discussed (people, shipments, establishments or whatever) as this can vary;
- specifying means, modes, medians or standard errors at the bottom of the tables, such as average number per user or spend per establishment;
- providing a mean number of responses per person, such as that on average, 2.1 brands are mentioned by respondents.

Early liaison with the field team and DP department or individual is essential (refer to the section on quantitative process, page 107), and provision of the table specification while the survey is in field saves time. Thinking about the data analysis at an early stage and in conjunction with developing a report template also helps shape the report. The tab spec gives instructions on how the tables should be set out: in other words what should be:

- The banner specification: those categories or sub-groups in addition to the total sample by which the results are to be examined (for example, small, medium and large establishments (definitions given)) along with the source questions that enable DP to identify these categories. Where sample sizes are known, these should also be given to DP. Guidance on abbreviations to be used is also time-saving. An example of a banner specification is given below.
- Table specification: an outline of which questions should be analysed by which sample breakdowns and what special 'filters' should be used, for example 'Q7 by Banner 1, 2, 3 but only for those who have advertised (Q6)'.

SAMPLE BANNER SPECIFICATION

This is a banner specification for a skills survey with SMEs. (Note that there would have been more than one banner, and TOTAL is repeated for each banner, with 24 columns usually the absolute maximum.)

Each sample breakdown would indicate the question number and the code attached to ensure that the DP staff correctly defined the subgroups required.

TOTAL

Gender
Male
Female

Title
Owner/Proprietor
Director
Manager

Business Type
Manufacturing
Retail
Construction
Tourism
Professional Services
Other Service

Location
Central
East
West
North
South

Size of Business (By Number of Employees)
Under 10
10–50
51–100
101–500
Over 500

Years in Operation
Under 3 years
3 years +

Training Budget
Yes
No

Company Training Plan
Yes
No

Average Number of Days Spent on Training per Employee
0
1–5
6+

Average p.a. Amount Training
0
Less than £200 (but more than 0)
£201–£500
£501–£1,000
£1,001+

% Staff Appraised Annually
0%
Under 50%
50+% employees

Business Plan
Yes
No

Respondent Ethnicity
White
Asian
Black
Other

In the sample banner specification, we see that the sample was broken down into 45 different sample cells that could extend over three pages of computer table breakdowns against each question. The client wanted the breakdown in this degree of detail. It was a large sample, with N = 1,500, respondents so such a detailed breakdown was feasible.

The data on tables from B2B questionnaires can be complex. Ideally, do not get too detailed or over-engineer specifications, but do anticipate needs as this can save time, allow the testing of hypotheses without ordering additional data runs, and be cost-effective in the long run. It is always possible to re-specify to get more depth later – typically, from a first run, already we have far more data than we can use.

An example of a page from the 'deck' of data tables is given in Table 7.8.

Example of banner and stub

The data in Table 7.8 relates to a survey with UK businesses concerning impediments to running their business, what training skills might be needed, and how a supplier of business services might be able to fill the gap in these unmet needs. The data presented here relate to an early survey question, 'What do you see as the main challenges or difficulties that are currently impeding your company's business growth?' It is analysed by business sector (using nine subsectors in all) and by the gender of the owner, as two examples of sample breakdowns that can often reveal interesting differences. The question was unprompted, and responses were post-coded into similar categories according to guidelines set out by the researcher and agreed by the client.

This data table illustrates several aspects of analysis and interpretation. Note:

- This is a multiple response question where respondents can mention more than one issue or problem.
- It is not a prompted question, so no list was presented – all answers are spontaneous.
- Answers are listed (see the first left-hand column) in most to least frequently mentioned (the data bureau will do this as per requested specifications for all relevant survey questions) with similar responses grouped.
- The three pages of responses are shown, though issues are mentioned very infrequently on pages 2 and 3.
- Data are rounded to the nearest whole number (percentage).

A quick look at the headings across the top of the table (the banner) shows how the data were analysed first by the full sample – 'Total Sample' (N = 1,210) – then by a second variable, 'Business Sector' ('Business' N = 496; 'Manufacturing' N = 108, 'Creative' N = 61 and so on) – and further using a third variable, the Gender of the business owner ('Male' N = 534, 'Female' N = 143, 'Mixed' N = 453). This allows researchers and the client the opportunity to determine if the experiences of respondents in the various business sectors differ (potentially there are different forces, pressures and needs in the different industries), and if perceptions or experiences differ according to the gender of the business owner. For clarification, the first sample cell 'Business' under the overall Business Sector variable related to a range of businesses such as those in finance, insurance, import/export and wholesale.

For each response, there are two lines of data. The first line of data shows the *number* of respondents giving that answer in each group (Total or 'Transport' and so on) and the second shows this as a *percentage*

Table 7.8 Sample banner and tab output for a quantitative survey

	Total	Business sector									Gender of ownership			
		Busi-ness	Manufact-uring	Creative	Tourism	Retail	Construct-ion	Tran-sport	Other services	Other	DK/NA	Male	Female	Mixed
Base	1210	496	108	61	77	72	38	28	191	115	24	534	143	453
Funding/finance/access to finance/funding	246 20%	103 21%	18 17%	19 31%	8 10%	12 17%	4 11%	4 14%	46 24%	27 23%	5 21%	95 18%	25 17%	108 24%
Staff (right staff)/right staff for the job/experienced	128 11%	55 11%	8 7%	3 5%	10 13%	4 6%	5 13%	2 7%	25 13%	14 12%	2 8%	58 11%	19 13%	42 9%
Marketing/sales and marketing	86 7%	35 7%	13 12%	3 5%	6 8%	8 11%	2 5%	1 4%	9 5%	7 6%	2 8%	52 10%	11 8%	22 5%
Competition	68 6%	17 3%	15 14%	5 8%	6 8%	8 11%	4 11%	2 7%	7 4%	4 3%	2 8%	33 6%	4 3%	30 7%
Market conditions	57 5%	27 5%	5 5%	3 5%	7 9%	3 4%	- -	2 7%	4 2%	5 4%	1 4%	34 6%	3 2%	19 4%
Skills/skills shortage (un spec)	55 5%	20 4%	10 9%	2 3%	- -	1 1%	4 11%	2 7%	10 5%	6 5%	- -	33 6%	4 3%	16 4%
Staff recruitment	51 4%	21 4%	2 2%	1 2%	6 8%	2 3%	1 3%	- -	14 7%	2 2%	2 8%	18 3%	8 6%	20 4%

Table 7.8 (*Continued*)

	Total	Business sector										Gender of ownership			
		Busi ness	Manufact- uring	Creative	Tourism	Retail	Construct- ion	Tran- sport	Other services	Other	DK/NA	Male	Female	Mixed
Obtaining new clients/ business	51 4%	26 5%	4 4%	4 7%	2 3%	4 6%	3 8%	- -	4 2%	4 3%	- -	24 4%	6 4%	20 4%
More space/ need more space/bigger premises	44 4%	20 4%	2 2%	2 3%	4 5%	4 6%	- -	2 7%	4 2%	6 5%	- -	17 3%	8 6%	15 3%
Economy	43 4%	22 4%	2 2%	1 2%	7 9%	7 10%	- -	- -	3 2%	- -	1 4%	19 4%	- -	24 5%
Managerial skills	42 3%	15 3%	1 1%	4 7%	4 5%	3 4%	4 11%	1 4%	4 2%	6 5%	- -	17 3%	6 4%	17 4%
Time/time management	33 3%	12 2%	2 2%	2 3%	2 3%	4 6%	- -	1 4%	6 3%	2 2%	2 8%	15 3%	5 3%	12 3%
Generating additional sales/new customers	29 2%	14 3%	2 2%	- -	1 1%	1 1%	2 5%	1 4%	7 4%	1 1%	- -	16 3%	4 3%	9 2%
Government legislation/ rules	29 2%	13 3%	1 1%	- -	- -	1 1%	2 5%	1 4%	7 4%	3 3%	1 4%	12 2%	4 3%	10 2%
Premises/ different/ location	28 2%	13 3%	2 2%	1 2%	3 4%	1 1%	- -	1 4%	3 2%	4 3%	- -	8 1%	3 2%	15 3%

Table 7.8 (Continued)

	Total	Business sector										Gender of ownership		
	Total	Busi-ness	Manufact-uring	Creative	Tourism	Retail	Construct-ion	Tran-sport	Other services	Other	DK/NA	Male	Female	Mixed
Clear objectives/ focus needed	27 2%	10 2%	4 4%	1 2%	2 3%	2 3%	2 5%	2 7%	3 2%	- -	1 4%	18 3%	1 1%	8 2%
Retention of staff	22 2%	8 2%	1 1%	- -	2 3%	1 1%	- -	- -	6 3%	3 3%	1 4%	7 1%	3 2%	9 2%
Sales growth	21 2%	11 2%	2 2%	1 2%	- -	3 4%	1 3%	1 4%	1 1%	1 1%	- -	13 2%	2 1%	6 1%
Fundraising (as a charity)	17 1%	12 2%	- -	- -	- -	- -	- -	- -	3 2%	2 2%	- -	1 *	4 3%	8 2%
Regulations (tech)	15 1%	8 2%	2 2%	- -	- -	- -	- -	1 4%	4 2%	- -	- -	11 2%	- -	4 1%
Inadequate government funding/ NHS budget etc/councils	15 1%	5 1%	- -	1 2%	- -	- -	- -	- -	3 2%	6 5%	- -	1 *	6 4%	7 2%
Red tape	15 1%	5 1%	2 2%	- -	1 1%	3 4%	- -	1 4%	2 1%	1 1%	- -	8 1%	5 3%	2 *
Cash flow	14 1%	7 1%	- -	1 2%	2 3%	- -	- -	1 4%	1 1%	1 1%	1 4%	7 1%	1 1%	6 1%

(%) in that group. (Often, this data line is referred to as a 'vertical percentage' because it works on the base (N =) listed at the top of each column or respondent category.) With fairly rare exceptions, it is the percentages that appear in reports.

We can see that across the full sample, 'Funding/Finance/Access to finance' is seen as the most common impediment to growth, with N = 246 respondents mentioning this – representing 20 per cent of the sample. Immediately, we can see that there are some differences in the degree to which this is seen as a problem according to the business sector – those in Manufacturing are slightly less likely to mention this (17 per cent) while those in Creative enterprises are more likely (31 per cent). Normally, a researcher would specify significance tests (not shown here) to the data processing bureau. Any differences across a variable (such as Business Sector or Gender) are calculated and annotated on the data table. These would then be noted and discussed as appropriate in the report.

As skills and the potential for assisting businesses to improve the skills base of their staff were the overall focus of the survey, it is interesting to note that 'Skills or skill shortage' is specifically (spontaneously) mentioned as a significant growth impediment and is the sixth most common answer (5 per cent of mentions overall). This, plus the second most common answer of 'Getting the right staff or experienced staff for the job' (11 per cent), showed there was a market, or at least a need for, the client's training services. This was explored further in other survey questions.

REPORTING

Finally this chapter looks at the output from the quantitative analysis – the analysis and interpretation and reporting via different mechanisms.

Analysis and interpretation

The process itself is no different from any other quantitative study, and the earlier comments on preparing qualitative reports are also valid here. However, for B2B quantitative studies, it is perhaps even more important to streamline the reporting and to always keep the 'big picture' in mind: What are the objectives? What does the client need to find out? What are the key surprising or actionable results? Generally, industrial or commercial-sector clients want insight as well as factual and attitudinal data from quantitative surveys. By contrast, governmental reporting may have more focus on facts and less on interpretation, and specific styles and formats are often needed for organizations associated with the government.

Some hints:

- Confirm with the client what is agreed and wanted in terms of output and by when (including any standard templates to be followed). Written reports are more rarely asked for.
- (Where possible) show the client the blank template (or indicate the structure and layout) you have drawn up for any slide presentation while the study was in field.
- Ensure the information you have to hand is what you need. Specify further information from DP if additional data runs are needed.
- Produce graphs and textual summaries that tell the story, using any tricks of the trade that improve clarity.
- Send output over to the client company's research sponsor ahead of the date of any debrief or final reporting so that he/she can review it and make any changes before exposure to key business audiences.
- Be prepared to do a cut-down version or customized presentation and/or a follow-up presentation to discuss strategy in more detail or via a workshop. Do not try to cram everything into one deliverable; nowadays business clients often choose to have data 'staggered' so that there is a one-page summary for the board and a longer debrief for those closer to the issue.

Reporting formats

While sometimes a quantitative report is 'stand alone' if no prior desk research or qualitative work has been done, more commonly a presentation combining other research is required. Here, particularly, the sheer amount of data can be overwhelming, and it will be important to prioritize the findings in terms of the business objectives that must be addressed. I had a boss who, before any presentation was finalized, would sit us down and say, 'Tell me the story'. This was a good discipline for B2B research as it ensured you had to think about what the key messages were ahead of time. In this situation, showing where the qualitative and quantitative results are saying the same things (or where the quant clarifies the qual), and where there are any differences between the two, is what is needed.

The most usual forms of reporting are:

- written summary and executive report;
- set of computer tables on file, computer disc (CD), or in hard copy (if international and the sample is sufficiently sizeable, there may be different sets of tables for each country as well as one 'Total' set);
- debrief – presentation often using PowerPoint slides or charts prepared via some other form of graphic package.

Other possibilities in terms of B2B quantified reporting include:

- workshops;
- web-based reporting (becoming increasingly usual);
- client feedback reports (sent individually and/or summary posted on the website).

These different reporting issues are now covered in more detail.

Charting tips

By now, you will have a fair idea of the sophistication of your client (in numeric, market research and other terms). As mentioned in the qualitative report section, ask your contacts about their internal audience needs. Also think of those who may be reading the charts after the presentation – ensure that data and implications are clear for all who see them afterwards without the benefit of the researcher's on-the-spot explanation. As always, the key is achieving the right tone. It may not be a good idea to prepare a market research report at the kindergarten level, as the clients to whom we present are more often than not used to digesting large quantities of complex financial information and data for business planning that might make our toes curl. But more often clients are not highly skilled research professionals, and many who are exposed to the report will be non-research professionals. Think about the type of publications they would use as reference material (industry magazines, *Bloomberg News*, *Fortune*, *Forbes*, *BRW*, *Financial Times*, *Wall Street Journal*), and see if you can borrow some presentation ideas.

Some sample output charts are included at the end of the chapter.

Include some introduction or annotation as to how to read charts – this is especially useful for a B2B client audience that does not deal regularly with market research. We tend not to pay enough attention to explaining how to read research data, but it can be done. Add simple explanatory notes about what 'base' means, what are 'top/bottom 2 box' scores (as an aside, an episode of the television series *West Wing* used the term 'top 2 box score' and even discussed 'balance' in framing questions), how a significantly higher or lower figure is annotated in the charts (typically using circles and squares around chart figures), what 95 per cent significance means in practice, how a scale works, how to read and interpret an image/perceptual/positioning map, what a regression technique does and what it shows, how to interpret correlations, or how to interpret findings from multinomial logistic regression.

- Use present tense, not past tense – unlike academic publications, this should be the norm for market research and shows the currency of the information.
- Don't present pages and pages of repetitive graphs. Different elements of the story you are building can be presented simultaneously if this is not overly difficult. Where appropriate, bring variety to the presentation using different sorts of chart – bar charts, pie charts (only for single response questions where responses add to 100 per cent), GANTT charts, trend lines, 'spider' charts, histograms and 'maps'
- Make the title interpretative or actionable rather than descriptive – instead of 'Awareness of products X, Y and Z' use 'Increasing awareness of products X and Y'.
- Include a short word interpretation of the key finding or implication from the data in each main chart. For example: 'Cost controls dominate as the main business priority for those in **non-IT** roles. For **IT** functions, customer service issues are almost as important as cost controls.'
- Include sporadic summing up of key sections in point form to ensure the plot is not lost and the key findings and implications are showing through.
- Incorporate qualitative work or answers to open-ended questions in the body of the presentation, especially where this backs up the theme or 'story' of the presentation.
- Annotate the sample being referred to (the 'base') and its size, for example Car Dealers N = 150. Note that it is a requirement of all market research societies that this information be included.
- Use legends to explain grids or columns, such as red = Importers, blue = Exporters. Maintain consistency and logic (for example, consistently use orange for IT respondents and yellow for Non-IT respondents). As for scales, label scales to show the direction 1 = Least important and 5 = Most important. Clearly label axes. If results are all in the 0 to 50 per cent range, draw the chart with percentages going up to 60 or 70 per cent (but don't vary this too much across charts – try for a happy medium).
- When choosing colours, don't go for brightness and contrast but think about how the colour separation choices (for example, in some charts, you may need five colours for a five-point scale) will print in greyscale for black and white copies and be easily differentiated when reproduced by photocopying. Think about using textures ('hashing') as well as colours to differentiate. When doing trend lines that track more than one product/brand/image item on the same graph, make sure that the lines can be differentiated easily in black and white as well as colour, and on paper as well as on the screen. (Too often dots and dashes are indistinct or the legend cannot be

read.) In business, presentations may often be sent on to others electronically, but not uncommonly they will print off in black and white.

■ Provide deliverables that look good (go for elegant rather than splashy) as well as those that will last. For special reporting, produce shorter reports on glossier paper/card or laminate them, get special sleeves made for computer disks carrying the data, and so on. Label everything clearly and well.

Above all else, once the analysis and interpretation has been done, do step back and check that the main points the commissioning client needs to know are covered in sufficient but not excessive detail – for example, whether to introduce a new application, how the different segments of its customer base are reacting, what likely uptake and penetration will be, what might be the barriers or pitfalls, what market entry strategies seem to be best, how to communicate effectively with the market place, to anticipate and counter what competitors might do or are doing now.

Workshops

Client workshops can also be an especially useful tool to make the most of research, particularly for complex research and where the client has invested a great deal and wants to really understand the implications in order to develop constructive action plans. As much as we try to communicate the research nuggets in the presentation, there is still a lot in our heads, and working together with clients can produce a better strategy overall.

CASE STUDY: CUSTOMER SATISFACTION WORKSHOPS

Main message

Active research, active planning, and demonstrating how workshops can be especially useful where the users of the research are people who are not involved with the process of research, but do need to understand it to implement the findings.

Respondent definition

Customers in Europe who used BP Chemicals products in a manufacturing process.

Details

Some years ago, BP Chemicals undertook annual customer satisfaction studies with customers who used their products in a manufacturing process. Customers were represented in many different user industries around Europe (paint companies, adhesives, cosmetics and so on). Extensive semi-structured interviewing took place in local languages, and as the study continued over some years, some identical questions were asked year on year to allow comparisons over time relating to performance, satisfaction, needs and so on.

Every year, BP Chemicals had an annual get-together with all the key sales staff across Europe. This was a good occasion for the results of the annual survey to be presented and for those present to brainstorm the implications of the findings (in total and relative to their country). This annual meeting meant that the results were used actively by the sales teams. They could see where they were doing well and badly, could compare themselves with up-and-coming competitors, and develop strategies together and collaboratively that would address the issues of note.

Unfortunately, after some years of very useful workshops where the research undertaken underpinned the basis of their implementation plans, the company decided to undertake much of the research in-house. So our visits to Chamonix and Antibes came to an end!

Web-based reporting and client feedback reports

Interactive web-based reporting mechanisms with data and tables for internal client audiences via an intranet are becoming more common, reflecting a growing use of research at the grassroots. At the click of a mouse, local site managers, dealers and others can examine their own results. Web-based reports can be added to a client's website but only where results are for public consumption.

Charting: some examples of quantitative reporting

Below are some examples of typical slides, showing how key issues commonly explored in research can be depicted, and how, in particular, quantitative data can be collapsed down into manageable 'bites'.

Figure 7.1 looks at business attitudes to energy, and demonstrates how a lot of information can be included on one chart by using colour and boxing, with a text summary to highlight the key finding. It can be noted that significant differences between regions are shown with boxes around the relevant data points.

Figure 7.2 demonstrates how, given that all the percentages are under 60 per cent, the percentage scale is up to 60 only and does not go up to 100. (To go to 100 would make the resulting bars much smaller and so lose the impact of the differences between the issues). On the other hand, some argue that it is better always to have a standard axis throughout the presentation, as some readers will sometimes just compare the length of bars.

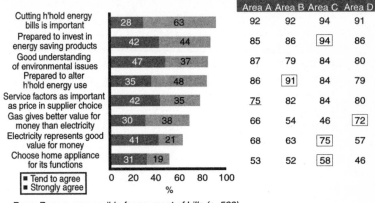

ATTITUDES TOWARDS ENERGY

There is interest in cost saving and some willingness to act to achieve this, possibly under an environmental platform also.

		Area A	Area B	Area C	Area D
Cutting h'hold energy bills is important	28 / 63	92	92	94	91
Prepared to invest in energy saving products	42 / 44	85	86	94	86
Good understanding of environmental issues	47 / 37	87	79	84	80
Prepared to alter h'hold energy use	35 / 48	86	91	84	79
Service factors as important as price in supplier choice	42 / 35	75	82	84	80
Gas gives better value for money than electricity	30 / 38	66	54	46	72
Electricity represents good value for money	41 / 21	68	63	75	57
Choose home appliance for its functions	31 / 19	53	52	58	46

■ Tend to agree
■ Strongly agree

Base: Person responsible for payment of bills (n=523)

Figure 7.1 *Attitudes towards energy segmented by major regions of company operations*

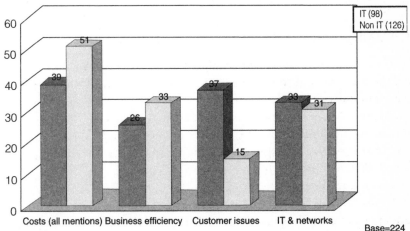

Main Business Priorities – by IT/non IT (Q1)

IT (98)
Non IT (126)

	Costs (all mentions)	Business efficiency	Customer issues	IT & networks
IT	39	26	37	33
Non IT	51	33	15	31

Base=224

Figure 7.2 *Business priorities for the main customer groups*

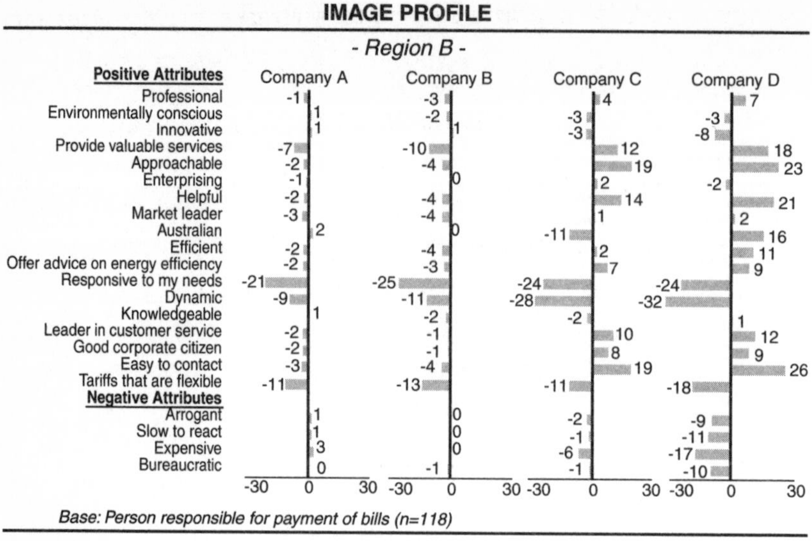

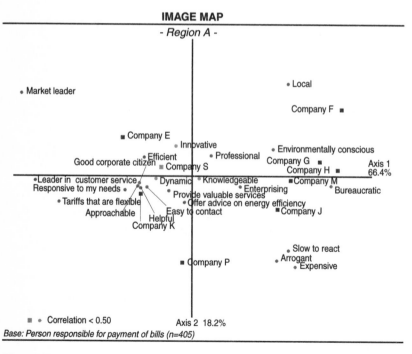

Figure 7.3 *An image profiling example*

Figure 7.4 *An image mapping example*

Figures 7.3 and 7.4 show image profiling and image mapping examples.

SUMMARY

When reporting B2B research, keep your wits about you, think of the 'big picture', and don't get overwhelmed by detail. At all times, keep the objectives firmly in mind and use your skills and experience to meet the specific needs of the assignment – it is all doable.

8 Costing: guidelines on the cost of projects

This chapter looks at what to take into account when asking for quotes from agencies for business to business research, or, if you are an agency, what costs need to be allowed for.

FIRST CONSIDERATIONS

Costing projects 'correctly' is important whichever side of the fence you sit – the client side or the agency side. Typically, costing B2B projects is more difficult than FMCG or B2C costing:

- Consumer research has more predictable and 'standard' pricing. Indeed, many MR and fieldwork agencies have 'rate cards' that can provide quick estimates for interviews with consumers of different demographics at different interview lengths. No such facility is usually available for B2B, although many experienced researchers have a 'rule of thumb'.
- Consumer research has easier to define and find respondent groups – for example, finding N = 200 men aged 34–44 or N = 2,000 nationally representative men and women aged between 21 and 65.
- Typically, incidences are better known or easier to estimate for consumer research.
- Consumer research is less affected by market changes (fewer respondent categories being in over-interviewed markets).

There are some short articles on costing issues, called *Counting the Cost*, in the library section of the AQR (Association of Qualitative Researchers): website www.aqr.org.uk. These may be helpful in qualitative costing, but generally there is no industry standard price for B2B.

COSTING BASICS – FACTORS INFLUENCING COSTS

The biggest issue for B2B is the diversity and range of the universes involved. There are:

- different sectors;
- different functions;
- different levels;
- different sizes of the populations;
- varying levels of difficulty in recruitment;
- issues that must be resolved regarding incentives.

Factors to take into account

What needs to be taken into account when costing out research with business samples? The basic factors, included below, should be a useful guide for agency researchers and those on the client side alike. From the client's perspective, being aware of these issues can guide the development of the brief, or RFP, and may suggest where upfront compromises can be made to the requirements of the research supplier. They can also help to set expectations for the client's internal audience:

- Respondent incidence, for example size of universe, size of sample wanted.
- Respondent definition (complexity of the criteria, the type and number of different categories of respondent).
- Length of interview or session.
- Quotas – several or few; easy or difficult. Note that it is much easier to find people in non-interlocking quotas than for interlocking quotas (that is, where a respondent has to fit the quotas but does not have to conform to a specific combination of the quotas), especially for business interviewing.
- Respondent availability/contactability/resistance or acceptance of research.
- Sample availability, accuracy and format.
- Methodology: preferred approach, for example single or multimode using different data collection methods.

- Location of the work: national, single-city; multi or single country. If it is multi country, which ones? Which languages (there are concomitant translation costs of the questionnaire, of technical language and terms, code frames and open-ended questions)?
- Time frame allowed for fieldwork:
  - If the results are needed in a shorter period, this will require additional staff to interview and reduce the ability to call back those who are unavailable during a specified time frame.
  - If respondents are unavailable during parts of the typical 'interviewing day' when a field team is likely to operate – for example, finding professional bakers at work.
- Techniques being used (or not) that might add cost, such as multivariate or regression analysis or segmentation.
- Subject area: directly relevant to the respondent or more peripheral.
- Scheduling of interviews: appointments, call backs, pre-contact via fax, e-mail or letter prior to any survey.
- Incentives.
- Reporting needs – brief or extensive, including any feedback promised for participants; written report in addition to presentation materials; additional tailored presentations to different parts of the client's company.

Often, a research design comprises interviews with a mix of respondent groups, which entails different interviewing costs across the groups. In all, costs have to be derived for each separate element. For example, obtaining a quote on a sample of $N = 100$ opinion formers comprising 30 legislators, 20 top business leaders, 10 media commentators and 40 key corporate relations directors in major customers across North America is not something anyone can pull out of a hat like a rabbit. Each part of the sample has to be considered in terms of the size of the universe (how many there are) and in terms of difficulty to recruit, for example whether such people are historically pro or anti research, and what is happening in terms of political activity that might make it easier or more problematic.

Depending on the availability of e-mail addresses for the chosen sample, internet research will cost more or less – it is most expensive when addresses are not available or up to date, and least expensive if e-mail addresses are readily available. The internet is not always the optimum interviewing medium. Sometimes we need to persuade clients who are enamoured with the internet to allocate a bigger budget so that other, or additional, approaches more appropriate can be used. The growing problem of spam (unsolicited e-mail), especially in a business context, is a major barrier to undertaking research that has not previously been sanctioned or introduced by the client (owing to an existing relationship with the respondent). Many corporate companies have sophisticated spam filters (or firewalls), and it is unlikely that mail from an unknown research agency will get through.

Implications

Taking the above into consideration, we can note that obtaining quotes for B2B work and preparing a proposal can take longer than for other types of research. In particular, in the case of international work, reference to local agencies is often needed, and this takes additional turn-around time. Clients should take this into consideration in their project planning schedules.

Discussion of some of these issues with the person responsible for the brief (RFP) is recommended. For example, it might be considered how the methodology could be adjusted to maximize response, whether the criteria could be widened to include some less senior people, or whether or not in international work there is some flexibility in the mix of countries to be included. (Some can be twice as expensive as others.) It can be useful, too, to ask if there is a budget limit – clients are usually unwilling to give this, but it can be enormously helpful when trying to design a project that is the 'right' kind of size (remember Goldilocks and the three bears). In particular, for business samples, getting an idea from the client of the incidence of respondents or an estimate of market penetration can be a useful precursor to obtaining costs; for instance, 'the number of actuaries in Germany' or 'the penetration of gas in Swedish businesses'. If a study were being undertaken on gas central heating in Scandinavia, a useful start for obtaining quotes would be to know the current penetration of gas and how many plumbers/central heating engineers might have experience in gas installation.

Many a researcher has had the experience of attempting to discuss issues such as these to help prepare a proposal and associated costing, and the client has been unwilling or unable to help. Indeed, some just want to know how much the project is going to cost. In these circumstances (and where detailed or full information is not available), the best approach is to make, and to clearly list, all assumptions. If the client does not want to get into deep discussion, the most important thing is to understand how he/she is defining the market.

As researchers typically have to collect quotes for some part of the research process from external agencies (or even from a field force that is internal to the research agency), finding out as much as you can before obtaining quotes from others can save a lot of time.

On a per unit (per interview) cost basis, B2B research is more expensive than consumer research. Usually, this is driven far more by the cost of recruitment (and associated incidence) than by other factors. As a guide, face-to-face B2B interviews can cost easily twice as much as B2C interviews. The cost of telephone interviews is affected by how many times it takes for an interviewer to get in contact with a respondent in the first place (four or more calls would not be unusual), and how difficult it is to arrange the interview (and how many call backs, even after an agreement has been made to do the interview, because of changes in the respondent's schedule and other problems).

Cost considerations from the agency side

Normally, a research supplier (an agency) will have to include the following when costing:

- How many executives will be needed, at what levels of experience and seniority. Is any particular expertise required? What is the likely time that will be spent on each stage of the project?
- Has similar work been done before that can act as a 'bridge' or where some elements will already be a 'given' (some of the questions in a questionnaire, for example)?
- How 'difficult' will the client or subject matter be? Is it a very complicated or unknown area that will need extensive familiarization and briefing (of the executive team in charge and those undertaking the fieldwork)?
- How much time will be needed in sourcing suitable B2B recruiters or fieldwork agencies to work with (especially if international) and to obtain cost quotes from them?
- How much time will be needed for project set-up, project management, analysis and reporting?
- What are the recruitment, fieldwork and translation costs?
- Data processing costs (if conducted in house or by external suppliers) and any other analysis costs outside executive costs.
- Other 'out of pocket' costs such as travel, hotels, telephone and other miscellaneous or associated costs (often best presented as an estimate rather than a set fixed amount).

When sourcing external agencies, choosing those who know about B2B research can prevent major project headaches – specialist B2B agencies or departments in agencies, consultants who major on B2B, fieldwork agencies that are, at least in part, dedicated to business research and that have trained interviewers who know how to handle business people. They know more about the characteristics of the market, the quirks of the different sectors, and the ways to maximize recruitment. Specialist agencies in particular fields such as medical recruitment may have relatively higher charges but they bring to the project a knowledge of their specialism and (possibly) databases that can save a great deal of time in the long run. If there is a slight premium to pay for such additional expertise, often it may be worth it to avoid future problems.

CONTAINING PROJECT COSTS

How can costs be reduced? Generally, in terms of B2B by the following:

- Keeping samples as low as practicable, for example not undertaking 500 interviews if 250 will provide 'sufficient' validation.
- Choosing the most cost-effective data collection methods, or mix of methods, to achieve objectives.
- Ensuring the client helps as much as possible with any provision of sample and 'warming' of respondents (for example, an introductory letter, e-mail or fax, where appropriate) – invaluable in B2B research.
- Keeping an eye on travel and other costs, for example can we communicate by videoconferencing, and do the debriefs need to be in Basel and New York?

Sometimes it is legitimate to try to reduce costs. At other times, if research quality is to be jeopardized by this, the researchers should 'stick to their guns' and uphold the proposed research approach, and/or clearly set out the implications of the reduction. In B2B, it is important that quality and professionalism are not put at risk. Often, short cuts are counter-productive.

SUMMARY

The cost of B2B research can be considerable, so it is important to think carefully about potential action plans as a result of the study, where the critical respondent groups are whose views need to be assessed, and sample size. Often, B2B costs are loaded by the 'front end' – the costs of finding the sample, recruiting people, and project set-up. Costing B2B projects is as much an art as a science. The 'art' comes from knowing what has gone before, being creative, having a 'sense' of the market, and the 'science' comes from tight briefs and proposals, methodically gathered assumptions and costing spreadsheets. Both are important if we are to get the costs right and deliver work at an affordable price.

9 Overviews of the business respondent, sectors and research applications

This chapter gives a series of short reviews – of the business respondent, of the different market sectors and of the different research applications.

THE BUSINESS RESPONDENT

They are human, too

Earlier sections have touched upon likely titles and particular characteristics of business respondents – that they are likely to be knowledgeable, businesslike and short of time. Business respondents are not dissimilar to consumers and often will unavoidably wear a 'consumer hat' as well as a business one if the area of exploration is one where they have both business and everyday experience of the product or service. This is worth remembering if some questions about personal interaction with the brand are included as well as business-oriented questions – for example, in mobile phone or PC use. It is less an issue if the interview is talking strictly about manufacturing production systems.

However, the main point to remember is that the individual being interviewed is driven by all the normal considerations and psychology that motivate us all. Understanding the psychology of the business respondent is as important as it is in any form of research (see case study).

CASE STUDY: BRAINSTORMING SESSION WITH PHARMACEUTICAL MARKETING EXECUTIVES

Main message(s)

Pharmaceutical companies needed to rethink the way they were communicating to doctors about their products and services. Prior campaigns focused on doctors as neutral absorbers of facts in their professional role rather than recognizing that they are, in effect, consumers.

Respondent definition

Marketing and research staff of a global pharmaceutical company and research staff of a leading market research company.

Detail

A half-day strategy session was undertaken to discuss the issues affecting the pharmaceutical industry worldwide, and in Australia in particular. The research team did a semi-formal presentation of a range of techniques and models that are commonly applied in consumer research to business issues, and outlined some potential applications in the current and proposed marketing programme of the client company. The client used the brainstorming session to better understand the rationale behind the techniques, their principles, and how the results are interpreted and made actionable in future communication initiative applications.

The main change in thinking was to recognize that, in many cases, doctors could be thought of in largely 'consumer terms', and this meant that the thrust of future research could be altered in order to gain a better understanding of their needs. Traditional techniques of consumer research, for example emotive and rational influences on choice behaviour, barriers and facilitators, brand relationships and brand building, could be placed on the table. The hope was that future brand launches and communications would benefit from this new understanding.

Further evidence of this was given in a paper at the 2004 Market Research Conference in London by Richard Gilmore of Insight International. Entitled 'Doctors eat ice cream, too', it looked at how to engage doctors in exploring what lies behind their motivations and gave parallels with the consumer experience.

Understanding the business respondent

Again, as touched on in earlier chapters, it is common for some information to be collected about respondents as 'individuals' in addition to their role in relation to the business. What are the sorts of information it is useful to collect from the business respondent? The most usual categories are:

- background information (title, responsibilities, years in the role);
- personal details (age, and occasionally education);
- needs;
- perceptions;
- role in decision making;
- current and likely future behaviour (in purchasing, preferred suppliers);
- awareness/experience (of brand, competitors, services).

Also sometimes asked about are:

- attitudes (personal and related to the business);
- disposition (past history/favourability in the future) and preferences;
- brand relationships;
- communication channels and receptiveness (used, preferred);
- business environment, trends.

If detailed attitudinal profiles are needed in addition to more basic demographic data, it is appropriate to give a quick but accurate explanation of why these are needed. This may not always be possible in interviews that have limited time or are being conducted remotely. How this need for attitudinal information is handled is important, as some respondents may consider this type of information to be somewhat 'frivolous'.

Approaching the business respondent

To reiterate, a certain formality in approach may be maintained in acknowledgement of the business person's role and relationship with the sponsoring client – a current customer, a lapsed or potential customer – so conducting the research professionally is important. Make sure respondents enjoy the interview, and do not take up more of their time than necessary. As B2B researchers, we are fortunate to come in contact with so many interesting people in so many diverse occupations; we can learn so much and maintain the profile of research as a discipline. Sometimes we find ourselves in the uniquely privileged position of having a significant tranche of time with people who play a key role in leading business and industry. Let us ensure that they feel it is as worthwhile as we do.

The business respondent is not the only one whose psychology and position should be borne in mind – those who work with him or her are also important. They are often the 'gate keepers' and can sometimes provide helpful additional information.

Finally, be aware of the different culture and background of the respondent. Adopt the niceties in procedure, such as the way business cards are handed out in Asia, the handshake in Europe, the strong accent on keeping to time in the United States, the no-nonsense approach in Australia. Our business respondents are our treasure chest, so we need to be sure to treat them with courtesy and understanding.

OVERVIEW OF SECTORS

It is not possible to do justice to all the many and varied sectors that come under the B2B research umbrella, but here is a brief run-through of the key sectors that employ B2B market research (also see Chapters 1, 10 and 12). Each poses somewhat different challenges, some of which are outlined. All those who have worked in each sector will know about particular idiosyncrasies and ways to overcome or take advantage of them. Despite differences, business research is more similar than dissimilar across the sectors. Some sectors' key characteristics and typical studies within each are given below. These are not comprehensive, but describe some of the more common areas of B2B research for each sector.

Sectors looked at in some detail are:

- IT and telecoms;
- financial services;
- transport;
- manufacturing/industry/chemicals;
- energy companies and utilities (water, electricity, gas, oil);
- professional services;
- pharmaceutical.

IT and telecoms

IT and telecoms share many characteristics:

- They are fast moving. Clients need results quickly, with short and speedy reporting mechanisms, and rarely want full written reports – just the presentation charts.
- Knowledge is quickly out of date so it is necessary to undertake ongoing research in order to maintain the leading edge (client and agency-side).

- Companies in these sectors are committed to truly using research.
- It is often highly technical research, with lots of jargon needed to be absorbed and communicated.
- While both products and services are researched, since the mid-1990s the latter have been even more so, and with the growth of e-business (for example, IBM now generates 50 per cent of sales from services rather than products – *BusinessWeek*, 2 August 2004), 'e-'platforms for just about everything are on the research agenda.
- With global acquisitions occurring in mobile telephony, there are fewer clients but often the footprint of their businesses is larger, so any research is more widespread geographically.
- The PC, laptop, mobile phone, and personal organizer categories are such that there is a lot of overlap between B2B and consumer (sometimes going via SOHO – the small office/home office category on the way). This can present particular challenges in defining a sample, determining where to 'cut off' the eligibility for interview, and sourcing lists.
- Purchasing/decision making can equally be highly centralized or dispersed.
- Clients and respondents are 'at home' with telephone and internet research – research channels that use approaches close to their own ways of doing business. Automated project management tools, web-based questionnaires and web reporting all fit well with their way of doing business.
- Because there are many over-researched respondents in IT roles (in IT/telecoms companies or managing IT/telecoms in other sorts of company), we must take care to interview as widely as possible in the industry so that too much burden is not placed upon the more senior people. As the group is so over-researched, we also need to be aware of the danger of the 'professional' questionnaire answerer.
- An additional feature is that, often, the contract sizes are massive and key customers have an enormous weight. In some areas, there may be such a small customer base that a census is viable.
- Respondents may often be known to each other (which can lead to an interesting group dynamic); they are well aware of the value of their time and expect appropriate compensation, although at times a summary report can be more interesting than a personal incentive.
- Metrics from customer satisfaction studies may be used to reward employee performance, including bonus allocation or a portion thereof (for example, sales teams dealing with operators, wholesalers, retailers).

Typical studies

- Ad hoc/NPD and innovation work.
- Numbers-oriented and competitor-aware tracking of business performance and brand health, customer satisfaction and churn.
- Retail and distribution studies – for example, focus groups with those working in the company in retail roles.
- Competitor analysis and 'watching' (including desk research) to keep an eye on moving markets and innovation.

Financial services

This is also a broad area, encompassing corporate finance, mergers and acquisitions, business banking and insurance, reinsurance, broking and other intermediary services, asset management, and many business-linked financial products and services:

- While more financial resources might be devoted to consumer research, the financial services business market is substantial and does attract detailed research.
- A considerable amount of financial research is undertaken with people in business such as stockbrokers, traders, dealers, venture capitalists, COOs (operations), and finance directors. The role of the intermediary is also critical to many ventures, so intermediaries such as insurance and mortgage brokers, financial planners or IFAs (Independent Financial Advisers) and others are researched. For the small business market, business owners, managers, accountants and financial controllers make up the respondent base.
- This can be highly specialist, so it needs sector knowledge or a willingness to learn the jargon and be comfortable working in non-concrete terms. There are no jars of product on the shelf here.
- More research is commissioned domestically (in country – and often done to a template for global players) rather than internationally although the trend, as in all B2B, is towards international research. The growing significance of global players with companies extending their reach into non-domestic markets influences international thinking: for example, HSBC's acquisitions of Republic Bank and Household International as inroads into the United States.
- A wide variety of research methods are used: face to face (good for highly financially or commercially sensitive interviewing), telephone and internet.
- Ad hoc and continuous tracking, qualitative and quantitative research are done. Some companies in the finance field commissioning research feel more comfortable with (at least some) statistics and hard data.

- This sector tends not to be as fast moving as IT/Telecoms research, though this is changing. Some international markets are 'ahead' of others (in deregulation, technological sophistication and so on), so it is often the case that the same issues, products and services are researched in one country several years prior to another. Very similar research is also undertaken by the major players (again, often at different times).
- There are some sophisticated clients in terms of both marketing and market research active here – for example, American Express, MasterCard, Citibank, HSBC and many others.

Typical studies

- Ad hoc qualitative and small scale quantitative research on reactions to new services and products, for example loans, business credit lines and credit cards, business information services, online services.
- Advertising and communications research; reactions to differing publications material/press advertisements.
- Quantitative brand health and corporate image tracking.
- Segmentation of customers and 'future/current share of spend/ portfolio' studies.
- Customer satisfaction – loyalty, 'likelihood to recommend'.

Transport

This sector covers transport in its widest form – commercial vehicles, freight, distribution, commercial carriers, and transport used solely for business use:

- Automakers and freight companies are large users of all forms of research, if primarily with consumers rather than with business buyers and users. There is, however, a large commercial vehicle manufacturing base and transport infrastructure, including courier companies and farm equipment manufacturers which have undertaken extensive B2B research for many years.
- Substantial research is undertaken in the business field, in particular via specialist transport/automotive research agencies.
- Some transport areas (mainly rail) focus on their domestic market whereas many others, such as aviation, international freight and containers, involve a wider perspective. Much research is undertaken internationally (many companies export and manufacture in numerous countries), so there are international research needs.
- Frequently, purchasing and procurement departments have the final say in which research agencies to use.

- Recent consolidation in the automotive area means increasing issues of brand portfolio management for the leading manufacturers.
- Some marketing and market research-savvy clients are active in this sector, for example DHL, FedEx, and others such as Ford or General Motors (and the Japanese auto makers that are known for their long-term market research planning) that have a foot in the business and consumer camp.

Typical studies

- 'Clinics' for the airline business user with reference to a whole range of issues, for example seat comfort, meal services, check-in procedures, e-ticketing.
- 'Auto/farm equipment clinics' – desired features and optional add-ons; future trends/uptake, branding, drive/ride on sessions for, for example, John Deere tractors.
- Frequent business flyer or frequent user studies (qual/quant), including customer satisfaction and new service development and loyalty programme research.
- Quantitative performance tracking, brand image and competitor perception studies.
- Customer satisfaction regarding commercial vehicles/transport systems; detailed tracking studies for domestic, international couriers/freight and logistics.

Manufacturing/industry/chemicals

In this sector B2B research takes centre stage, as typically little work is done with the ultimate consumer. As indicated in the section on the history of B2B research, these companies were the mainstay of its origins, but are less so now. Characteristics are:

- New product development and Innovation are now more in the limelight than production and manufacturing research issues.
- This is less time pressed than many other sectors (so research can be better paced – often a longer commissioning cycle, also).
- Recently there has been a trend to taking the research 'in house' or using small specialist agencies. For instance, in the chemicals field, Dow, BP Chemicals and many others now undertake much research by using their own research departments rather than buying from outside – but this may be cyclical. The upside is that this is cost-effective; the downside that there is too much introspection and insufficient learning from outside.
- Traditionally, the sector is good at using the information acquired. Those commissioning often have little background in marketing/

market research so often have regarded research more reverentially than some others, and so, oddly, may have used it more.

Typical studies

- Desk research on possible market/export opportunities and distribution options.
- Semi-structured interviews on logistics and optimum processes.
- Quantitative research on service level agreements and quality assurance.
- Combination research to assess market sizing, market penetration for products and so on.
- Customer satisfaction, medium and major clients, regarding logistics, supply and demand, on time and accurate delivery, technical and after sales support and so on.
- Quantitative surveys on staff morale.

Energy companies and utilities (water, electricity, gas, oil)

- While there has traditionally been more emphasis on B2C than B2B, market forces such as deregulation have made historic markets vulnerable to brand switching (and business customers make up a sizeable portion of their customer base).
- Regulators, opinion formers and those influencing government opinion and 'licence to operate' are an additional respondent audience.
- Research nowadays is often international in scope, not just domestic. Most of these companies, with heavy merger and acquisition activity over recent years and deregulation of utility markets, are either predator or prey.
- This sector is increasingly sophisticated in terms of marketing because of competition, with a knock-on effect on the sorts of research wanted.
- There was more emphasis in the past maybe on quantitative than on qualitative work in these sectors, but qualitative work is increasingly being included in the research repertoire.

Typical studies

- Focus groups with tradespeople or with commercial transport users (new fuels, new systems, 'new build').
- Qualitative interviews with stakeholders such as energy analysts/media commentators/NGOs regarding market trends.

■ Quantitative studies on pricing or trade-off studies, competitor perception studies and benchmarking, customer commitment and satisfaction.

Professional services

This includes business firms such as accountants, lawyers, chartered surveyors, trade associations, public relations companies and management consultancies. The sector is characterized by:

■ Growing use of B2B market research, if from a small base.
■ Larger groups tend to be international but much research is still done at national level (with some autonomy for national units).
■ Firms rarely have their own research departments. They tend to like using the big research agencies because of their 'name'/recognition factor when using the research results for publicity.
■ Clients welcome the objectivity of the outside researcher.
■ Note – some ad agencies, PR and management consultancies will commission research on behalf of their clients: Boston Consulting, Accenture, Interbrand, Fleishman-Hillard and many others.

Typical studies

■ In-depth interviews with key clients regarding customer satisfaction; likely reactions to diversification, new services and pricing protocols.
■ Large quantitative studies on image/perception and/or performance assessment (their own and competitor context).
■ E-mail surveys with business clients on current market moves and trends (sometimes for publicity purposes).

Pharmaceutical

■ This is often not strictly classified as 'business to business', but there is much research with health professionals (medical, dental, optometry, pharmacy) and intermediaries (procurement officers and hospital managers). It shares many characteristics with other B2B sectors, but is highly specialized.
■ The emphasis is moving from new products/applications in the pipeline to more market research understanding motivation and decision making in the medical field. In the United States particularly, and increasingly elsewhere, there is more attention to data mining, identifying and understanding market place trends, segmentation studies and estimating ROI (return on investment).

175

- The deregulation of many drugs from Rx (prescription) to OTC (over the counter), including government encouragement of such moves (for example, with plans to introduce lipid-lowering drugs as OTC) has meant a change in direction in the nature of the research, with patients nearly always also included in key pieces of research to establish the full picture. Especially in the United States, there is heavy spend in direct consumer marketing by the pharmaceutical industry. B2B and B2C is often the issue here, not just B2B.
- They are very heavy users of research; pharmaceutical companies are some of the largest spenders.
- Much research, whether consumer or B2B, is undertaken internationally, often with specialist healthcare agencies/medical market research experts or with MR agencies with a devoted medical/pharmaceutical subgroup.
- Preventive medicine and government-sponsored programmes mean that patients are having a growing influence on the medical profession, and any marketing by the pharmaceutical industry generally (for example, Quit Smoking campaigns, obesity), so this is a growing area of research. In B2B terms, the research tends to be on the communications side, involving professionals as well as consumers.

Typical studies

- Historically, in some countries this was a qualitative stronghold (with small universes, critical decision makers, high cost of market entry and failure), although tracking studies are common for long-term 'big drug' programmes, for example for heart disease, cholesterol management, impotence and diabetes.
- Qualitative research with medical practitioners, practice nurses and others on new drug introductions (reactions/barriers) and on communication messages/platforms and preferred channels for communication; consumer health programmes and website information is offered via the GP or primary care physician.
- Studies with representatives on different sales aids/approaches.
- Quantitative surveys (e-mail and other approaches) on trends in therapy areas; quantitative doctor panel press readership and reactions to new medical press advertising campaigns; research on new healthcare systems and delivery.

Other sectors

There are many other sectors engaging in B2B research. Primarily these represent B2B enterprises themselves (construction, engineering and so on) but many tend to think of research only sporadically and do not invest heavily in it. Some sectors such as the media are beginning to use research more and more as the basis for finding out what the business person is interested in, and to use their extensive subscription database as a relatively effortless way of canvassing opinion internationally.

Growth and decline in market research tends to follow growth and decline in the sectors (see Chapter 3). Researchers should maintain awareness of such shifting patterns and help the different sectors learn from each other. Many of the issues addressed (knowledge management, distribution, logistics, innovation and customer relationship management) are shared by the different sectors. One of the advantages of generalist B2B researchers is that they can bring such expertise from researching one sector into others and so help cross-fertilize. This can be helpful for business sectors that may not be very marketing literate, may not have their own in-house research expertise, and may operate in a rather isolated environment.

APPLICATIONS OF MARKET RESEARCH

The final overview section in this chapter looks in more detail at the different sorts of research that address the various business problems and issues motivating research commissioning.

Combining research topics in B2B research

In research topics, it is common for research to address more than one aspect of the marketing mix rather than exclusively focusing on just one issue. For example, questions on brand or corporate image and perceptions might be included in customer satisfaction work, or pricing questions in usage and attitude studies or NPD.

Techniques such as market segmentation are used where companies have a fully fledged segmentation philosophy in their marketing plan, or as a useful diagnostic to help tease out the nuances of how to execute most effectively a product or service launch.

> ### CASE STUDY: SEGMENTATION STUDY OF SMALL AND MEDIUM ENTERPRISES
>
> #### Main message
> Thoughtful and well conducted segmentation analysis can provide extra diagnostics to other research even in a market context that, historically, is regarded as difficult to research.

Method

Quantitative research undertaken with 300 decision makers in firms with between 10 and 150 employees (SMEs) was followed by 20 in-depth interviews, and finally filming of a selection of SME decision makers talking about their experiences dealing with large suppliers.

Detail

The SME market is often overlooked in research terms and targeting is difficult. The purpose of this 2004 study was to develop and implement a segmentation approach that could be routinely applied to this market in the future. SMEs account for 52 per cent of British turnover, and understanding how the SME market in the UK segmented into different types was important.

From the results four key factors; namely, Independence, Involvement, Identification, and Intensity were isolated as the major determinants of SME decision makers' attitudes to their company and its suppliers. The research identified five major segments: 'Dedicated advice seekers', 'Impatient pragmatists', 'Owner controllers', 'Corner defenders' and 'Wary delegators'. A bank of five simple questions determined any decision maker's score on the four 'I's and predicted with 87 per cent certainty which of the five segments he or she fell into. Other clients could use these questions to understand how their customer base divides into these segments, allowing future communication to be more relevant and targeted to the different types of business.

Source: Research International and Ogilvy, 'Are you talking to SME?' 2004.

More rarely, competitor analysis is undertaken as a stand-alone output rather than as an ongoing addition to whatever research is being done. It can be useful to take the measure of the competitor market place when conducting a customer satisfaction or loyalty survey, or when finding out about market sizing or market opportunities. Business direction and trend prediction occur in many surveys. On occasion they are the main focus of the interview, but more often they are added to provide a fuller picture of the research context. Very commonly in B2B research, decision-making processes are also asked, and form the introduction to many a screening or main stage questionnaire. Finally, questions on how companies store and share information and exchange knowledge (knowledge management) are not infrequent additions to B2B interviews today. As B2B respondents are often so short of time, it makes good research sense to combine question areas when one *does* have the opportunity to speak or meet with them in an interview.

A change in emphasis

The trend of the last 50 years in developed nations from manufacture to technology, from production to service industry, with much of the manufacturing output now coming from countries outside Europe and North America, has also had implications for the type of B2B research undertaken.

The historic accent of B2B research on the more functional, production-driven areas of logistics and supply and demand has had to change to embrace these other key variables in today's economy. Importantly, the emphasis on using technology effectively and knowledge management – the acquisition of knowledge and effective sharing of critical information, the ability to communicate most effectively using new communications methods – mean that research topics are very different from what they were in the 1950s and 1960s. This shift in emphasis is likely to continue, and we must ensure that due weight is given to addressing the business issues and problems that emerge, if we are to be able to research effectively the newer ways businesses keep ahead. All affect the main applications of B2B research.

Common research areas

Different B2B research techniques have already been touched on. Here are some that are particularly relevant to certain areas of research, with particular characteristics that tend to favour different research approaches based on the nature of the questions being asked. The following areas are covered:

- new product development and innovation;
- market sizing/market configuration research;
- measurement techniques and models;
- pricing;
- customer satisfaction/customer relations management research;
- advertising and marketing communications research;
- evaluating e-communications and e-interactions;
- corporate image and branding research.

New product development and innovation

The two main motivators for undertaking NPD research are responding to a threat (rival company activity, a demoralized sales force, falling market share or a declining market overall) or seizing a perceived opportunity (identifying an unmet market need or niche, seeking to better manage a product/service portfolio, taking advantage of a potential innovation, responding to – or anticipating – market needs and trends). Typical questions might be:

179

- Where is there a gap in the market?
- How can we bring to market the new product that our R&D department has developed?
- What would be the reactions to our new service application? Who is likely to find it most attractive? What features should it have?
- How can we differentiate it from what is already there?
- What is its USP (unique selling point) and how should we communicate this?

It is critical for organizations to identify new products, services or new applications of existing products or services in order to keep their place in the market and not become dinosaurs. Business books and marketing texts are full of stories of companies that failed to adapt, or grow organically, or did not capitalize on an idea or product. Early testing of new ideas and concepts, maintaining awareness of technological change, market movements and trends are all essential to a prosperous business. Research can play a part in each of these.

The 'normal' framework for research in the NPD cycle is:

- Have an idea; test out the concept; validate that there is a market for it; refine and re-test; launch; review and modify.
- Make a go/no go decision (possibly with some additional disaster check or communications/positioning research).
- Launch.
- Monitor the launch and initial period of product performance; review and modify as needed.

The researcher's skill set is to encourage the creativity in business respondents, and have the ability to spot opportunities/market gaps, for example by understanding the market, listening for latent needs, hearing key words, and recommending turnkey solutions.

First, desk research, internet trawls, competitor analyses via looking at competitors' websites, and sales and marketing material (audits) should be undertaken periodically. This should not just be done by researchers in the company or those who are externally commissioned, but ideally by all those responsible for watching out for changes and innovation.

Second, qualitative research should be a regular part of any company's armoury, allowing the company to maintain a close dialogue with its customers or others such as industry experts to enquire about innovation trends and what others in the market are doing. External B2B researchers who can ask such questions in an objective and unbiased way play a useful role here. Creative brainstorming sessions as well as more traditional qualitative methods can also contribute to uncovering what may be 'latent' requirements.

Qualitative NPD research has a vital early-stage validation role to test out early concepts, ideas or prototypes with business customers – either in tandem with or before consumer (B2C) research. A good example is that gas companies will not want to test out new heating systems for householders without prior testing of the views of the plumbers and fitters responsible for fitting them – since they have already identified the fact that often this group is a gate keeper and decision maker for the householder regarding heating systems. Branding, packaging and price point research is relevant for NPD and over the life cycle of products. A company such as Castrol undertakes considerable ongoing research to update its product look and specification. Such work may involve not just major customers but those such as the truck drivers distributing the larger Castrol cans and barrels who work with the product day to day.

NPD research with internal personnel such as the production engineers, sales force, national accounts managers or customer service advisers can provide many ideas on what might be developed and how this can be best executed. Looking internally for advice and business opportunities, building on the specialist knowledge of those within the company, is a good first step in research. As Jeffrey Peel of Quadriga Consulting said at a recent conference: 'Work with the management teams. Don't only sound out the external perspective, but work with the internal organization to develop superlative brands.'

Third, quantitative research would be used if a major investment is being made in a product or service that is entirely B2B, or strongly B2B-dependent or B2B-orientated. Greater demand for making a firm business case before commencing with the expenditure required by NPD means that more quantitative research is likely to follow any initial qualitative exercise.

Typically, the format of such an NPD research programme might look as shown in Table 9.1, with the B2B element commonly taking much more of a role in the earlier exploratory research stages and then quantitative research sometimes (though not always solely) being more focused on the B2C side.

In NPD (as in market sizing – see the next section), disclosure of client identity is a particularly important issue. Do you disclose who the client is upfront? Is this going to alert others to your interest in the market/product/service/innovation? How much are the estimates of take-up being made influenced by the brand (or company)? Additionally, where questions are asked about competitors, commissioning clients may not always want to 'show their hand'. Sometimes a lower response rate is a price worth paying if a company does not want to reveal its identity or interest too early.

Table 9.1 *Stages and tasks undertaken in a typical NPD programme involving B2B elements*

Research type	Tasks
Desk research	
Secondary sources, including internet trawl	Ongoing eye on innovation in the sector and competitor activity. Some creative brainstorming to help spot market gaps and opportunities.
Qualitative research	
Stage 1: Exploring the new concept	Sketch out market opportunities, broad basis of product features and benefits. Qualitative research with sales force/ internal experts and with 'friendly' customers to determine likely acceptability.
Stage 2: Detailed product research	Possible in-depth interviews with industry experts/analysts. Refine the concept via images, prototypes, mock-ups, and hone down key features and communications platform/s. Gauge reactions and acceptability, prioritize further development efforts on most appealing features, identify positioning and perceived competitive set.
Quantitative research	
	Produce quantitative estimates of demand and take-up, determine market positioning, test out alternative communications propositions.

CASE STUDY: NPD RESEARCH WITH PLUMBERS AND FITTERS AND CONSUMERS IN HOUSEHOLD APPLIANCES

Main messages

Market research conducted early in the NPD process with business users and consumers can prevent costly failure.

A business community may be seen as key to success in a broader market context, thus this requires an understanding of its motivations and likely behaviours as well as the bigger ultimate audience.

Respondent definition

Plumbers and fitters accredited to deal with gas appliances.
Consumer decision makers about household appliances.

Details

In 2000, an energy client was developing a new form of central heating and water heating/boiler system. One European country was chosen for a research pilot to test likely reactions from both plumbers (who install the central heating) and consumers. B2B research and B2C research was undertaken in tandem.

B2B research comprised two-hour focus groups with plumbers and fitters accredited to deal with gas appliances. They were asked what features they would like and what features they felt the consumers would like. Features the *plumbers* would like were:

- thermostatic control;
- central heating;
- water temperature;
- remote access/control;
- telephone control;
- linked to alarm clock.

Plumbers thought *consumers* would like the following:

- information on a display screen;
- the ability to change the time on household appliances (and get them to work, even if remotely);
- programming of other appliances.

However, *consumers* told us that they really did not see the benefit of the last three items. Remote control of other household appliances would be 'nice to have', but basically they did not want to feel overwhelmed by technical wizardry, and the simpler options had more appeal.

Had only the B2B research been conducted, a product might have been designed that would have been 'over-engineered' from the point of view of the ultimate consumer. The plumbers gave useful guidance on what were the features they are looking for (and they frequently are the major advice source for home-owners looking to replace old boilers), but they could not give the whole answer. To develop the 'perfect' new heating system, research with both installers and the ultimate consumer, the householder, was needed.

Market sizing/market configuration research

When B2B was dominated by the industrial sector, market sizing and measurement was one of the major forms of research undertaken. Typically, questions asked are:

- How big might the market for X be in Y region of the world?
- What sort of price could we sell X at in order to achieve critical mass?
- Who are the major competitors? What are their offers in this field?
- How long would it take us to reach a sustainable sales level?
- Where, in which countries and with which type of customer, might there be most opportunity?
- How do we best position ourselves to gain these sales?

Desk research using publications and the internet is often used at the early stage to build up a bank of statistics that give some background to the current market – which the big customers are, which are the big suppliers. Sometimes government statistics or a published report will supply some of the missing information, but not always. Interviewing experts to begin to map out the market is a good place to start as they are often up to date in terms of current trends, if less knowledgeable about details such as tonnage, capacities and specifications. In many cases, primary research with B2B customers themselves is the only way to achieve any reliable evidence of market size, building up from individual information. How much do they buy, from which suppliers, for what uses, at what price? Their responses will help to determine if there appears to be a market for the new product or specification and whether further work is justified.

I have the impression that market sizing and estimation work is less common than it used to be. It used to be a primary source of revenue for large agencies, but now seems to be less so. Is this because markets that are investing a lot in research such as IT/telecoms and hi-tech are in such a fast-moving world that they do not have time to do the background 'due diligence' via research prior to launch? Do they just prefer to launch while there is a window of opportunity and see what happens, rather than risk not being first in market? If this is the case, it is incumbent on us as B2B researchers to provide the validation research offers by speeding up our processes or finding alternative methods of providing speedy feedback.

Quantitative volume forecasting research models are offered by some of the larger market research agencies (in particular in this instance Burke with BASES and Research International with MicroTest sm), that claim to provide accurate estimation of likely market size if the client can provide quality input data on likely distribution, marketing spend and plans. Investment in models of this nature for B2B forecasting is relatively rare as a large budget is required for the research and modelling. Instead, often more modest research is undertaken with smaller samples of existing or potential business customers. Gabor Granger is a tried and tested non-proprietary technique for market forecasting – simply put, 'Will you definitely buy, possibly buy, probably not buy, definitely not buy?' And, for those who do say they will buy, 'How much will you buy and at what frequency?' Although not state of the art in terms of volume forecasting, in B2B where samples might sometimes be small, such estimates are useful in determining a company's future action in terms of launching, or not launching, a new product. Frequency of purchase, which is often less frequent in B2B than in consumer markets, presents an issue, but even so this is a technique which is not infrequently used as it requires smaller samples than conjoint to be robust.

In a sizing survey, questions normally relate not just to present and recent past behaviour (What is being bought now/this month/this year? What has been purchased in the recent past?) but also to future actions. (What is the likely demand for the product next year/in the next three or five years? What is the future buying or the replacement cycle: how often do you need new printers, how often do you update your accountancy software, how frequently do you refurbish your offices, how often are production lines changed, how often do you arrange hospitality trips to reward your sales force?) All this – plus how clients perceive the effect of external factors on their business – helps to determine market uptake.

Some aspects that help in undertaking successful market sizing include:

- Ensure that the sample is reasonably large and accurately represents and reflects the market place. Ideally, a stratified random sample is best.
- Be careful if over-sampling larger establishments or those that are particularly influential in terms of spend that they are accurately represented in the sample frame. Re-weighting may be needed to estimate full market size.
- Check respondent credentials and alert them in advance to the content so that they can prepare to have ready access to data.
- Ask about competitor suppliers – strong and weak points and what makes any 'best in class'.
- Look for factors that affect usage, such as seasonality, order taking, pricing structures, offers, discounts, distribution, back office support and technical support.

- Provide ranges on key numerics (such as purchasing data, respondents' market volume estimates) or allow for maximums and minimums to help the respondent answer (exact figures are rarely needed, ranges are usually fine).
- Ensure that respondents and clients recognize that total accuracy in estimating a market is not possible.

The normal framework for market sizing work includes:

- desk research (public information available about the markets, though often less available than we would like);
- expert interviews (opportunities, issues);
- qualitative and/or quantitative research to determine likely market volume (this is sometimes undertaken simultaneously with a larger consumer sample).

The skill set required includes an ability to find out data from obscure sources; an ability to cross-compare figures from different sources, knowledge of questions and scaling parameters typically used to estimate potential, and the mathematical ability to compare and extrapolate figures.

Pricing

Principles

Typically, pricing investigations are taken in conjunction with other business issues, most commonly when:

- New products, services or applications need to be priced at a level to maximize take-up and profitability.
- The market is shifting – new introductions are causing re-examination of the market (for example, increased use of mobile telephony affecting landline use and the different pricing scenarios to combat defection).
- One company suddenly changing pricing strategy.
- Cost pressures cause a reappraisal of pricing regimes.
- There is restructuring of a division as a profit and loss rather than cost centre. Suddenly, there is the issue of whether people will pay (and how much) for what they previously had been offered free.

Pricing can be a complicated area to explore in the business situation because the issues are rarely as straightforward as 'What would you pay for X or Y?' Frequently, pricing involves basic price regimes as well as (at one end) discounts depending on quantity bought, other products or services purchased, special deals according to occasion or special relationships and so forth, and (at the other extreme) premium charges for add-on services, advanced or special features. Once a purchasing director in a paints company described to me how negotiating with his chemical supplier was 'like an elaborate rain dance'. Doing the research can be intellectually challenging, but it is all the more gratifying to help develop pricing tactics and strategies where even small differences in recommendation can result in success or failure.

When pricing of existing ranges of products is explored, respondents are likely to answer confidently and straightforwardly. By contrast, pricing new products or services is made more difficult by the need to describe the concept, where it might fit, and its details prior to exploring possible price scenarios. Ideally, some early research should be undertaken qualitatively to assess possible pricing ranges before any quantitative work is done. Validating possible pricing protocols via some external research before going to market can save a company's bacon, and internal advice should be listened to from those close to customers such as the sales management.

CASE STUDY: PRICING RESEARCH FOR A GOVERNMENT SERVICE FOR FARMERS

Main message

By undertaking the right kind of research, businesses can pitch and price their services to meet the specific needs and expectations of customers and remain a viable concern.

Respondent definition

UK farmers, including a subgroup of lowland and hill farmers.

Details

Over recent years, the UK government has implemented its policy of floating services that previously had been freely provided and obliging certain divisions or agencies to be financially self-supporting. One of these was a service providing advice on agriculture and livestock to farmers in England, Scotland, Wales and Northern Ireland. No one in this government-run service had had much commercial experience, nor did they know how much could be charged for such an agricultural advisory service.

Hence, surveys to assess pricing elasticity were commissioned. The views of lowland and hill farmers (often less wealthy than their arable colleagues and so more prone to question whether to pay for advice) were sought via focus group discussions, with a broader group of farmers across the land interviewed face to face in a quantitative survey.

The main subject under discussion was the price that farmers might pay for the service and how they might like to do so – by the hour or by the project – and how a price for remote advice versus personal visits might be derived. A fairly straightforward question-naire was developed using the Gabor Granger pricing technique to help develop a pricing strategy (for example: How much would you pay? What amount of advice would you buy? How often?). Ultimately the service was relaunched as a commercial operation with pricing by the hour for advice and by the project for longer engagements. It has flourished as an autonomous self-supporting organization ever since.

Some pricing research is predicated on respondents' reactions to various scenarios. For example, a study was conducted with UK GPs relating to what they would expect to pay for a series of vaccines for those travelling abroad if the UK government decided to make these 'paid for' rather than free government-subsidized items. This necessitated some complex modelling work, presenting the GPs via face-to-face interview with different scenarios to which they were asked to react.

There are simple pricing techniques such as price sensitivity monitor that calculate (across a sample) appropriate price thresholds by assessing maximum, minimum and expected prices (expected because that is what the respondent feels something is worth; minimum because, if priced too cheaply, there are doubts about efficacy or quality, and maximum where this cost becomes so high that the respondent is unlikely to purchase). Modelling is useful where the market is relatively unknown. A slightly more sophisticated approach segments business customers into groups that are more or less price conscious/value-driven or more brand loyal or quality-focused, and so on (using a form of factor analysis on a battery of agree/disagree scales and/or other items). Then it is possible to chart up the differences in price that would be paid by the various segments. However, sometimes business samples are not large enough. At the most complex, a large or more sophisticated study can undertake price modelling using techniques such as brand price trade-off, a form of conjoint analysis. This would be most appropriate for high-ticket items, a risky product entry, where there is fierce competition, or when the business cost of making a wrong decision is high.

Lakshman Krishamurthi (2001) gives a useful review of (first principles) issues, outlining factors affecting the pricing process, a discussion of the concept of 'value', and outlines briefly how a full monitoring pro-gramme can be implemented that measures the effect of pricing changes.

A typical pricing research framework will include:

- Qualitative exploratory work with those purchasing a product to discover price elasticity and acceptable levels.
- Later quantitative work (rarely on its own in B2B but more often combined with other usage and attitude information) testing out the most acceptable prices or pricing packages.

Skills needed are qualitatively, an ability to talk turkey on numbers in a way that does not frighten the respondent; and quantitatively, a facil-ity with manipulating numbers and extrapolating figures and an abil-ity to undertake different configurations depending on sometimes complex scenarios.

Reporting techniques for pricing research

Normally, reporting will give ranges of prices with the average price acceptable for the general sample. Different average prices might be in evidence from 'customers' versus 'potential customers', or across seg-ments (as described above). Figure 9.1 shows how pricing scenarios were displayed for one survey.

Customer satisfaction/customer relations management (CRM) research

Principles

This is one of the major types of B2B research carried out by clients, both those in purely B2B organizations and also companies like multi-national consumer goods manufacturers which need to know what the purchasing directors in retail chains think of the service they are receiv-ing. CRM research is an important part of corporate health assessment. Over the last two decades, the interest in CRM has grown due to the:

- recognition of the role of relationships in developing business;
- use of balanced score sheets and other forms of performance track-ing where customer satisfaction results are one of the key perfor-mance indicators (KPIs);
- linking of bonuses and management reward systems to customer satisfaction scores.

Typically, the sponsoring client is revealed upfront (ensuring a higher response rate and data that reflect the true 'context') and often the respondents (usually customers but sometimes lapsed customers or

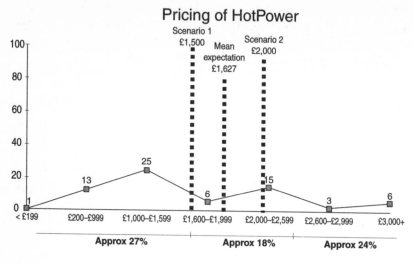

Figure 9.1 *Pricing scenarios for energy*

potential customers) are asked whether they are willing for their answers to be passed back in attributed form. Many business clients are happy to agree to this as often they want their views to be heard, and there may be particular issues raised in interview that they would be happy to see addressed as a result.

Qualitative research with business audiences is usually with a select number of (often) key players such as the principal buyers or equivalents of 'national accounts' via in-depth interviews using a topic guide. Qualitative work can serve three purposes. First, it can flag up changing needs and expectations from clients and allow the client to keep abreast of new requirements and unmet needs. Second, it can act as a 'dipstick' to show the relationship between perceived performance and satisfaction. Third, it can ensure that what is being monitored via quantitative research is still valid. (For example, should the ability of call centre staff outsourced to a foreign country to understand English and to understand the nuances of a customer query or complaint, be new attributes that should be added?)

CASE STUDY: USING MARKET RESEARCH TO SUPPORT A BUSINESS CASE – RE-TENDERING FOR A GOVERNMENT CONTRACT

Main messages

Information on performance and customer satisfaction can significantly contribute to future business strategies.

Disraeli's 'lies, dammed lies, and statistics' did not apply in this case – the numbers spoke for themselves, and the tender was won.

Respondent definition

Business subscribers and registrants to the TPS and FPS ('do not call') services in the UK.

Details

The Telephone Preference Service (TPS) and the Fax Preference Service (FPS) are the central 'opt-out'/'do not call' services required by the Telecommunications (Data Protection and Privacy) Regulation 1999, whereby it is unlawful to make unsolicited sales and marketing telephone calls to any number registered with the TPS or FPS. The incumbent manager of these services was Telephone Preference Service Ltd (TPS Ltd), a subsidiary of the Direct Marketing Association.

In 2003, with a year to go before re-tendering for the government contract to manage the services, TPS Ltd wanted an independent assessment of its performance from its customers (registrants and business subscribers) in order to include this in its re-tender bid. NOP was commissioned to do the research.

Subscriber research

As this service was the sole source of income for TPS Ltd, subscribers' views were particularly important. Many of the 280-odd customers who pay to receive the 'no call' data files are marketing or market research companies and computer bureaux. Direct marketing is highly competitive, and NOP World felt there might be some resistance to open and honest discussion about possibly competitive activity. The sample was extremely regionally dispersed. Additionally, the subject matter required a considered and individual reaction.

Hence, qualitative research, and specifically in-depth interviews rather than focus groups, was proposed for subscribers. NOP conducted N = 21 one-hour interviews with two different types of subscriber: key decision makers (who decide whether or not to subscribe to TPS services), and technical administrators (who use the data on a day-to-day basis). Interviews were conducted across London, the South East and the Midlands at the respondent's place of business.

Specific research objectives for subscribers included exploring views of the methods by which the files can be received, rating the service, the pricing structure and whether subscribers would prefer the Direct Mailing Association (via TPS Ltd) or a commercial company to manage the services.

The results showed that TPS Ltd was providing a high-quality service that was considered fast and efficient, and helped to keep their end-customers happy, as well as ensuring that their own companies were complying with the law. (A typical subscriber comment: 'To be honest, we just wish other things that we had to do were as hassle free. It's an example of something that has been set up to fulfil a need that works.')

Over the past year the results have been incorporated into TPS Ltd's tender, have informed lobbying efforts on telemarketing issues, and helped to improve communications with subscribers.

Registrant research

A quantitative survey of registrants was also undertaken. TPS Ltd incorporated into its tender document the high satisfaction rates recorded by those who had registered with the service, as well as the fact that consumers' expectations of registering with the services had been met.

The findings were so positive that there was no requirement by the government for any radical service changes. However, as a result of subscribers' comments, a regular e-mail newsletter is now sent to subscribers informing them of legislation and updates.

The result? TPS Ltd won its re-tender bid.

Source: Marketing Research Awards, July 2004. NOP World won a Commendation in the 'Business and Professional' category for this entry.

As with qualitative research, quantitative customer satisfaction research assesses the whole 'service experience' across all those major interfaces/areas/dimensions the company has with a customer (products and services, accounts/billing, company staff, ordering and delivery, company communications, marketing and advertising and so on) and then on key sub-elements of each of the major dimensions – drilling down, for example, on completeness and timeliness of delivery. The difference is that there is much more detail and numeric scores are obtained. Typically, company image data are also collected, as well as competitive set analysis and 'best in class' or best practice, generally regardless of category in which the company operates. This is a growing trend. Overall scores on excellence, quality, some loyalty or commitment measures, and likelihood to 'remain a customer' or 'to recommend' are also key items. Examples of some simple quantitative customer satisfaction questions are shown in Appendix 6.

Customer satisfaction measurement techniques and models

Customer satisfaction research is one area where research companies and consultancies have developed proprietary models and techniques, so the content and approach will vary. Some customization of proprietary models is undertaken to accurately reflect details of the industry or company, but the basic framework of the particular model is retained at all times. Some market research companies use statistical modelling techniques to determine the key drivers of customer satisfaction. By applying regression (indirectly assessing the relative 'importance' of the various performance factors) or other techniques, those key areas/dimensions that can be leveraged in order to produce changes (improvements) in a company's scores are identified. Other approaches directly ask respondents the importance of factors in a simplistic way using traditional rating scales. Some models specifically include direct performance comparisons with competitors as a standard way of gathering performance indicators. Others set up measurements so as to be able to compare current service provided against desired levels of service (gap analysis).

For some CRM (Customer Relationship Management) models with sufficient depth and history of studies, norms are available so that clients can compare (or benchmark) their performance with an 'industry or category average' (banking or pharmaceuticals as broad categories, or insurance as a more specific field). One of the most commonly asked questions from clients is 'My score on this is 60 per cent – how good/poor is that?' The provision of norms goes a long way to addressing this information need.

Of course, using a CRM model in the research process is only possible where samples are sufficiently large and clients have budgets that allow either a detailed one-shot strategic analysis of the health of the business or – more commonly, where investment in detailed models is concerned – a larger strategic study and then tracking over time to determine whether the changes in company practices have been successful in producing the desired outcomes. After all, there is no real point in undertaking a major investment of this type, making changes in company practices and then not checking to see if they are working. (Of course, secondary independent data like sales may partly fulfil this role.)

Whether or not a model is used, if customer satisfaction results are tracked in a B2B context, this might only be every six months, annually, or (perhaps more commonly) every two to three years. In the latter case, a shorter survey than an original ad hoc initial survey might be used. Nevertheless, items should be as identical as possible in form and content so that comparability is maintained. (A small change in phrasing can produce significantly different results.) The repeat frequency is determined by the size of the population, how often respondents (decision makers) change jobs, the changing pace of the market (if fast-moving or not), and how quickly companies can implement changes in processes and practices. There is no point upsetting 20 major clients in key markets by insisting on carrying out customer service surveys with them every year if this can have a negative effect. In particular, if business respondents are not told what actions have been taken as a result of the previous round of research, or if they decide (for example, after several rounds) that nothing is improving, this will produce customer resistance and (potentially) an even more negative evaluation.

CASE STUDY: CUSTOMER SATISFACTION FOR PHARMACEUTICAL COMPANY

Main message

A superior product was designed that better met the needs of users as a consequence of the market research programme, and this stabilized sales against a very competitive market.

Respondent definition

Key personnel in UK hospitals in charge of waste management, needle exchange, distributors and blood transfusion services.

Details

Daniels Healthcare sells hospital products, manufacturing needles ('sharps'), scalpels and clinical waste containers for private clinics, NHS hospitals and blood transfusion services. Despite a good market position, the company faced strong competition.

In 2000, the company commissioned M&E Consultants to carry out customer satisfaction research with key personnel in hospitals in charge of waste management, needle exchange, distributors and blood transfusion services. A two-stage programme of qualitative and quantitative research (N = 100 telephone interviews) was undertaken, examining factors influencing purchasing and satisfaction.

High scores were obtained in all areas relating to service and product satisfaction apart from one attribute: the product attribute 'Not easily over-filled'. Since the qualitative research found that safe use of sharps containers was a key motivation factor in choosing a supplier, this was an important quantitative finding.

Consequently, Daniels Healthcare went back to the drawing board. In 2003, the company launched successfully a newly designed container, called 'SHARPSGUARD[r]' that could not be over-filled. The customer satisfaction research had highlighted a problem that might not have come to light without asking detailed questions of those who actually use the containers. Perhaps more importantly, it enabled the company to take preventive action before its sales declined. It remains a market leader.

The normal framework for customer relationship work is:

- qualitative research with customers, often via in-depth interviews or mini groups;
- quantitative ad hoc assessment of performance and determination of priorities (reasonably lengthy);

- quantitative repeated tracking over time (generally shorter questionnaire for this).

The research skills needed include an ability to talk sensitively to customers about their needs and service performance; an ability to be alert to small changes in the market that may have a major effect on clients' expectations; an ability to bring anecdotes to life; a gift to communicate complex performance messages and to handle the psychological dynamics where client (or division) performance is at stake; understanding of statistical techniques; experience of CRM across a number of different markets; and a technological facility to provide data, in as real time and to as wide an audience as possible.

Reporting for B2B customer satisfaction research

Reporting of customer satisfaction results is often multi-layered. With so much on the line, it is important to make the results understandable, provide interpretation and show the implications. The same amount of thought needs to be allocated to the client presentation as is given to the research process. Many members of staff may be involved in customer service provision, and the client may 'cascade' the results through the ranks to make them accessible and actionable. So reports need to be appropriate for the different audiences (perhaps the customer services director and team, sales personnel, front of office/call centre staff); selective – so that staff can manipulate some of the data themselves, ask questions and feel they can 'use' the results (back-end, web-based reporting is invaluable here); and as close to 'real time' as possible so that findings have impact and problems can be addressed immediately.

There are many ways results can be presented, with real anecdotes on service being particularly potent in qualitative reporting. In quantitative reporting, quadrant charts (comparing performance against service priorities) are particularly effective, as shown in Figure 9.2.

Advertising and marketing communications research

Often these are combined in B2B research, but some of the issues pertaining to each are different.

Advertising research

In recent years, advertising to corporates and advertising related to B2B markets has become more sophisticated (as has marketing in general). Larger firms can afford television advertising of the sort seen on CNN/Bloomberg communicating the 'corporate message', but many others undertake press campaigns in newspapers and magazines that are read by the business community. Sometimes, advertising at the corporate

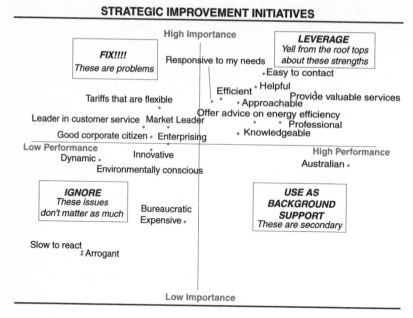

Figure 9.2 *Corporate performance matrix*

level is undertaken to try to boost the image of the company after a scandal or market difficulty (such as a product withdrawal, or failure of a drug test), associated with an upcoming sponsorship (for example, proud to be a sponsor of the Olympic Team), or following a merger or acquisition and possible rebranding (for example, Accenture/Andersen Consulting). Whatever the expenditure (and why), clients should know if and how it is working, and in particular, whether it is having the desired effect on the target group(s), which often include influential business and opinion former groups.

By contrast with the extensive (expensive, very often sophisticated, and quantitative) advertising research in consumer markets, qualitative research has traditionally been a more usual approach in B2B, particularly focus group work. Primarily, this has tested executions and impact rather than early advertising development work – often considered a luxury, especially when total spend on advertising may be low. In-depth questions can cover what sort of advertising in the sector is preferred, which channels work best, what press is read or respected, plus examination of the specific 'draft' advertisements – messages conveyed, the format (images used, copy, tone), and overall effect. Observing respondents' non-verbal reactions (keeping a watchful eye out for an emotional or non-verbal response – the raised eyebrow, slight frown or subtle smile – that otherwise would be under-reported) as well as verbal comments or rational responses can provide additional value. Sometimes, in-depth interviews are conducted – as the case study shows.

CASE STUDY: DEVELOPMENT OF ADVERTISING TO BOLSTER CORPORATE IMAGE RE SOCIAL RESPONSIBILITY

Main messages

By undertaking a small-scale but effective pre-test, the risk of spending significant money on ad development and media spend inappropriately (if a wrongly pitched message and execution had been chosen) was averted.

The company was able to move more quickly towards its repositioning as a result of thoughtful preparation and market testing.

Respondent definition

Key audiences – business journalists writing for well-known broadsheet newspapers, and NGOs including charities who were involved in campaigning in the client's area.

Details

At a critical juncture in the company's history, an oil company wished to run an advertising campaign using press and television to help negate negative publicity and to promote a new corporate responsibility platform. In order to assess various messages and different forms of execution, an advertising pre-testing research programme was initiated.

The method used was a sample of 12 face-to-face in-depth interviews with key audiences including business journalists writing for well-known broadsheet newspapers and NGOs that had a particular interest in energy consumption and sustainability. Interviews were conducted at respondents' place of work. Slightly different emphases in message and different forms of execution (for example, 'big, bold, and assertive' versus 'more gentle and reassuring') were developed on concept boards and tested (12 concepts in total). The mock-ups were shown, in a random different order, across respondents and reactions noted. The research executives were able to make recommendations on the:

- most credible and forceful message/s;
- preferred tone of execution;
- preferred visual execution;
- effective media channels (newspapers, other publications, television).

The resultant campaign was hugely successful. A great deal of work had gone into it but this thorough early testing and refinement meant that it 'hit the button'.

Measurement techniques and models

Advertising tracking has not been a big area of B2B research as a stand-alone exercise, but very often B2B companies or those operating in B2B as well as B2C environments will have some form of overall 'brand health' tracker that incorporates quantitative questions covering brand image, advertising and communications at the same time. The sorts of questions asked include what advertising has been seen (spontaneous and prompted – very often for the client and a 'competitor set'), where or on what occasion (media channel), and what was remembered about it (recall). Image attributes and the extent to which the communication is attributed to the 'correct' brand are also included so that an assessment of the level of 'cut-through' (messages effectively received and correctly branded) can be made.

Specific tests of the ad or other communication include measures such as 'likeability', 'applicability' and potential 'wear-out' (those advertisements that grate after a few exposures). Again, this is an area where many market research suppliers have developed proprietary models to measure advertising effectiveness, and the principles of advertising research for consumer brands apply equally well to ads that focus on the corporate as a whole.

The normal framework for advertising research is:

- qualitative precursor interviewing or post campaign;
- quantitative advertising research, if conducted at all, is usually conducted in combination with any other brand tracker that is carried out with the business public.

Skills needed for advertising research include an awareness of media generally and its terminology, and an ability to present data in an exciting way (media presentation standards are often higher than other forms of research presentation).

Advertising and market communications

The growth of integrated communications (advertising, PR, below the line marketing) and the need to evaluate the contribution of each is leading to some research tools being developed that measure more than just advertising efficacy. One example is the 'i to i tracker' (impact and influence) that assesses the effectiveness on the customer (business or consumer) of disparate marketing communications such as advertising, direct mail, public relations and sponsorships. Depending on the respondent definition and population, this can be done cost effectively using a B2B omnibus or, at more expense, an ad hoc quantitative survey. Other such vehicles integrating several measurements are likely to find an audience in B2B, where it is prohibitively expensive to undertake large stand-alone ad hoc or tracking exercises.

Maximizing the opportunity of time with a CEO, divisional head or owner of a small business is a key need in B2B research, and 'rolled up' surveys covering several topics at a time (customer satisfaction, corporate image, communications preferences) can, as mentioned earlier in the chapter, provide useful alternatives to projects on a sole subject. As syndicated work is often not feasible in the B2B world, looking for other ways to maximize the client's research budget must always be in our thoughts.

Marketing communications: evaluating e-communications and e-interactions

With the advent of the internet as a key channel of communication and business (e-business), knowing how the website works and how effective it is are necessities for many businesses. This applies equally to business or consumer publics – for firms that operate in both the business (B2B) and consumer environment (B2C). Although there are often separate sections for business publics with passwords for those who subscribe (paid or unpaid), websites service both markets and often are researched with both respondent categories, an example of where there is increasing interchangeability between the two constituencies.

Much qualitative work, often using the internet as a tool itself, is conducted with business audiences about websites. Typical issues are:

- Ease of navigation, organization, hierarchy of pages – 'how easy is it to get round the site?'
- Content: 'Is it easy to find out what you want to know?' 'How comprehensive and clear is it?'
- Ease of doing business via the website (undertake transactions, payment methods and options, information on delivery and tracking delivery, terms of business and conditions) – 'Could you price/compare/buy/execute or whatever as you wanted?'
- Corporate messages given.
- Comparison with competitor websites.
- Overall satisfaction with the site.
- Suggestions for improvement.

CASE STUDY: THE ROLE OF QUALITATIVE RESEARCH IN COMMUNICATIONS RESEARCH

Main messages

Bon mots from a key witness can do much to highlight what the client's priorities should be.

Sometimes, this can be more insightful than hundreds of interviews with those not so immediately involved in an issue.

Respondent definition

Senior executives in the IT/telecoms area.

Details

As part of a qualitative research project to examine the effectiveness of communications of the client company, a personal interview with a European head of IT, telecoms and facilities manager in a law firm revealed, in just a few minutes, some of his major priorities. When asked about preferred communication routes, he said what mattered to him was:

> More electronic updates and less paper or post. What I want is more relevant and less irrelevant material. I'm not interested in picture phones but in examples, case studies, new-technology road maps saying 'This is where we are headed with X.' You used to be able to go on the website to find out where the BlackBerry would work but with the 'improved' website, the 'map' has gone, and you cannot find this out yourself!

Alongside all the other information collected, this allowed the client company to pick up on both the large and small things in communications of concern to their clients and to address them accordingly.

Evaluating written and visual communications

Communications research is one of the most interesting areas of market research – finding out what resonates with business people in terms of content, form and channel of communication, and reporting on this to the client. It is one of the areas where sensitivity to language, awareness of visual representation, and the ability to make recommendations can make a very real difference. (See the chapter by Tony Allen and John Simmons on 'Visual and Verbal identity' in Economist 2003.)

Communications work encompasses more than just the internet, and the internet encompasses more than just websites. Communications work encompasses all form of communications, and B2B communication, particularly regarding opinion formers, is a major concern for many companies and other organizations. Research for these can be quantitative as well as qualitative, and frequently is so, for organizations that live or die by the quality of their communication.

In terms of refining other forms of written publication or communication such as company brochures, annual reports, company newsletter, lecture or seminar programmes, qualitative work can play a useful role. Annual reports are often the 'showcase' of an organization and are read by those in positions of influence (corporate investors, fund managers, stockbrokers). Their messages, their visuals, their tone and what they say about the company are all areas it may be useful to test out in discussion with some people in positions of influence before sending out to the wider market. Does the publication reflect the essence of the company, is it compatible with its goals and vision, does it impart clearly the key messages? Furthermore, increasingly, companies (for instance, energy companies) in sectors where practices are under review or regulation is pending, are bringing out reports for stakeholders talking about what efforts they are making, geographically or in terms of business process, to be more environmentally and socially responsible. Special Public or opinion former interviews can provide a useful guide in terms of direction.

A trade association commissioned a quantitative telephone interview with European opinion formers including association member companies (part of the questionnaire is reproduced in Appendix 7) as part of a tracking study over three-year intervals in order to assess the effect of changes in communications priorities and to get a feel for how well the different forms of communications were working. One unique aspect of this survey was that most of the interviews were quantitative in nature, but a small number were selected for a deeper, more qualitative approach that extended and explored motivations and rationale. (These more detailed interviews were undertaken by market research project executives rather than the fieldwork agency.) This further probing allowed the team to further explain the data, to clarify the rationale for respondents' answers, and so better interpret the total information obtained into strategy.

The normal framework for communications research is:

- qualitative research with business people/opinion formers, in-depth or mini-group;
- periodic quantitative follow-up research (particularly if the organization is one that is solely communications-oriented).

Skills needed are sensitivity to, and experience in, marketing communication (visuals, language, tone of voice); an ability to interview at senior levels; and an aptitude for explaining results to non-researchers.

CASE STUDY: TRACKING EFFECTIVENESS OF PUBLIC RELATIONS CAMPAIGNS IN THE FINANCE INDUSTRY

Main messages

Traditional research techniques can be applied successfully (in non-traditional areas) to quantify the effectiveness of communications activity.

Sometimes, a combination of primary research and data from other sources is required to fully answer the business question at hand.

Respondent definition

Managers of small businesses.

Details

A PR campaign was conducted on behalf of the Banks Automated Clearing System (BACS), with the objective of educating business about the benefits of using direct credit for B2B payments. BACS's core service line, direct credit, known as direct deposit in the United States, is the means by which an organization can transfer funds electronically, directly into a specified bank or building society account.

Research was needed to measure the effectiveness of the campaign, and it was evaluated using the i to i tracker[r] model (measuring 'impact' and 'influence' of the PR on attitudes, perceptions, behaviour and so on). Both media audit and primary research were undertaken.

A media audit (secondary analysis) of the public relations campaign was undertaken using the coverage list retrospectively to go from 'gross impressions' to actual reach (what proportion of the target audience was exposed to the campaign) and frequency figures (how many times were they exposed to something). Using the British Businessmen Readership Survey (BBRS), it was estimated that:

- 84% of large businesses had been reached, with an average of 3.4 opportunities to see or hear (OTS/H);
- 79% of small businesses had been reached, with an average of 3.4 OTS/H.

Primary quantitative research was then conducted via omnibus with small and large businesses. The results showed that 30 per cent of all small businesses surveyed recalled seeing an element of the campaign. It also showed that the key messages covered in the media had been picked up by those who had seen the coverage: 35 per cent recalled messages related to 'convenience'; 22 per cent to 'cost effectiveness'; 15 per cent to 'business benefits'; 11 per cent to the 'efficiency of direct credit'.

This had also had some influence on the overall usage of direct credit, with 32 per cent of all businesses (29 per cent amongst small business) now adding bank details to their invoices, enabling their clients to pay them by direct credit – a much higher figure than for those who had not seen the PR coverage. Not only had the message got across but some measure of behavioural change also resulted. The effectiveness of the campaign was ultimately to be based on whether it successfully raised awareness of direct credit and whether the number of small businesses putting bank details on invoices increased. In the year following the campaign and the research, the actual number of payments made via direct credit increased by 6.4 per cent (to 993 million, compared with 933 million the year before).

Corporate image and branding research

Principles

The motivations for undertaking corporate image or branding research are similar – to understand the role and power of the corporate brand to enhance the business overall. Corporate image research is more about how the public, whether business or consumer, 'feels' about the company and its role in the business community and society in general: it is at the corporate level rather than at the brand or product level. Nevertheless, for the majority of B2B situations, the corporate name is also the primary brand name – for example, Shell, American Express, Dell, Boeing, FedEx and GE. By contrast, consumer goods companies have a plethora of (typically) well-known brand names (Procter & Gamble has Pampers, Pantene, Ariel and so on), and it is harder to assess how the (umbrella) corporate itself is perceived.

As Scott Bedbury argues in *A New Brand World* (2002), brand research is all about understanding a company's 'DNA' – the strength of the brand, its attributes and its competitive potential in the market place – and then leveraging these attributes. Typically, B2B branding research is motivated by strategic concerns and is numbers-focused, paralleling the traditional brand health investigations of consumer research. It can be undertaken for the corporate brand and also for those with an identity independent of the wider 'corporate umbrella'. For example, different brands of ICI Paints include Dulux as the main paint brand, Alabastine the main 'preparation' product, and CIMSEC for tiling and grouting.

Brands have value, global reach and power. The recent trend to attempt to place a monetary value on brands, and indeed to include this on a company's balance sheet, appears to have its origins with the wave of brand acquisitions or mergers in the mid-1980s. As Jan Lindemann points out in a chapter called 'Brand evaluation' in *Brands and Branding* (Economist 2003), in takeovers there was a considerable mismatch between the amount of money being paid for companies and what showed on the balance sheet, largely owing to inability of existing accounting standards for goodwill to account for the growing value of intangible assets. Whilst in part this has been recognized, acquired assets are still treated differently from 'home grown' brands in a company's balance sheets.

Some independent analyses of the 'power' of major brands are published – for example, Interbrand's Business Week Global Brand Scoreboard. The most recent report is quoted in *BusinessWeek*, 2 August 2004. This index estimates value, ranks, and tracks the brand value, annotating factors contributing to a brand's growth or decline. (Estimated brand value and changes since 2003 include Apple: US $6.87 billion, up 24 per cent; amazon.com US $4.16 billion, up 24 per cent; AOL US $3.248 billion, down 18 per cent.) Corporate perceptions within the business community can provide a useful input to these brand valuations.

Often, corporate image or branding work (whether qualitative, or ad hoc quantitative or tracking) is combined with other research such as tracking vehicles, or research on other topics of interest to the company. In particular, corporate reputation research often links with communication research, as there is substantial overlap in the kinds of issues involved. For example, what do business investors or analysts think of the organization, and how can it best communicate its corporate messages to them? As well as understanding corporate image and positioning, different communication platforms and channels can be evaluated.

Sometimes corporate image research can utilize syndicated fieldwork resources. For example, MORI UK researches opinion formers' views of a range of companies across different sectors. However, more commonly, individually commissioned corporate or brand image work is needed with privately reported results.

Examples of situations where research can play a useful role include when a company:

- has acquired or merged with another group (CitiGroup after a host of acquisitions including Travellers, adapting the Traveller's umbrella logo in the process);
- is reviewing its image status and 'what it stands for' (KFC not Kentucky Fried Chicken to overcome negative press regarding the healthiness of its food);
- is considering a major revamp of its brand or corporate livery: logo, tag line, visual statement, letterheads, uniforms, everything that sends a message out about the company (BP to bp);
- is reinventing the company, augmenting, or extending its portfolio of products and services (Apple iPod launch).

It is usual to undertake some qualitative exploration with key stake-holders and publics to consider what is the best direction, how a rein-vention of the company could be phased, and what needs to be done in their eyes to shift the company image.

Individual interviews are more common than focus groups for corporate image work, although focus groups are common in rebranding research, particularly when there are visual stimuli or a complex business plan is under consideration. Gathering senior people together for such research is the challenge. Telephone is used as much as, if not more than, face-to-face interviewing in qualitative exploration. For any quantitative phase, e-mail surveys are becoming more current as a quick way of establishing image norms with the business audience although a telephone interview provides a more in-depth approach and is more appropriate where the sample is more highly selected and when individuals have a lot to say.

Benefits of corporate image research

Having a good corporate image, a strong name or reputation can establish and maintain a market place advantage, make staff feel better about themselves and take pride in their association with the company, enable sales staff to 'get a foot in the door' with clients, and, generally, act as an asset to the company in all its spheres of operation. With good reason, companies are continuing to invest in corporate reputation research – as companies such as AOL (the 'busy signal' issue), Exxon (Valdez scenario), Shell (revised estimates of oil reserves), Arthur Andersen (company accounting audits) and others know. Making use of research to remain alert to the company's image and to what is enforcing or weakening its identity in the business community is a wise step in today's competitive world.

Perceptions of companies are formed through the influence of multiple channels – experience of the product, press, editorial, word of mouth, advertising, sponsorship programmes, expert reviews, the company's website and internet 'chatter' about the company, the activities of special interest groups (such as Greenpeace and the Sierra Club). When undertaking research, it is often useful to try to identify the respective influences, and in particular, to pinpoint their media habits. In addition, although organizations will be assessed in terms of overall 'headings' (such as 'Known for its innovation'), the issues underlying these will also need to be examined in detail to find out exactly what it is that is driving perception. For example, in recent work with a chemicals organization, it was important to assess the extent of negative perception about chemical reactions and polystyrene window frames, and whether this was in any way influencing business (rather than consumer) perception.

In *A New Brand World* (2002), Scott Bedbury gives many examples of companies' efforts to better understand, refine and communicate the company 'DNA'. While many of these relate to consumer markets, the case studies give interesting insights that are worth reviewing for their relevance in the B2B context. IBM's re-engineering of its corporate image under the leadership of Louis Gerstner is cited commonly as a strategically-led rebranding case study, and concerns both the B2B and consumer markets. IBM's move was deemed necessary as the growing PC business had not been well integrated into a grand brand plan, and corporate communications had become fragmented. The resulting new strategy, 'The spirit and letter of IBM', developed an unambiguous, unified and understandable brand platform. This communicated directly IBM's brand identity to customers, assisted brand choice, supported price premiums, and easily accommodated future IBM business ventures. The company's more recent advertising for IBM consulting and e-business services are an extension of this earlier transformation of 'Big Blue'. See also Tony Allen and John Simmons's chapter in *Brands and Branding* (Economist 2003), which discusses British Airways' attempts to rebrand as a global carrier (affecting both visual and verbal identity) and the account taken of various audiences.

In many countries, there is also more focus on corporate 'social equity' or 'social responsibility', or indeed the 'social value' of brands. To date, not a great deal of research has been conducted in a strictly B2B context – the end-consumer has tended to have attracted the most research attention. Some small-scale work has been done but no major long-term tracking studies. However, this is likely to change with companies' growing recognition that maintaining a responsible profile in the world can be a differentiator (and potentially adds value to the business and its balance sheet).

Rarely is corporate image research undertaken solely with only one group in mind. Rather it is conducted in a single 'shot' that covers different groups (shareholders, consuming public, customers, potential customers, opinion formers and so on). The research conducted with opinion formers (which usually includes many who are in business) is the main focus here. In this sort of work, it is not unusual to draw up a wide-ranging sample based on important influencers including:

- industry experts such as media analysts, journalists, industry commentators, trade associations, those who know the sector and have a 'helicopter' view;
- investor groups such as current shareholders, fund managers, large equity holders, hedge funds, associations representing investors;

- those in government, regulators, and NGOs (or lobbyist groups in the United States);
- other companies (competitor organizations or those supplying the sector);
- others such as head hunters/recruitment specialists, career advisers at universities, or others that may have dealings with the sector and who often have an in-depth knowledge of how companies are seen;
- employees (often added to employee research, although a separate study may be needed if a total revamp of the company is about to happen).

Typical questions asked include:

- What is the overall image and perception of the company? (Familiarity/favourability are often key questions – how well do you know the company, what are your opinions of it overall in terms of negative/positive, how strong is the management, leadership and sense of purpose?)
- What helped form this image?
- How are individual aspects contributing or contributing differently to the way the company is seen?
- How is perception changing over time?
- Where does this organization sit compared with competitor organizations?

Keeping up to date

As with customer satisfaction research, corporate image and branding research findings can rapidly become out of date. In tracking studies, attributes need to be revalidated. (For example, with an expanded product range, should we examine perceptions of British Gas just in terms of gas or as a wider energy company? As it is a leading provider of e-business services, can we afford to only look at IBM's image as a computer manufacturer? No, the survey must move with the times.) However (as noted earlier), we must be attuned to the fact that changes in attribute wording and the set of attributes used can produce different results, just due to the change. Typical items common to different industries and studies cover aspects (see also the discussion in the customer satisfaction section) to do with overall excellence, having a clear vision or direction, commitment to quality, product and service range, innovation, leadership in field, meeting customer needs, training and knowledge of staff. However, the majority of items will be customized to the company, its industry and the key platforms, and any 'vision statement'. In selecting attributes, some care needs to be taken to avoid 'woolly' concepts and 'motherhood' statements and hone in on really differentiating attributes.

Reporting

Here, reporting of B2B results can allow for some descriptive and imaginative presentation methods. Include some verbatim quotes if qualitative research has been done. The most usual data presentation methods are quadrant charts that map results on two key indices simultaneously (such as familiarity and favourability; *importance* of image attributes compared with the company's *performance* on each) – and (where undertaken) comparing companies on the two dimensions, charts outlining a SWOT analysis (strengths, weaknesses, opportunities, threats), and line chart maps of the company's key image attributes (possibly also comparing ratings against competitors).

Figure 9.3 demonstrates a strategic improvement matrix (akin to what is used in customer satisfaction research) where the company's performance on each is mapped with importance of image attributes. These data come from an annual quantitative corporate image study with opinion formers in a number of countries for a large multinational. The chart provides an easy guide to the company on where efforts need to be focused:

- leverage attributes (top right-hand quadrant): high Importance where Performance is also high;
- fix (bottom right-hand quadrant): high Importance and Performance is poor;
- secondary support (top left-hand quadrant): high Performance but the variables are less important'
- ignore (bottom left-hand quadrant): Performance is poor but the variables are less important.

In this case, we see that Emotional Values and Financial Reputation are of relatively low importance in the scheme of things even if company performance was good – therefore, a platform based strongly on this would not be recommended. Vision and Leadership is relatively important and yet performance is rather weak – the client should be encouraged to move quickly on improving this. No areas are in the 'danger' box, with high importance and pathetic performance, so this is better news for our client.

A typical framework for corporate reputation research is:

- qualitative work with opinion formers and influencers, usually telephone in-depth interviews;

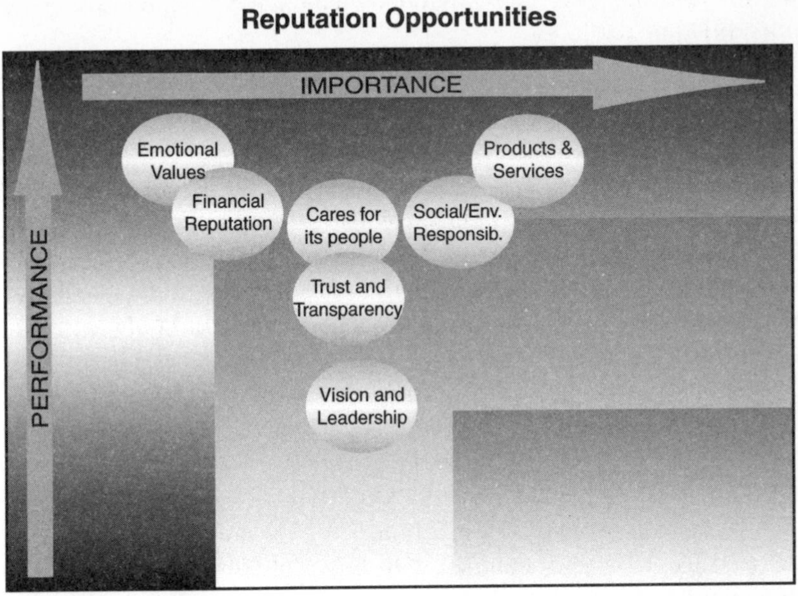

Reputation Opportunities

Figure 9.3 *Strategic improvement matrix*

■ larger-scale quantitative periodic research or buy-in to a syndicated Special Public survey with appropriate respondent groups.

Research skills needed include an understanding of business issues and what drives business health; an ability to capture wider issues but in addition identify the smaller details driving perceptions; and a facility for capturing the market mood and sense of whether a company is on the rise or decline from relatively few, if key, interviews.

CASE STUDY: DEVELOPING A BRAND IDENTITY

Main messages

Real improvements in the corporate image or brand identity can be gained, resulting in better sales opportunities if the re-engineering is founded on good research as input to a quality design team.

Research firms and design agencies can well work hand in hand – a research and implementation strategy.

Respondent definition

Customers of Andor Technology, manufacturers of scientific imaging equipment.

Details

Andor Technology is a leading developer of scientific imaging products. Its products include highly sensitive digital cameras, spectroscopy products, x-ray imaging systems and time-resolve imaging systems used by scientists in biochemistry, space research and physics. Despite the products being aimed at a highly specialized technical buying audience, branding plays an important part in the decision-making process. Andor had been hampered in selling the full extent of its product portfolio to a number of customers because it was often perceived to be a 'niche' player rather than a 'portfolio' player. In addition, it did not have the necessary processes in place to police its branding, appearing to be 'less professional' than some of its peers in terms of branding gravitas and overall 'look and feel'.

Quadriga Consulting Ltd, a research and marketing consultancy, was appointed to work very closely with the senior management team in order to agree on a broad marketing strategy. The management team was encouraged to define Andor's brand identity. Quadriga set about establishing a redefined set of brand image concepts via customer research from which a new brand platform could be selected.

Given the geographical spread of the customers, web survey techniques were invaluable. Web survey tools were used to evaluate the current Andor brand within a competitive context, the proposed amendments to the branding approach, and finally copy conventions, tag lines and so on.

As a result of the research and design work, a 'brand imaging system' has become the 'bible' for the company in terms of graphic guidelines including logo treatment, approved copy conventions and tag lines. The broad thrust of the image system has been extended into advertising and public relations platforms to define the tone of voice for the company and the visual representation of the brand.

SUMMARY

In summary, research of virtually every sort is done in B2B. Some kinds, such as market sizing, acquisition research and business prediction, tend to be B2B specialisms, while others, such as customer satisfaction, corporate/brand image research and finance and mobile communications (those with business and consumer applications), are conducted frequently as B2B and B2C. There is a great deal of variety for the business researcher, and there is the chance to undertake strategic and fascinating research.

10 Regional differences and comparisons in B2B research

This chapter examines regional differences in B2B research. Although it is by no means comprehensive, the aim is to highlight some of the main characteristics by market, in particular selecting areas of difference that are particularly relevant in the B2B research process. Some market size information is given in Chapter 1, but regrettably there is little firm information on this. Here the nature of the B2B market, its international scope, its focus, the type of work done and the business environment are the major aspects covered. It should be noted that comments in the 'Environment' section refer to the state of the market research industry (in general) in that region in order to provide a relevant context as well as any points made specifically about B2B market research.

REGIONAL REVIEW

Great Britain

Market size

Great Britain is a large, flourishing market with a long B2B research tradition, but nonetheless small compared with the consumer research market place.

International

As well as undertaking domestic projects, UK research agencies buy and coordinate much international research on behalf of clients, in particular because of the English language and closeness to European political and commercial centres.

Type of work

Much of the work is small-scale qualitative and consultancy, but many of the larger quantitative business trackers are run out of Great Britain via panel, online and telephone field methods.

B2B focus

This can be characterized by flourishing industry forums dedicated to B2B research, and the fact that most large agencies have specialist business departments with researchers who are dedicated to B2B and B2C research.

Environment

This is a cooperative business community educated in research and generally happy to commit to being research respondents. There is good library and statistical information provision, with sound governmental statistics to provide a backbone to information collection, with access to good research resources at every level for all elements of the research process.

United States

Market size

By world standards, this is large, and overlaps with the B2C market.

International

US clients commission some multi-country B2B studies out of the United States. These types of studies sometimes include two or three countries, but can sometimes include 10 or more. The location, time zone, and English (and Spanish for South America) favour the United States as a master unit for coordinating international studies. Research agencies with offices on the West Coast have the advantage of office hours overlapping with most of the world. In multi-country studies, usually larger research agencies use their local offices or affiliate agencies throughout the world to conduct the local research or to subcontract to local agencies, especially in B2B where local knowledge is often so important. On occasion, for very large studies, US research agencies may use coordination hubs, for example the UK as a hub to coordinate

Europe, and Singapore, Hong Kong or Australia as a hub to coordinate Asia. Whilst it is more common for international qualitative studies to use a local moderator who is an expert researcher in that country and who understands all the nuances of the culture and the language, occasionally bilingual researchers from the United States are sent. This is particularly advantageous if it is a very specialized market and it is difficult to find a moderator in the local country with the relevant expertise. At times, a simultaneous translator is used in these other international markets. Large B2B studies may be more common generally in and from the United States than elsewhere – often these are for areas where there is considerable B2C overlap (such as IT) and/or where the role of professional intermediaries is important (finance, transport/hospitality industry, beverages).

Type of work

In the United States, B2B work is very varied. The size of the projects varies considerably – from small qualitative studies with 5–10 depth interviews to large multi-stage projects comprising desk research, qualitative research and quantitative research stages. Because of the size of the market, there is considerable opportunity for large quantitative studies and complex analysis (more so than is the case in Europe and elsewhere). Often companies require considerable depth in research topic coverage and demand a high degree of (statistical) confidence in the results (in order to make a business case, for example) and considerable detail in reporting. It is not uncommon for advanced techniques (such as regression modelling to determine drivers or perceptual mapping) to be utilized in B2B, albeit with guidelines on interpretation provided.

B2B focus

This can be characterized by:

- The US B2B market being relatively more mature, in the sense that every client is likely to have been a respondent in some context at some time (for example, for American Express, MasterCard, a hotel chain or an airline). While generally this means greater sophistication in understanding the role of research, it has not always led to a better understanding among researchers of the need for shorter, tighter questionnaires that recognize the respondent's time shortage.
- Some larger client companies have dedicated B2B research managers who are generally very skilled in market research principles and techniques. (For example, in the United States it is not unusual to have to weight data or report on boost samples separately.)

- Most large agencies have departments that specialize in broad industry sectors, and within these departments there are researchers who are experienced in B2B and B2C.
- In the United States, conventions of response confidentiality, to which European researchers conform, tend to be less strictly adhered to. Customer relationship management clients are often anxious to use the findings to directly repair relationship problems, and some B2B researchers deal with this by offering response confidentiality as an option.
- The United States has led the way in the development of relationship modelling. Since the late 1980s, there have been good working models of the causative relationship between business practices and customer loyalty. A number of formal models of customer satisfaction were 'born' in the United States, and CRM, employee satisfaction (or 'climate research'), and quality assurance research are well embedded as research programmes in many different sectors. Generally, major client research buyers expect research techniques to be offered in packages that come with their own software and/or interactive online reporting process. These approaches are especially attractive to multi-country research buyers who are looking at 'between country' comparisons or research-based performance indices.
- Loyalty programme research is well established with business markets, with an increasing focus on the small business market (credit card, airlines, hotel, and travel industries) – with some B2B although much of this is B2C.
- With many developments in technology originating from the United States, new product and service work in IT and telecoms is common, as is branding/competitive positioning research.

Environment

The United States is technologically equipped (although technology is not always optimized to improve efficiency) and e-mail enabled (although most companies' systems are not prepared for the future level in demand for e-business and business e-mail as reported by the ePolicy Institute, August 2004). E-mails from unknown parties – for example, research agencies – are likely to hit spam filters or (for larger organizations) company firewalls. There is considerable respondent 'wear-out' in some sectors (IT from Y2K research and so on).

Canada

Whilst Canada is a smaller market than the United States, it shares very similar characteristics in terms of infrastructure and approach to research. Agencies in Canada are less likely to be called on to act as a coordinating centre for multinational B2B studies.

Asia

Any attempt to generalize regarding Asia as a region is fraught with danger: the very idea of 'Asia' is a term of convenience that has been thrust upon the region, and belies the complexity of cultural difference and centuries of traditional perspectives that often dictate the approach to business in different countries. Most marketers to the region work on the basis of a rough grouping of key markets based on their relative maturity/sophistication/infrastructure as follows:

- most mature: Hong Kong, Singapore, the Philippines, Korea and Taiwan;
- less mature: Malaysia, Indonesia, China and Thailand;
- developing maturity: Vietnam, Cambodia, Laos and Myanmar.

Market size

Relative to Europe and North America, a lower volume of B2B research is conducted. However, a growth of B2B research may be anticipated with the historically strong research tradition in Japan (often with amazingly long planning times in anticipating the need for research results – for example, the automotive industry) and growth of economies such as China, India, South Korea, Vietnam and elsewhere. The GDP of China is now as large as that of the UK, and is likely to reach that of the United States by 2040 (source: McKinsey, 2004). Although B2B research has not been a large element of much work done to date in China, this is likely soon to change.

International

Some work in Asia is coordinated out of Europe, some out of Australia, and some is coordinated internally via hubs within the region (such as Hong Kong).

B2B focus

Work is commissioned as required on a rather ad hoc basis, although continuous studies may become more usual with the market developing. The focus is likely to be very different from country to country depending on the principal industries and economic drivers.

As Herve Turpault, a former colleague of mine working in Research International Japan, said recently, 'Everything is fairly similar in Japan compared to the UK in terms of the way B2B research is conducted from recruitment to discussion content to incentive.' Three exceptions can be noted. In the business context, Japanese business people, who tend to work in a more reserved culture when talking about money and finance, may be less open to discussions touching on financial issues. In terms of incentives in Japan, although book tokens are not unusual as an incentive for B2B respondents, there is no real practice of donation to charity. B2B incentives are usually in the form of a gift rather than cash. Often, it is difficult to conduct longer telephone interviews with business respondents – it is considered not very polite. (Note: in a consumer context, traditionally focus group discussions take longer, with a longer introduction than we are accustomed to. My colleague's experience is that the above may be overcome with a good moderator who is heavily coached, as can the issue of not being open about financial matters.)

When undertaking B2B work in Asia, it is important to solicit local advice the further away the country is in terms of what is familiar – norms, protocols and mentality can be very different in many other countries.

Type of work

This is similar to B2B work elsewhere. Investors will commission studies to discover more about market, market size and potential, particularly in growing markets like China. 'Infrastructure-focused multinationals that sell products from electronics to subway systems are finding China to be their most important market for growth' (source: McKinsey, 2004). Multinationals are likely to elect to do some market research before taking the plunge.

Research into NPD or new applications is expected to grow, particularly with the establishment of more research and development functions in countries such as China. Similarly, with the increase in 'back office' work being done in Asian countries, performance monitoring and customer satisfaction research are likely to become a more common part of the research portfolio.

Currently, fewer corporate reputation or 'opinion leader' type studies are conducted in this area, with more research focusing on the viability of, and demand for, actual products and services (plus how to tailor provision/delivery to the specific market).

Environment

Burgeoning economies, growth in dynamic sectors such as IT and call centres in India, growth in the technology industries in China, 'relaxing' governmental attitudes – including the likely changes in the structure of the banking industry, the move in many cases from public to private industry, general investment in industry and a 'can do' philosophy, all lead to an environment where B2B research is likely to flourish in the long term.

Two helpful publications on doing business and research in Asia are *Kiss, Bow or Shake Hands: How to Do Business in Sixty Countries* by Terri Morrison, Wayne A Conaway and George A Borden (1994) and a McKinsey Consulting report, 'Guide to doing business in China', an article from one of the 2004 editions of the McKinsey Quarterly (www.mckinseyquarterly.com).

Europe

The European market has many similarities to the UK, but in some ways it has a less formalized infrastructure. Many research agencies have staff who undertake B2B work but there are fewer with divisions dedicated to it or with large numbers working in B2B. (Of course the UK is part of Europe, but as a separate section has been devoted to the UK there is a need to look at Europe as a distinct entity here.) Again, as with Asia, there is considerable cross-country diversity.

International

Some international work is commissioned out of the larger West European (for example Germany, France) and East European centres, particularly if the UK is not one of the areas to be researched. However, most B2B research is still conducted 'in country'.

Type of work and B2B focus

This can be characterized as follows:

- All sorts of B2B work is conducted, again driven in part by the country-specific industry focus, industrial tradition, technology innovation, the local economy, and research tradition.
- The industrial heartlands of the Rhine in Germany and those of Central Europe and now in newer centres such as Toulouse in south-west France (a centre for the air and aerospace industries) mean that B2B research may be conducted as much outside major European capital cities as within them.
- Work in Scandinavia tends to straddle Norway, Sweden, Denmark and Finland, although of the four countries, Sweden tends to be the country where most work is done as it is the largest Scandinavian market.
- In France, there is a stronger tradition of longer focus groups and more use of more experimental approaches such as 'enabling techniques' for qualitative work, even in the B2B context.

Environment

Again, country-specific conditions need to be noted. For example, in Germany data protection legislation and its enforcement are particularly strong, so awareness of the market research guidelines and additional rules by which one must abide is essential for B2B researchers. Respondents know their rights, so one must tread especially carefully. (See the Code of Conduct and ethics issues in Chapter 12.)

A useful publication for understanding the European Union is from the Economist series *Guide to the European Union* (see www.bloomberg. com/economistbooks).

Australia

In the past 20 years or so, more B2B research has been undertaken than might be expected:

- Historically, the region is a testing ground for new technology.
- Typically, Australians are 'early adopters'.
- Earlier industry deregulation than in many other countries provided substantial opportunities for products and services with a strong overlap between B2B and B2C markets.
- The market is very open and competitive.
- Increasing trade with Asia (China in particular) means that businesses seek to replicate their local market knowledge in foreign markets.

The B2B landscape is characterized by the facts that by world standards, there are very few large companies, markets are concentrated in most sectors – there are a few dominant players (brands) with many other smaller companies – and there is a very strong geographic concentration of industry and commerce (three major cities, two of which contain most companies' head offices).

International

Australian agencies can be called upon to act as coordinator for research in the Asia–Pacific region for both local and international companies, or to participate in regional studies that are run out of London or Hong Kong. This work comprises research (for example) in financial services (business services, credit cards, smart cards), IT and technology (mobile communications, GSM, wireless), tourism, economic studies, media, transport and freight, plastics and paper packaging, building products and construction.

Type of work and B2B focus

The type of work and the B2B focus are characterized as follows:

- All types of B2B research are undertaken.
- The service economy is well developed, and the proportion of GDP represented by manufactured products has declined. Correspondingly, now much B2B work is service-oriented, although for the industrial sector a core research base remains (often with syndicated studies examining the size, state of, and future potential for a market).
- Many global businesses have a strong representation in the region, and Australian operations are included in their benchmark and tracking performance studies.
- B2B studies using advanced modelling techniques (brand health/equity, CSM, employee commitment), behavioural models (demand and pricing modelling), or statistical analysis (market positioning, driver, needs analysis) are not uncommon, particularly among global clients.

Environment

The Australian Bureau of Statistics provides excellent data for market sizing and activity, and ASIC codes were revised to provide more detail for service categories. In the late 1980s and early 1990s the tech sector was over-researched with significant respondent wear-out, and it is showing signs of being so again. Generally, business respondents are open to research requests, and qualitative workshops or groups with catering and/or a good venue are still seen as a bit of a 'treat'.

The MR industry has a diverse structure and is generally mature, sophisticated, open to change, and keen to adopt 'best practice'. Internationals like AC Nielsen, Millward Brown and TNS have sought a strategic position in the local market through acquisitions, local expansion and licensing of research models. Additionally, there are numerous state-based players, many small agencies which typically are specialized (by technique, sector, or access to proprietary models), and some B2B or 'industrial' specialists. However, compared with agencies in the United States, for example, research companies tend to have a more diversified business base.

SUMMARY

In many ways, regional differences in the way research is conducted impact similarly on B2B to the way they impact on B2C and consumer market research. The history of industrial and technological development in a country and region, as well as the market research tradition, will have shaped the way it looks today. Generally, there is more similarity than dissimilarity across the world in the way B2B research is undertaken (for example, in terms of sample size, respondent type, type of work done and deliverables). Despite this, there are idiosyncrasies. The main operational issues for business researchers to look out for are local protocols in terms of respondent contact – how should business respondents be addressed, what are the 'no nos' in terms of the setting up and conduct of interviews, what incentives are (or are not) appropriate? Here, contact with local clients or agencies can, and should, guide us.

11 What it is like being a B2B client and B2B researcher

Many who commission B2B research have specialist knowledge of their sector or industry but relatively little direct experience of B2B research or of the potential benefits, drawbacks or pitfalls of market research in general. Larger companies such as American Express, FedEx, Dell, Microsoft, Nokia and HSBC are likely to have in-house B2B market research specialists (and perhaps sector specialists within the B2B market). However, many companies – even sizeable ones (in industrial sectors, for example) – do not have staff with this expertise. Hence, it is a good idea for those undertaking B2B research to gain some understanding of the research process and what might be achieved. In particular, if external agencies are used, it is important that they feel they are 'in good hands'.

WHAT IT IS LIKE BEING A B2B CLIENT

Many B2B clients are not themselves researchers, and often feel rather in the dark about what is expected of them and what they should do. For example, one of my recent projects is for a government-affiliated agency operating across the world. The IT department wrote the brief (RFP, or request for proposal) and is sponsoring the research, but has no intimate knowledge of research practice. In circumstances like these, it is critical that the proposal is clear, that it outlines the design and assumptions, the expected outcomes, and that it explains the technical terms used. The proposal should provide process charts with 'who does what' (client or researcher) laid out clearly so there is no mistaking what the research will be covering, what the different roles/responsibilities are, and what the likely output and timetable will be.

Responsibilities of the B2B client

What are the steps and tasks that the B2B client needs to look after? The main responsibilities are covered below:

1. Explore with the internal client the main reasons for undertaking the research (qualification of the problem or business issue at hand), and what, if any, budget limitations or timelines may apply.
2. Draw up a brief (or RFP), with due internal consultation. It must explain clearly the background to the issue, what the issue is, and give information on any previous relevant research, known limitations, and any suggestions about how the research might be best approached: for example, 'We would suggest adopting a qualitative approach here as the sample is so small and individuals are difficult to get hold of.'
3. If external help is required select individuals or agencies from whom a proposal is requested.
4. Assess incoming proposals in response to the brief in relation to criteria such as understanding (not just restating) the specific concerns and issues at hand, knowledge shown of the sector or market and previous experience (of this or analogous problems in a different category), research design, suggested techniques to assist an understanding of the issue at hand, and ability to undertake the project in time and on budget.
5. Commission the research and coordinate paperwork with internal accounts; sort out and pre-book currency if the research is multinational and this is an issue.
6. Allocate a single contact point for market research liaison (and sometimes a specific team in the client company whose input can be used). This individual will be responsible for coordinating input to the process, reviewing, and approving things like the final research design, screening criteria, topic guide, questionnaires developed, expert briefing papers (on language, technical terms etc). He or she should attend any briefing to interviewers (if desired), and ask for regular updates from the agency in terms of field process, such as number of interviews completed and reporting progress.

For very large projects, different coordinating 'hubs' may be needed regionally or divisionally instead of just one single contact point. A corporate-wide employee commitment study undertaken by an Australian colleague provides a good example. At the beginning of the project, a steering committee was established comprising the MR manager, the HR manager, and four members representing key business divisions and separately operating company units. Further, project leaders were chosen in each division to facilitate information about the research project and to encourage questionnaire return. (Several prizes were awarded for a high response rate – in this case, it was typically over 80 per cent.)

7. Agree analysis formats (reviewing a report template if submitted by the agency) and outputs with the agency.
8. Review any presentation drafts before delivery to the final internal audience, so that appropriate language or terminology can be used, and there are no surprises.
9. Arrange a presentation or debrief with relevant staff to suit the internal audience and attend the debrief (including helping with any equipment needs).
10. Ensure the results are communicated to any external audiences, to internal audiences such as the board, the management team, those working in the call centres, NPD and so on, in as accessible a format as possible – including, for example, notes on a website. Here the medium is as important as the message – keep it short and make people *want* to know the results.

In all, work throughout the project as the representative of the company with the research agency to ensure it understands the brief, is on track, and is delivering what was agreed (barring serious complications). As much as you can, ensure the research findings are used and that any survey contributes to company policy and action rather than gathering dust on a shelf (or taking up file space). It is important to ensure that staff understand the findings and implications, manage the knowledge gained and use the research to leverage the brand's DNA.

There are some key aspects worthy of special attention that will expedite the whole process and assist in producing quality outcomes. As a B2B client, if you can, familiarize yourself with the basics of research and have an idea of the sort of work that might be required. Have an idea of the size of project you might need (small, medium, large; single or multi-country) and what you can pay for (limited budget or whatever it needs, because of the magnitude of the issue).

Work out:

- What are the key business issues or questions to which you want answers, ideally via internal consultation with those who are involved in needing the research to be conducted.
- Whether it is possible to develop some hypotheses for inclusion in the study about the possible reasons for, causes of, or contributing factors to the issue/problem at hand, and if there are any special groups whose reaction/views might be somewhat different. For example, do you suspect that the high-spending, technologically advanced customers will be likely to be twice as willing to try the new service as the lapsed?
- Who should be interviewed and what are the sampling issues associated with that? For example, can the company provide sample (contact) list and in what ratio, with what facility? Are there any key segments that need to be included?
- What actions might be taken if a given result is found ('action standards') – to understand if different possible outcomes mean different types of action and to determine if the company can (or will) act on information gathered? (Action standards are more commonly used in consumer research but can play a role in B2B at times.)
- Are there any analogies with other industries/businesses/brands from which lessons can be learnt?
- Can any B2B research be combined with any other sources of data, for instance customer research feedback aligned with churn statistics or numbers of complaints received or sales records, so that the total is greater than the sum of the parts?
- What are the internal time frames that allow a realistic timescale for the research whilst meeting internal deadlines? For example, a research executive summary might be needed by 15 September for input to next year's budgeting process to allow for tooling up early in the New Year; more detailed findings can follow.

It is good B2B research practice to ask questions and request advice from others (internal team and external agency), and this is even more important where the person charged with undertaking a study is not a dedicated research practitioner. Ask the agency if it wants to know more in order to better address the business needs at hand. And ask questions about the research and any terms or techniques you would like explained – a research buyer who is not completely au fait with the process should not hold back from asking for explanations of the process and 'next steps'. Do not be macho in not admitting where you are not skilled.

Skills the B2B client brings to the table

Particular skills of B2B clients include the following:

- The ability to build a bridge between the business side and the research professionals:
  - Liaise with external agencies that may have little knowledge of the specific product area at issue.
  - Liaise with internal clients who may be remote from marketing and market research and may have technical, R&D or production experience and speak this language.
  - Act as a reference point for queries and problem resolution throughout the project.
- The ability to translate knowledge of the business and the category, including complex technical or industrial knowledge, into terms that will be understood by researchers, fieldworkers and respondents alike. This includes the provision of a glossary of terms or index that can act as reference material.
- The ability to represent the company's position in checking that the correct terminology and reference points are used in the final reporting. Let the report speak for itself (your role is not to edit the findings) but ensure that the information is framed in such a way as to maximize internal audience understanding and improve the likelihood of action being taken. In this way, internal clients do not lose faith in the researchers through their unintentional misuse of language or terms. For example, if a research executive reporting on a study muddles 'chlorate' and 'chloride', or does not understand the nature of the distributor network, credibility can suffer.

Preparing B2B research briefs

B2B research briefs should include sufficient background to enable the supplier to write a proposal in response with reasonable confidence that he or she has the facts right, understands the basic parameters of the situation, and that suggested approaches address the key issues. Generally, give the agency at least two weeks to respond – preferably more if the likely work is complex and/or if it has an international component. (Obtaining quotes from local field agencies in the relevant countries takes more time than obtaining home country quotes.) The following should be included in any brief (RFP):

- Details of background (this may be more extensive than for other forms of research), including any prior relevant research or market knowledge.

- Why the research is needed – overall and individual business and research objectives.
- Who the major sponsors of the research are, for example marketing, IT department, quality assurance, CRM or the board.
- How any primary or secondary research will fit in, or need to fit in, with other information or output.
- Who the respondents are likely to be, likely sample, and sample sources.
- What research output ('deliverable') is required, including additional presentations anticipated with sub-divisions or special internal clients.
- When the research results are needed by.
- If a face-to-face meeting or teleconference is wanted after the brief has been sent out.
- In what format the proposals should be delivered (as written proposals, in PowerPoint, via a presentation or any combination of these).
- Contact details for the main point of contact: postal and e-mail address, phone numbers.

How to choose a B2B research supplier

Choosing a B2B research supplier is one of the most important tasks of those commissioning B2B research. Some agencies have a specific reputation as consumer agencies, whilst some are known for both B2B and B2C. It is useful to know which of these you are dealing with before you begin. Generally, it is advisable to send a brief out to between two and four agencies – maybe one or two whom you know and one or two who are new or recommended to you.

Maureen Duck, researcher at the *Financial Times*, quoted that in a survey she had conducted in 2004, 59 per cent of clients chose their 'preferred suppliers' in research agency pitches, and the figure was slightly higher for the B2B clients surveyed. In B2B, preferred suppliers play a useful role where there is an accumulation of understanding about clients' markets and briefing new agencies would require more effort for the client. Of course, teams can change and those with expertise can leave. The main criteria clients gave in the above survey for choosing agencies are 'dependability, understanding of the business and of the influence of the decision-making process, appreciating how information is presented back internally, the delivery of the best strategic insight and finally, the ability to develop the client/agency team to become a problem solver and partner'.

When comparing B2B proposals in response to a brief, these aspects can be considered:

- The understanding demonstrated of the client needs, objectives and market place.
- How well such knowledge was applied to the case in hand.
- Questions asked or accuracy of assumptions made; for instance, did the agency ask sensible and thoughtful questions or make assumptions that were inaccurate or skewed?
- The interests and skills of the individuals involved.
- A clear outline of how the agency would go about the work.
- Demonstration of how the work might be used by the client to 'solve' the issue or act on the findings.
- Did the agency pass the 'Goldilocks' test (is it just right?) in terms of research design and sample size. Was it practicable, did it make sense?
- Did the agency add appropriate value in terms of talking about how appropriate techniques, models and norms might contribute to the project?
- And did it:
  - show how the team will work with the client: teamwork, clear division of responsibility?
  - present a realistic time line for the project phases (remember, what is desired and what is 'do-able' might differ)?
  - provide an acceptable, well argued and 'transparent' price?

Sometimes it is useful to allocate marks for each of these aspects, so that the proposals can be judged objectively as well as subjectively. It is also useful to have several pairs of eyes look at the proposals if possible – what is your combined view on who presented the best proposals, and which you feel most comfortable with? It is also important to try, as much as possible, to compare 'apples with apples' and to not make decisions based on numeric calculations related to the proposal price that have spurious value.

A special case is when researchers are proposing to employ particular techniques or models to address the business issue at hand. For instance, when a client wishes to commission a CRM study or a full branding study, it might be faced with choosing among several alternative philosophies, CRM or branding models. Clients could review the considerable literature and published case studies on CRM, examine the fundamentals of, and justification for, each approach presented to them, inspect anonymized examples of recent studies and the reporting framework, determine how appropriate the standard (proprietary) elements of the measurement systems are to their industry or company, compare models on key features and benefits (for example, whether norms are provided), and ask about the experience of the team that will undertake the research. At the end of the day, the choice of supplier has to 'feel right'.

Clients should attempt to do some homework and work closely with whoever is conducting the research to get the most out of it. Undertaking B2B research can be an enjoyable activity when client and agency teams work well together. The client can learn a lot very quickly about the process of research and how to get the most out of it, and the researcher can enjoy working with someone who is new to the process and can be guided through it, or alternatively with a sophisticated client who 'knows the ropes' and is clear about what he or she wants from the research.

WHAT IT IS LIKE BEING A B2B RESEARCHER

The life of a B2B researcher is one of challenge and change. As a July 2002 article in MrWeb, a UK market research digest and newsletter, expressed it:

> The differences between the role of the B2B researcher and that of consumer researchers? There are lots, although there are plenty in common too. It could be summed up by saying that most of the skills are common but most experiences are different – you may have the same training and the same type of brain as a consumer researcher but you do different things with them when you are working among people who buy for business.

There are many sorts of B2B researcher working within research agencies or operating independently: executives with client contact who design research, manage projects, analyse and report on data; fieldwork interviewers; those who enter data; coders; specialist computer programmers who manipulate data analysis software; data processors; and those who undertake special analyses such as advanced statistical analysis or modelling. Those most affected by the fact that the research is B2B as opposed to any other type are the executives and fieldwork interviewers. It is they who, in particular, need to know about the particularities of the market place, the characteristics of the respondent, and the exigencies of the business clients commissioning the research.

Skills B2B researchers need are diplomacy, an ability to speak at senior levels, and an eternal interest in a wide variety of different business areas or areas outside the routine of our normal daily life. Also useful is the skill to absorb lots of rather detailed information like a sponge and distil it into meaningful results. Double- and triple-checking everything – with different sets of eyes – is not a bad practice to foster also. Other skills relating to individual types of research (CSM and the like) or to particular sectors (IT/telecoms and so on) are described in Chapter 9.

Being able to work with clients throughout the full stages of the project is important too. For example, some clients may not be aware fully of the 'real' deadlines associated with submitting a questionnaire to the field force, especially when a translation (or translations) is needed – each change requires new questionnaire versions, new translations and sometimes new briefing notes. Often, it requires patience and some flexibility to meet client needs, especially when the deadline is 'stretched' by further rounds of requested changes. This is where initial good communication (especially about client/agency tasks and timelines) and strong project management skills can come in very handy.

CASE STUDY: A SUMMARY OF B2B CONSIDERATIONS FOR THE RESEARCHER

This is how a July 2002 article in MrWeb outlined the differences between B2B research and other types of research, described some of the skills a B2B researcher needed, and mentioned particular issues to take into account.

Sampling

'Sampling, weighting, grossing up – an altogether different process – knowledge of how to use them is crucial.' Apart from the complexity of getting a sample that represents all sizes, types and locations of business, do you want to talk to companies or sites? Does a branch office count or should it just be head offices? And then there is the question, is the person who buys, the person who uses it?

Interviewing technique

Likely to be very different where big companies are concerned as opposed to small businesses that may make individual judgements and are similar to consumers. B2B interviewers are likely to need more gravitas although that does not mean they don't need to be friendly. Respondents should be given more scope in choosing what they think is most important to discuss but there is also more room for interviewers to throw in their own suggestions or challenge answers to provoke interesting responses.

Politics

The internal politics of a company are a factor in drawing up project plans. For example, it may be advisable to interview some of the client's staff first to get their perspective or to encourage their 'buy in'.

Recruitment emphasis

Business services markets are now a major proportion of the economy, and include such diverse areas as company training, cleaning, catering, telecoms supply, consultancy and outplacement counselling. These are 'small universe' projects where a tiny number of key respondents will not only suffice for a snapshot but actually cover the entire market. A good recruitment strike rate can be the number one concern. Clients may specifically request identified responses from particular companies: this needs to be addressed in interviews with respondents or 'squared' with the Market Research Society Code of Conduct.

Questionnaire structure

This needs to establish both the corporate and personal context in which a person works; may need to get a rounded corporate view; may need to probe into technical areas or into different areas for each respondent dependent on the company's focus or policy.

Competition

Competition and secrecy are more established facts of B2B with more 'sensitive' information (budget and confidential future plans) making up for the lack of 'personal' questions.

International work

This is common in B2B research so cultural issues and local sampling issues must be considered.

Source: MrWeb.

Let's turn now to the different sorts of jobs in B2B research.

Research executives

Research executives who enjoy working in a business as opposed to a consumer world will relish the career of B2B researcher. It is difficult to know whether you will like it, though, unless you try it; generally, the larger agencies will allow younger researchers to have a period in both research spheres on request. Some love it; some do not. Once a researcher has had experience of the business world (whether B2B or B2C), it is common to have a different perspective on consumer projects, which can be more repetitive and more of a 'known quantity'. Some researchers prefer what is known and familiar to them – discussing with consumers subjects of which they know something themselves and undertaking extensive qualitative exploration of consumers' buying behaviour and attitudes. By contrast, the business researcher may have less time for psychological investigation and may be working with topics that are remote from his or her own sphere of knowledge. It can be a bit of a challenge, but one that someone who likes variety and is not fearful to tread in unknown fields may relish.

A university qualification of some sort (in Europe, a degree in psychology) is not unusual for a B2B researcher. It is not uncommon for business researchers to have experience of some other form of research or to have direct business experience prior to joining a specialist B2B research team. Some have training following a degree in business studies, law or medicine, and can bring expert background knowledge to their research.

The B2B researcher in the course of a normal week's work usually will be involved in several projects and in many different stages of project. These may include the following (possibly on different projects):

- Questioning a client about its market and the issues arising from a recent brief, for example what are the particular market characteristics that need to be taken account of, and what are the particular sensitivities, if any?
- Deciding on the optimum sample size given the (often) very low incidence of some respondent categories of respondent (and budget considerations).
- Obtaining quotes from an internal field force, 'sister' or associated agencies (domestic and/or abroad) with known expertise in B2B interviewing.
- Asking the client for more information on the particular translation of technical terms that may not be commonly known by the translation agency.
- Checking up with agencies elsewhere about success in recruiting difficult-to-find samples – how many interviews completed, how many yet to do. Discussing options if the sample cannot be achieved in full – could some additional interviews be conducted with some other categories of respondent? Could minimum and maximum quotas be allocated rather than just one set quota size?
- Finalizing a topic guide for a client in one rather unusual sector and sending it off to the client asking him or her to suggest any additions or changes needed.

- Arranging to conduct a personal interview with a senior executive for a study involving a small number of qualitative interviews.
- Double-checking on recruitment for a luncheon mini-group of intermediaries.
- Checking the data processing specifications on a quantitative ad hoc project.
- Drawing up the template for reporting and/or web-based information dissemination.
- Attending an evening B2B 'forum' meeting with other B2B researchers.

In the course of their career, some B2B research executives will work 'client-side' as well as for market research agencies or consultancies. This can be helpful if they then return later to agency 'life' in providing an insight as to how larger companies work, in increasing specialist knowledge, and in understanding how to make research more usable. Many researchers are generalists – commonly working in different sectors, although sometimes with a speciality – while others are much more specialized and only work in one area such as transportation or healthcare. In this case, researchers tend to stay longer in that sector. Normally, the precursor to a B2B career is working in an agency with B2B expertise and gaining good (general) market research qualifications. Interestingly, B2B is one area where commonly a researcher will undertake both qualitative and quantitative research. This allows both the left and the right side of the brain (sensitive 'quallie' and more numerate 'quantie') skills to be drawn on; again, this reinforces the message that B2B research is the natural home for people who like variety and challenge.

The business executive or director in a research agency often has a close relationship with people (many of whom are not researchers) in the client company hierarchy. His or her contribution, drawing as he/she does on wide experience, often of other sectors, other markets but similar business issues, means that he or she may be asked to talk about research results in a very wide context, often acting as a management consultant as much as a researcher. An executive can promote research up the value chain, contributing analysis, interpretation, knowledge from research and other sources to what the research tells him or her. Intelligence gathering, data fusion with data drawn from many sources, interpretation, are all skills that B2B researchers can, and do, bring to their clients. We repeat, intelligence gathering is now often as much the focus as primary market research. The B2B executive often brings a wider perspective to the client company and acts as a trusted adviser as well as a research partner.

A B2B fieldworker (telephone interviewer)

Much B2B work is done by telephone so the B2B telephone interviewer plays an important role. Typically, B2B research requires specialist interviewers who undertake nothing but business research or also some B2C research. Often they are mature and well qualified, and have a degree or some other higher qualification that gives them confidence in speaking with business respondents. Typically, interviewing is not their main occupation but provides some cash flow. Some are fluent in one or more additional languages, and in an international study this is essential if the subtlety of technical or complex language is not to be lost. As noted earlier, B2B interviewers must be well trained, have an authoritative manner and voice, and be prepared to persevere in the face of some initial respondent (or gate keeper) rejection or hesitancy. Telephone interviewers may never meet those they interview, and must be able to be as convincing with, as interested in and as enthusiastic to hear the responses of their twentieth client as of their first. They must know when and how to probe, and be able to ask questions and record answers (some of which will be verbatim) at the same time. Maintaining the impetus and pace of the interview is important to maintain respondent interest. They must be 'a cut above' in every way and should be rewarded accordingly. Finally, on occasion a telephone business interviewer must be prepared to put in long and unsociable hours: for example, interviewing in a different time zone from a central location or contacting tradespeople outside normal hours. Interviews must be conducted when our respondents are available.

A typical day may include:

- A morning briefing with a client where a series of internet sites are displayed and the market background is discussed, for instance tourism in the hotel sector.
- At the briefing, a discussion follows where the client and agency personnel involved are there to answer questions and 'walk through' the questionnaire.
- Spend half an hour absorbing the questionnaire and picking out what may be the issues arising. Familiarize oneself with the glossary of terms.
- Do first interviews – set up several for the following day and for the following week but manage to do one with a respondent who happens to be there and wants to do the interview immediately.
- Fill in contact forms and report back to supervisor. Discuss one problem that is arising on the recruitment eligibility (for instance, are

motels allowed in the sample or not?). Check with what supervisor and/or researcher and/or client said about SIC codes and eligibility.
- Leave to go home and dress up for night, doing some extra work in a totally different field (acting in a fringe play)!

Telephone interviewers can make or break a B2B telephone survey. A professional manner and approach can make a huge difference. If studies come back with lots of 'questions unanswered' or many 'don't knows', one must always look at the quality of the questionnaire and of the sample in the first place, but in the second, at the quality and briefing of the interviewers. Often, lots of unanswered questions (or uncoded responses that turn out to have been on the pre-code list after all) suggest that interviewing quality has not been as high as it should be. Go for the specialist interviewers whenever possible; skimping on quality in B2B fieldwork is never a good option.

B2B recruiters

B2B recruiters who set up face-to-face qualitative interviews, telephone interviews – or, on occasion, mini focus groups or full group discussions – are often a very special sort of person who share many of the characteristics of the previous categories of business researchers. Good business recruiters are few and far between, and when you find some, look after them. These people can recruit to the most demanding specifications; but this is not easy, and it takes time and skill. They need to be exceptionally persuasive, to know when to put pressure on and when to back off, and tend to have a good voice, patience and a convincing manner. Very often, the best recruiters have experience in some other field before 'falling into' their jobs in recruiting (again, sometimes not their 'main' career) – a happy accident.

Other roles

Other people engaged in B2B research include those who specialize in desk research, transcribers of tapes from focus groups and in-depth interviews, data entry staff, those who code up questionnaires, and those in data processing and analysis. Common to these roles is a need for a meticulous attention to detail and ability to translate the complex into the simple. The business researcher is often at the cutting edge in terms of business developments worldwide: a privileged position. As Scott Adams said, 'Creativity is allowing you to make mistakes. Art is knowing which ones to keep' – the Dilbert principle.

SUMMARY

Business researchers are rarely there by initial volition; many find their way to business research as they are attracted by its diversity and eclecticism. There tends to be somewhat more emphasis on ad hoc research and somewhat less on tracking research. The audiences to whom business researchers are speaking are often people with intimate knowledge of complex, and sometimes arcane, areas. We must sometimes encourage others who do not have a tradition of research to take risks and to have the courage of their convictions based on what we know is solid and good research. Business researchers are often aware of trends, of new business thinking, and of leaps forward in new product and design development well ahead of others. We are in a situation of both privilege and responsibility. Let's respect and enjoy it.

12 Training, organizations and ethics in B2B research

Briefly, this chapter covers three big issues. The first issue is training for B2B research – what is available and from where. The second discusses some organizations that are involved in B2B research and what they do. The third examines ethics associated with conducting B2B research: areas B2B researchers need to be particularly aware of in terms of the way they do their work, including data protection aspects. Some of the organizations mentioned in the second section will also be useful sources of information regarding the third.

TRAINING

To date, there is no body dedicated to training in B2B market research, nor are there any particular qualifications offered exclusively for working in the B2B research area. In the UK, for example, The Market Research Society (MRS) provides Introductory and Advanced Certificates and a Diploma in Market Research. These are general qualifications with minimal reference to B2B research but extensive reference to general market research principles, many of which of course underlie B2B practice. Every two years or so, the Business Intelligence Group (BIG) arranges a two-day training course that focuses entirely on B2B research.

Both within the UK and elsewhere, some individual research agencies allocate some time in their training programmes for junior staff, but learning about B2B research is more often done 'on the job' than in the classroom. Some coverage of market research is available of course via universities, business schools and other bodies under the 'marketing' heading, but the business-specific angle is more usually just part of the mix rather than the key focus.

In the United States, it is a similar situation. B2B training is included in more general research training, but not in great detail. There are two well-known sources of market research training courses: The Burke Institute (www.burkeinstitute.com) has a range of courses delineated by technique or method, and the RIVA Training Institute specializes in qualitative research and encompasses both B2C and B2B (www.rivainc.com). There are a number of MBA Marketing Research courses. Examples include the University of Wisconsin-Madison School of Business, University of Texas-Arlington, University of Georgia-Atlanta and University of Chicago. Most courses will include some element of B2B.

If you are interested in a career in B2B research, the best option is to join a client company that has significant B2B revenue (and does research) or a research agency with people devoted to work outside the consumer arena, usually a division or unit devoted to B2B and B2C research.

ORGANIZATIONS

Many organizations focus on marketing, many on market research, and relatively few relate to B2B activities or purely to B2B market research. These organizations perform a variety of functions. They are there primarily to serve their members – they act as foci for their members, they enable the sharing of information and news of our industry, and they provide networking opportunities. In addition, they perform a useful role acting as industry spokespeople and ensuring that our business is understood and that regulators and the legislature are well informed. They act as a repository of non-sectarian information for all of us and as a useful source of information on events, research news, and guidance on industry guidelines and data protection. As a B2B researcher, get to know your overall industry body as well as any B2B-specific network.

To look first at useful organizations geographically, some of the major organizations that encompass B2B market research, while not focusing solely on it, are listed in Table 12.1. The website www.quirks.com provides a list of market research, marketing, advertising, industry associations, quality organizations and statistical groups across a number of countries. Quirks also provides very useful market research reviews, some of which are mentioned in the References and further reading on page 299.

Some brief descriptions of some key bodies follow, although, as stated above, most have a much wider focus than just B2B research.

AIMRI (international, mainly Europe)

AIMRI was formed in 1991 and is based in London, although it represents an international constituency of market research agencies. Its aim is to promote business development for aligned agencies, whatever the nature of their specialism.

AMA (United States)

The AMA has market research and B2B marketing sections on its website. The B2B marketing articles can give a general feel for topical issues of interest. The market research section provides short advisory pieces on subjects such as quantitative research and focus group principles. These can be useful but at a rather broad level and without necessarily being focused on just B2B.

ARF (United States)

The ARF is a general organization but offers some guidance on B2B.

CASRO (United States and elsewhere)

CASRO is a trade association of research agencies, representing companies primarily in the United States, Canada and Mexico. It convenes annual educational conferences aimed at practitioners.

EFAMRO (Europe)

Formed in 1992, EFAMRO is an international federation of market research agency associations within the European Union. It provides extensive guidance on general data protection and ethical issues.

ESOMAR (international)

ESOMAR describes itself as European by origin, worldwide in activities, with a network of representatives in more than 70 countries globally. It is the largest market research-specific body. It holds a regular annual congress as well as seminars and conferences throughout the year, some of which are dedicated to specific areas that touch on B2B. These may include subject areas such as customer service or more specific sectors such as the automotive industry or pharmaceuticals, many of which may include papers of relevance to the B2B audience. ESOMAR also produces various publications and an annual Directory, which is a useful source of information on agencies and their specialization in most countries of the world. This can be useful when searching for B2B specialists.

IPA (UK)

The IPA is less market research-orientated but provides details of advertising and marketing practitioners in the UK. It is helpful because it provides a listing of around 25 marketing agencies for which over 50 per cent of their revenue is derived from B2B work. It is often difficult to find B2B specialists, so it is useful to be able to pinpoint them via such a general site. Although they are not market researchers first and foremost, finding other marketing/advertising agencies with a B2B specialism can be valuable.

MRS (UK and elsewhere)

MRS is the largest research industry body, representing all in market research, on both the client and agency side, although many agencies also belong to BMRA (the British Market Research Association). It operates well beyond the UK as it has over 8,000 members in more than 50 countries.

B2B research specialist industry bodies (UK)

BIG and the BIG Conference are two organizations in the UK dedicated to B2B market research.

BIG (Business Intelligence Group)

- BIG is dedicated to supporting and promoting the interests of individuals involved in any aspect of business intelligence and market research, whether as information users or suppliers.
- It produces a regular newsletter, *The Big Times*, and holds regular evening forum meetings in London dedicated to B2B research topics.
- All involved in B2B research in the UK should consider membership.
- The website has details via MrWeb of all main worldwide market research organizations, a useful link.

Table 12.1 *Market research organizations*

Region	Organization	Acronym	Contact details
Europe and international	European Society of Opinion and Market Research	ESOMAR	www.esomar.org Tel: +31 20 664 2141
	European Federation of Associations of Market Research Organisations	EFAMRO	www.efamro.org 26 Chester Close North, Regent's Park, London NW1 4JE Tel/fax: +44 20 7224 3873
	Alliance of International Market Research Institutes	AIMRI – used to be AEMRI	www.aemri.org 26 Granard Avenue, London SW15 6HJ Tel: +44 20 8780 3343
USA	American Marketing Association	AMA	www.marketing power.com
	Advertising Research Foundation	ARF	www.arfsite.org 641 Lexington Avenue, New York, NY 10022 Tel: +1 212 751 5656
	Market Research Association	MRA	www.mra-net.org 1344 Silas Deane Highway, Suite 306, Rocky Hill, CT 06067-1342 Tel: +1 860 257 4008
	Council of American Survey Organizations	Casro	www.casro.org 170 North Country Road, Suite 4, Port Jefferson, NY 11777 Tel: +1 631 928 6954 e-mail: casro@casro.org
UK	Market Research Society	MRS	www.mrs.org.uk 15 Northburgh St, London EC1V 0JR Tel:+44 (0) 20 7490 4911

	Institute of Practitioners in Advertising	IPA	www.ipa.co.uk
	Business Intelligence Group *	BIG	www. b2bresearch.org Contact Fiona Roberts-Miller, e-mail: fionarm@onetel. net.uk
			or tel: +44 1306 741368 or the BIG Chair, Claire Labrum, e-mail: Claire. labrum@synovate.com or tel: +44 207 923 6235
	BIG Conference *		www. bigconference.org Contact Pene Healey, e-mail: pene@clara.co.uk or tel: +44 20 8864 1834
Australia	Australian Market and Social Research Society	AMSRS	www.mra.com.au Level 1, 3 Queen Street Glebe, Sydney NSW Australia 2037 Tel: +61 2 9566 3102

* Two organizations, both based in the UK, that do specialize in B2B.

BIG Conference

- Autonomous in operation, though linked with BIG.
- Holds a conference in the UK in May each year with around 100 attending, client and agency side, providing an opportunity for B2B researchers and marketers to get together, hear papers, participate in training workshops and share news and views devoted to B2B and business issues.

■ Is becoming increasingly international and hopes, in the future, to provide *the* international forum for B2B research new thinking and discussion.

Other more specialist organizations

A few larger market sectors have their own organizations. Examples are PBIRG (Pharmaceutical Business and Intelligence Research Group, in the United States) and EphMRA (European Pharmaceutical Market Research Association). These are known for well-attended and well-focused conferences in the medical/pharmaceutical area, which is their main business focus.

ETHICS IN B2B RESEARCH

Codes of conduct

Codes of conduct in market research are intended to protect researchers, and more particularly, the public with whom we deal. The aim is to have guidelines in terms of behaviour to preserve the good name of the profession and to ensure that we maintain the respect of the business community we serve. Probably the best known international code of conduct is the ICC/ESOMAR International Code of Marketing and Social Research, available on the ESOMAR website. This provides not just guidelines on research in general but some that are particularly pertinent for the B2B researcher (for example, guidelines on customer satisfaction studies, on using the internet, on video recording and on particular sectors such as pharmaceutical market research).

Like ESOMAR, the UK-based MRS provides guidance on particular nominated areas: its guidelines on conducting online research for example are updated every two years as things can change so fast. EphMRA and PBIRG have guidelines on internet research particularly relating to pharmaceutical research on their website.

At present, there is no agreed code for B2B research in particular, although there used to be an IMRA/MRS code of conduct in the UK – last revised in 1983. Nowadays, we abide by the general research codes of conduct which cover the main issues germane to us as B2B researchers as well as to all others operating in the world of research.

The core codes are accessible readily via the industry organizations' websites as detailed earlier in this chapter. These cover:

- responsibilities to informants;
- the interaction between suppliers and users of market research;
- responsibilities to fieldworkers and other outside contractors;
- responsibilities to the general public, business community and other institutions;
- professional responsibilities.

In the United States, while there is no standard code of conduct, typically, ESOMAR or AMA guidelines are used as a reference source.

As B2B researchers, what do we need to particularly look out for? One of the main issues must be that no information should be attributable to a respondent personally or to a respondent's organization without a specific waiver. This requirement extends to the disclosure of identity by indirect as well as direct means – with small samples and easily distinguished characteristics, the business respondent may be more easily exposed by thoughtless description. Care must be taken always to prevent identification unless the respondent has given express agreement for his or her views to be known.

Respondents should be told that, as researchers and representing those who work with us, we *are* operating under a code of conduct. This is important in a world where 'sugging' (selling under the guise of market research) and other market research 'lookalikes' can undermine the reputation of genuine research in the home and workplace. Furthermore, in B2B research, when subjects are often highly confidential, with commercially useful information being revealed by the client and provided by our respondents, it is vital that respondents are reassured that the research is not part of any industrial espionage or that any sales calls will result. We have a duty to treat their information and goodwill with respect and to safeguard confidence in our profession.

Data protection

With the sorts of information with which we deal, having due regard to data protection is important for all of us in B2B research. Individual countries have specific data protection laws that must be obeyed. It is the duty of all researchers to acquaint themselves with, and to abide by, the data protection principles of the countries within which they operate. Also, some client companies have a compliance officer, and sometimes it is useful to make contact with this individual before undertaking any research to ensure there will be no repercussions. If in doubt, refer for guidance to your local country research trade organization or to a body such as the MRS' Professional Standards Committee and Codeline, which provides specific advice on request.

Particular European Union Directives include the Directive of the European Parliament and of the Council of Ministers of 24 October 1995 on the protection of individuals with regard to the processing of personal data and on the free movement of such data, and the Directive of the European Parliament and the Council of Ministers of November 1997 concerning the processing of personal data and the protection of privacy in the telecommunications sector.

In the UK, the MRS and BMRA provide information on their websites about the principles of the 1998 UK Data Protection Act (for more information, see the website www.dataprotection.gov.uk). See the end of the chapter for more information on the UK MRS guidelines – these should be relatively typical of 'official' guidelines in other countries.

Via its website, EFAMRO provides the Plain Man's Guide to Data Protection, which gives a useful overview in lay, and rather humorous, terms. Some extracts from this are given below:

> Tapes and videos must be regarded as personal data and you must follow the revised ESOMAR Guidelines on this subject relating to respondent permissions.
>
> Care must also be taken that even where the data is anonymous there is no element of identifiability (sic). By that it is meant that there is a low probability of an individual being recognized, for example in the way a lottery winner can be identified as being a blue eyed one legged Englishman with five cats living in Salerno.
>
> Clients will often not be aware of the Law and how it affects market research. Care must be taken to give the proper advice. Ignorance or action for a third party is not a defence.
>
> The Law covers the actions of all Companies in the EU and any transfer of data to other countries outside of the EU. Transferring completely anonymous data is OK, but personal data even a sampling frame must have the same rules observed by end users as if they were in the EU. The best way to ensure this is through the terms and conditions of your contracts.

One question for B2B market researchers is, 'Does everything have to be conducted according to our industry codes?' In fact, (in the UK) there is an exceptional circumstance where you *can* operate outside the code of conduct called 'Category Six' research (for example, if you want to use the market research data acquired for database building). This can only operate if the researcher does *not* say that any research is being conducted under the aegis of the MRS. However, to undertake this activity you need to be aware of the Direct Selling Directive and the Direct Marketing Guidelines; it is not without legislative implications of its own. If you are a B2B researcher who is an MRS member, for such research you must not mention the MRS or promise confidentiality – in other words, the respondent must not believe that the research is being undertaken as a market research project with the 'usual' protection offered. Category Six work may be useful on occasion in the B2B environment where a client wants to tidy up or add to its database while research is being conducted, but should not by any means be used to replace our normal way of working, which provides safeguards for the individual and keeps market research and direct marketing as very distinct disciplines.

SUMMARY

In summary, there are many organizations that offer help to B2B researchers. Both local and international organizations provide information and it may be useful to consider membership. There are a few B2B-specific organizations that can be particularly helpful. In such a relatively small industry as B2B research, knowing others who operate in the area and what latest thinking is can be important. These various organizations help us keep up to date and make us look outside our own 'small patch'. Behaving sensibly, professionally and with due regard to ethical and data protection considerations makes common sense. If in doubt, ask. Go on the web, look things up. Discuss with others. Do not 'wing it'.

Appendix 1

Sources for B2B market researchers

ONLINE SOURCES FOR DIFFERENT INDUSTRIES AND MARKET SECTORS

Online data searches can be overwhelming, as there is so much to choose from. Some websites that are particularly useful to the business researcher were mentioned in January 2004 by Nick Thomas of MrWeb and Trevor Wilkinson of Purple Market Research at a BIG Forum meeting (BIG is the Business Intelligence Group, the UK association of B2B market researchers). They, and some others, are listed here.

Published reports

Data Monitor (www.datamonitor.com)

Less easy to navigate than some of the other sites because reports are listed by sector (for instance technology, pharmaceuticals) rather than just alphabetically by subject name. However, this is a powerhouse of information if the report you are looking for is there. Some current ones listed are:

Table A1.1 *Useful websites*

Type of source or type of information	Website(s)	Description
Good general sources	www.google.com	Starting here or with another search engine such as yahoo.com is a good way to begin to filter the search. Watch sponsored links, as these are paid for and may not always be on spec
	www.Reuters.com	Business news and sector-specific bulletins
	www.bloomberg.com	Business news and sector-specific bulletins
	www.quirks.com	Marketing research review includes contact details for advertisers, trades bodies, associations and MR companies, statistics sources (worldwide)
	www.mrweb.co.uk	Sectors/SIC-based information and portals
	Economist series	
	Harvard Business Review series	
Journals, periodicals, media	www.ft.com www.economist.com www.bbc.co.uk www.wsj.com www.nypl.org Journal of Business to Business Marketing Brandweek Advertising Age Journal of Advertising Research Journal of Marketing Communication Research	Websites of major city newspapers and media outlets (eg Financial Times, Wall Street Journal Interactive, which provides useful business reviews) New York Public Library site

	Journal of Marketing Research	
	Marketing News	1987 **21** (1), p 14 has useful definition of market research in article entitled 'New marketing research definition approved'
	Marketing Science	
Government sites	GKsoft.com.govt	Comprehensive government information and statistics for all major countries
	www.Eurostat	European Union statistics
	www.statistics.gov.uk	UK national statistics
	www.sbs.gov.uk	UK Small business info (including by SIC code)
	www.tradepartners. gov.uk	
	www.dti.gov.uk	
	www.eef.org.uk	
	www.statisticks.bund	German statistics
	www.insee.fr	French statistics
	www.statcan.ca	Canadian statistics
	www.abs.gov.au	Australian statistics
	www.stats.govt.nz	New Zealand statistics
	www.stat.go.jp	Japanese statistics
	www.census.gov	United States: there is a cornucopia of stats from federal and state organizations
	www.census.gov/ stat_abstract	
	www.stat-usa.gov	Government info –
	www.fedstats.gov	economic, financial and trade data
	www.amstat.org	US statisticians' organization
	www.census.gov/ epcd/www/ naics.html	Info on the new US industry classification system

(Continued)

Table A1.1 *(Continued)*

Type of source or type of information	Website(s)	Description
Market and industry reports (Obviously, numerous, often country-specific)	www.hoovers.com	A–Z company profiles – top competitors and market shares
	www.keynote.co.uk	
	www.business.com	
	www.datamonitor.com	
	www.mintel.com	
	www.international businessstrategies.com	Agglomerated published information for different countries in PDF format across a range of relevant B2B subjects
	www.NationMaster. com	US site good for comparative stats and linked sources. Can make charts from it
	www.cia.gov	Central Intelligence Agency and producer of World Fact Book
	www.knowthis.com	A virtual marketing library run out of the United States
Technology/ innovation	www.globalwatchon-line.com	Latest developments in innovation
	www.silicon.com	Weekly technical round-up, streaming video, news
	www.triple-s.org	Technology news, software downloads, support
	www.research-live.com www.directory. google.com	Software reviews, daily research news, industry events
	www.brint.com	Reviews and describes software and technical

		services and gives links additional information and corporate websites
		The BizTech Network
Trade bodies and sector-specific sites (many mainly UK but will have equivalents elsewhere)	www.smmt.co.uk or www.mira.co.uk	UK Automotive
	www.cbi.org.uk	Confederation of British Industry
	www.cim.org.uk	Chartered Institute of Marketing
	www.riba.org	Architects
	www.architecture.com	Architects/construction
	www.oil.com	Oil industry
	www.totaltele.com	Telecommunications
	www.analysis.com	Telecommunications and others
Company lists (see also Market and industry reports)	www.dnb.com	Dun & Bradstreet – worldwide major supplier of lists and company information
	www.forbes.com	Sector reports plus links to other databases
	www.reedinfo.co.uk	

- Digital TV: The development of the Western Europe and US markets to 2008. Cost US $3,995.
- Technology spending plans in the German public sector. Cost US $2,295.

Key Note (www.keynote.co.uk)

Reports are listed in alphabetical order but the site does not say which jurisdictions they cover and only gives prices in pounds sterling. There are numerous reports to choose from. Some relating to the air industry, currently shown on the site as an example, include:

- aerospace, July 2003;
- air transport logistics, March 2003;
- air freight, December 2001.

Costs for these reports are around £350, making them considerably less costly than Mintel reports.

Mintel (www.mintel.com)

Reports are listed in alphabetical order and designate coverage of the United States, the UK or international jurisdictions. Many are relevant to B2B markets. For example, listed at present on the site are reports on:

- European hotel chain expansion, May 2004;
- food storage, United States, May 2004;
- telecoms retailing, UK, May 2004;
- energy supplements, United States, April 2004;
- redefining ecotourism, international, April 2004.

Euromonitor (www.euromonitor.com)

Reports may be less useful than some others to the B2B researcher as many of them concern food and drink, FMCG and retail issues. General reports are available, however: for example, there is currently one on major market share companies in Western Europe, April 2004, at a price of US $995. There are also some individual company reports (for example, Kirin Beverages at US $330), but even these tend to be biased to consumer goods concerns.

INDUSTRY-SPECIFIC PUBLISHED REPORTS

Industry-specific published reports are many and varied. Their availability can be sourced using industry associations, trade magazines and internet search engines. Here is just one example in the automotive field. The newly launched Used Truck Tracker provides market information for commercial OEMs, fleet and leasing companies, and aftermarket component (replacement parts) manufacturers. The source is called Used Truck MarketView; further information is available from Polk & Co on www.polk.com.

Two widely known commentators on technology markets are Forrester Research and the Gartner Group. Often these groups are sought out by the media to be spokespersons for new technology and trends – explaining innovations and change – and by venture capitalists to help assess investment strategies in the technology area.

THE BRITISH LIBRARY

The British Library provides a research service (details from its website, www.bl.uk or research@bl.uk). Areas it covers include:

- patents, trademarks and designs;
- biology and medicine;
- chemistry;
- engineering and technology;
- companies and markets;
- official publications.

All searches are carried out in strict confidence. It can also help in the following ways:

- tracking competitors: news, patents, product launches;
- accessing the latest scientific and technological developments;
- searching patent information;
- identifying opportunities to license new technologies;
- supplying copies of documents located during the search, using the British Library's collections.

Appendix 2
Sample screener questionnaire for in-depth interview

INTRODUCTION

Good morning/afternoon/evening. My name is... and I am calling you from Research IT Services, an independent market research company. We are carrying out a short survey on behalf of Mathilda ISP on the service your company gets from your Internet Service Provider. Please could I ask you a few questions?

> CE1 (CE – Category Exclusion) is designed to exclude (in this case) 'expert groups' whose opinions are not wanted in this study.

CE1   First of all, can I ask if your company is involved in any of the following? **READ LIST (EXCEPT NONE)**

Tourism	1	CONTINUE
Agriculture	2	CONTINUE
Telephone services	3	CLOSE
ISP services	4	CLOSE
None of these (DO NOT READ OUT)	X	CONTINUE

SCREENER QUESTIONS

S1a and S1b (S – Screener question) are designed to identify the most appropriate person to answer the questionnaire.

S1a   Can I also confirm that you are the person in your company in charge of handling user queries in regard to queries or problems with the internet?

Yes	1	CONTINUE
No	2	ASK TO BE TRANSFERRED TO RELEVANT PERSON & REPEAT INTRO
Don't know	3	ASK TO BE TRANSFERRED TO RELEVANT PERSON & REPEAT INTRO

S1b   Mathilda Telephones is interested specifically in improving its performance when dealing with calls related to technical issues: that is, effectively, queries that are NOT related to billing or promotional offers or the more everyday aspects of contacting customer service. Would you be able to answer questions in regard to this topic?

| Yes | 1 | CONTINUE |
| No | 2 | ASK TO BE TRANSFERRED TO RELEVANT PERSON & REPEAT INTRO |

S1c   Who provides your internet service (ie Who do you pay your bills to?) READ OUT. SINGLE CODE

Mathilda	1	CONTINUE
AOL	2	CLOSE
Freeserve	3	CLOSE
Wanadoo	4	CLOSE
Virgin	5	CLOSE

| BT | 6 | CLOSE |
| Tiscali | 7 | CLOSE |

S2   How long has your company been a customer of Mathilda? **READ OUT. SINGLE CODE**

| Less than 6 months | 1 | CHECK QUOTAS |
| More than 6 months | 2 | CHECK QUOTAS |

S3   When did you last phone Mathilda's customer service for any reason other than billing or to take advantage of a promotional/special offer? **READ OUT. SINGLE CODE**

Never phoned	1	CLOSE
6–12 months	2	CHECK QUOTAS
3–6 months	3	CHECK QUOTAS
Within the last 3 months	4	CHECK QUOTAS

S4   How many employees are there in your company? **WRITE   IN AND CODE. THREE DIGITS**

11–50	1	CHECK QUOTAS
51–100	2	CHECK QUOTAS
101–250	3	CHECK QUOTAS
251–500	4	CHECK QUOTAS
Over 500	5	CHECK QUOTAS

Appendix 3
Sample focus group recruitment questionnaire

Good morning, afternoon, evening. I am calling from XXX (**INSERT NAME OF AGENCY**), an independent market research company. We are conducting some research amongst tradespeople, which will be in the form of a group discussion/focus group (**FOR WHICH WE WILL PAY YOU/DONATE TO CHARITY/ETC... INSERT AS APPROPRI-ATE**). The subject of the discussion will be communications with suppliers (how do suppliers communicate with you).

    i. Would you be interested in taking part in a group discussion/focus group?

    ii. Could I confirm the trade you are in?

CHECK QUOTA REQUIRED

Yes	1 Continue
No	2 Thank respondent for their time and close

Roofer	1
Builder	2
Carpenter/joiner	3
Electrician	4
Plumber, Gas fitter/fitter	5

Q.1   Is this your own company, or are you employed by someone else?

Own company	1 Ask Q2
Employed by someone else	2 Thank respondent for their time and close

Q.2   Do you have any employees?

Yes	1 – Ask Q3
No	2

FOR PLUMBERS/GAS FITTERS/FITTERS, IF HAVE NO EMPLOY-EES, GO TO Q4

   FOR ANY OF THE OTHER TRADES, WHO DO NOT HAVE EMPLOYEES, SKIP TO QA

   ALL THOSE WHO HAVE EMPLOYEES, ASK Q3

   Q.3   How many employees do you have?

RESPONDENTS MUST EITHER BE SOLE TRADERS (NO EMPLOYEES) OR HAVE NO MORE THAN 10 EMPLOYEES

One	A
Two	B
Three to five	C
Six to ten	D
More than ten	E – Thank respondent and close

ASK PLUMBERS/GAS FITTERS/FITTERS ONLY – ALL OTHER TRADESMEN, GO TO QA

Q.4   Are you Corgi registered?

Yes	1 Ask QA
No	2 Ask QA

CHECK QUOTA REQUIRED.

ASK ALL

Q.A   Have you ever attended a market research group discussion or interview?

Yes	Ask QB
No	Skip to QE

Q.B   How long ago did you attend a market research group discussion or interview?

Within the last 6 months	Close Interview
6–12 months ago	Ask QC
1–2 years ago	Ask QC
Over 2 years ago	Ask QC

Q.C   How many group discussions/interviews have you ever attended?

One to two	Ask QD
Three or more	Close

Q.D   What was the subject of the group discussions/interviews you attended?

Write in_____

IF ON A SIMILAR SUBJECT – DO NOT RECRUIT

Q.E Does any member of your family or do any of your close friends work in any of the following occupations, either now or in the past two years?

Advertising	1 Close
Market research	2 Close
Public relations	3 Close
Journalism/TV/radio	4 Close
Media	5 Close
NONE OF THESE	6 Recruit according to quota

Appendix 4
Research snapshot as a reporting technique

Research conducted by: Company A, Project Research Executives X, and Y

Windy City Marketing Research & Consulting – Jack Kravitz, Managing Director

Date: October 2003

Aim: To understand the real needs and aspirations of the different customer groups in relation to use or possible use of natural gas fuel for their vehicles.

Method: Five group discussions were held – three with self-employed taxi drivers and two with self-employed Kombi drivers in Sao Paulo, Brazil; in addition, two depth interviews with taxi fleet owners.

Findings:

The great majority of the respondents desire the use of natural gas fuel.

There is a high level of awareness of the savings it could afford them and of the positive environmental effects the use of natural gas could bring about.

The main impediments to the usage of natural gas fuel are:

- Firstly, the price of the fuel cylinder installation. Tied to this, there is a general lack of understanding of which fuel cylinders were the most adequate for the price being asked.
- Secondly, the present fuelling situation, with very few filling stations available and long lines to wait for fuelling.

Of the possible benefits the most important ones are: free/reduced-price car washes/lube jobs; friendly and attentive service at the filling stations; little or no wait for fuelling; adequate fuelling pressure; current accounts for fuel payment; check-cashing privileges at the natural gas filling stations.

The frequent users' card and offers of free books and school material, tickets to sporting events, family days at amusement parks, etc are all found to be 'interesting', as long as this would afford customers the recognition they felt they deserved as frequent users.

The taxi fleet owners interviewed feel that the auto manufacturers should produce natural gas fuel vehicles from scratch, thus guaranteeing the usage of a minimum amount of trunk space, so important for taxis.

Appendix 5

Sample self-completion questionnaire (Business Link)

An example of a self-completion questionnaire is given here for reference.

FREE TRAINING FOR 5 STAFF MEMBERS

Business Link for London, the business support service for the capital is carrying out an Organisational Skills Survey of the training needs of small and medium sized companies in London – and we need your help. TAKE JUST TEN MINUTES TO COMPLETE ONE SIMPLE SET OF QUESTIONS AND YOU COULD WIN £5000 WORTH OF TRAINING for your staff or management as well as six months free support from a dedicated Business Link for London adviser.

Completing the Business Link for London training needs survey gives you five chances to win up to £5000 worth of training for your staff or management.

1ST –£5000   2ND –£3500   3RD –£2000
4TH –£1000   5TH –£500

And all prizes come with six month free support from a dedicated Business Link for London adviser.

By completing the survey you'll be helping us to get a picture of training needs across the capital and influence future provision, but even more importantly you'll be identifying how to get the best from your employees, right now and in the years to come. It's your chance to make your business more focused, more effective and more profitable than ever before. **You're just ten minutes away from a prize that could transform your business.**

SIMPLY COMPLETE THE QUESTIONNAIRE OVERLEAF AND HAND IT TO YOUR ADVISER, FAX IT TO US AT 020 8443 7270 OR POST IT TO US AT LINK HOUSE, 292-308 SOUTHBURY ROAD, ENFIELD, EN1 1TS.

FOR FURTHER INFORMATION
CALL 0845 6000 787 OR VISIT
WWW.BUSINESSLINK4LONDON.COM

BUSINESS LINK Learning+Skill council

ORGANISATIONAL SKILLS SURVEY:FAX IT TO BUSINESS LINK FOR
LONDON 020 8443 7270

Company name

Address and postcode

Tel no   Email

Your name   Position

Nature of business   Number of employees

Year established   Gender of ownership   MALE ◯   FEMALE ◯   MIXED ◯
Ethnicity of ownership of your company

WHITE ◯   MIXED ◯   ASIAN ◯   ASIAN BRITISH ◯   CHINESE ◯

BLACK ◯   BLACK BRITISH ◯   OTHER ◯   PREFER NOT TO SAY ◯

**1 Is your organisation prevented from meeting its business priorities in any way because of a
lack of any of the following skills?**
a Managerial   YES ◯   NO ◯
b Sales/Marketing   YES ◯   NO ◯
c IT   YES ◯   NO ◯
d Other technical (If yes please specify nature of skill/s)   YES ◯   NO ◯

e Financial   YES ◯   NO ◯
f Administrative   YES ◯   NO ◯
g Basic Skills e.g.Literacy and Numeracy   YES ◯   NO ◯
h Other skills (If yes please specify nature of skill/s)   YES ◯   NO ◯

2 Do you have a company training plan?   YES ◯   NO ◯

3 Have you set aside a budget for training?   YES ◯   NO ◯

FOR FURTHER INFORMATION
CALL 0845 6000 787 OR VISIT
WWW.BUSINESSLINK4LONDON.COM

BUSINESS LINK   Learning+Skill council

4 Are your managers offered training to improve their people management skills?
If yes, what do you offer?   YES ◯   NO ◯
_____
_____

5 Do you know what type of training your employees will need in the coming year?
If yes, please specify   YES ◯   NO ◯
_____
_____

6 What proportion of your employees received training in the last twelve months?
            NONE ◯   UP TO 10% ◯   10 % TO 50% ◯   OVER 50% ◯

7 Roughly how many days per year does the average employee spend on training?
                        NONE ◯   1-5 ◯   6 OR MORE ◯

8 Roughly how much did you spend on training and development per employee in the last twelve months?
NOTHING ◯   UP TO £200 ◯   £200 TO £500 ◯   £500 TO £1000 ◯   OVER £1000 ◯

9 Do you consider that training contributes to improving business performance?
If yes, how do you know?   YES ◯   NO ◯
_____
_____

10 What proportion of your employees has an annual appraisal?
                NONE ◯   UP TO 10% ◯   10%TO 50% ◯   OVER 50% ◯

11 Do you have any 16-23 year olds in your organisation?
If yes, what vocational training do you offer?   YES ◯   NO ◯
_____
_____

12 Are you an Investor in People organisation?   YES ◯   NO ◯

FOR FURTHER INFORMATION
CALL 0845 6000 787 OR VISIT
WWW.BUSINESSLINK4LONDON.COM

BUSINESS LINK   Learning+Skill council

13 Do you have a business plan with goals and objectives for the next twelve months or longer?

YES ○   NO ○

14 What do you consider to be the biggest challenges limiting the growth of your business?

15 Would you like a representative of Business Link for London
a to contact you to discuss how we could help you improve the skills of your people?

YES ○   NO ○

b a copy of the Organisational Skills Survey results   YES ○   NO ○

c free fortnightly e-newsletter   YES ○   NO ○

YOUR PERSONAL ACTION PLAN

What actions are you prepared to take to improve the skills of your staff over the next twelve months?

In the next three months?

In the following three months?

In the following six months?

Signature   Date

Terms and conditions

1 Any company completing a Business Link for London OSS will be entered into a draw to win one of the five prizes specified above.

2 A company can only qualify for entry into the draw once.

3 A participating company may only win one prize.

4 The competition is only open to companies based in the Greater London area.

5 The draw will take place on Friday 16th April 2004 at Business Link for London, 3rd floor, Centre Point,103 New Oxford Street, London, WC1A 1DP.

6 Winners will be notified within seven working days of the draw.

8 Winners will receive six months support from a Business Link for London adviser who will help you identify relevant effective training and validate the delivery. This will take the form of up to eight hours advice and support per month to be delivered in person, by telephone or by email as most appropriate.

9 All prizes must be taken within 12 months from the 31st March 2003. No cash alternative will be provided.

10 The adjuducator's decision is final and no correspondence will be entered into.

11 The prize draw is not open to any agents involved with the competition.

12 Proof of submitting an entry is not proof of receipt of an entry. Responsibility cannot be accepted for lost of undelivered entries.

FOR FURTHER INFORMATION CALL 0845 6000 787 OR
VISIT WWW.BUSINESSLINK4LONDON.COM

BUSINESS LINK   Learning+Skill council

Appendix 6

Sample customer satisfaction research quantitative questions

These are some of the sorts of questions that are asked in customer service research. First there is an overall service satisfaction question, then later come questions looking first at the importance of service attributes then at performance.

Overall question

Q   Thinking about all aspects of the service you get from **SUPPLIER**, including account management, price, coverage, customer service and handset availability, how satisfied would you say you were with **SUPPLIER? PLEASE TICK ONE RESPONSE ONLY**

Very satisfied   1
Fairly satisfied   2
Neither   3
Not very satisfied   4
Not at all satisfied   5
Don't know   6

Relative importance of different service factors

Q Thinking again about the last time you phoned **SUPPLIER** in regard to a technical issue (ie any issue not involved with billing or special offers), please can you say how important each of the following are.

PLEASE TICK THE RELEVANT BOX FOR EACH STATEMENT ROTATE.

Please use a scale of 5 down to 1, where 5 is extremely important and 1 is not at all important.

	Not at all important	Extremely important	D/K
Speed of answering the call	1 2 3 4 5		6
Time spent on hold	1 2 3 4 5		6
Manner of the staff	1 2 3 4 5		6
The automatic phone menu (eg the menu that you go through before speaking to a person)	1 2 3 4 5		6
Being passed to no more than two people	1 2 3 4 5		6
The knowledge of the staff	1 2 3 4 5		6
Length of time taken to resolve the query/problem	1 2 3 4 5		6
Updating you on progress of the call	1 2 3 4 5		6
Ability to resolve the query	1 2 3 4 5		6
Staff knowledge of your business	1 2 3 4 5		6

Performance against the different service factors

Q Thinking again about the last time you phoned **SUPPLIER** in regard to a technical issue (ie any issue not involved with billing or special offers), please can you say how well **SUPPLIER** performed on the issues we have just mentioned? Please use a scale of 5 down to 1 where 5 is excellent, 4 is very good, 3 is fair, 2 is poor and 1 is very poor.
ROTATE
PLEASE TICK THE RELEVANT BOX FOR EACH STATEMENT

	Very poor	Excellent	D/K
Speed of answering the call	1 2 3 4 5		6
Time spent on hold	1 2 3 4 5		6
Manner of the staff	1 2 3 4 5		6
The automatic phone menu (eg the menu that you go through before speaking to a person)	1 2 3 4 5		6
Being passed to no more than two people	1 2 3 4 5		6
The knowledge of the staff	1 2 3 4 5		6
Length of time taken to resolve the query/problem	1 2 3 4 5		6
Updating you on progress of the call	1 2 3 4 5		6
Ability to resolve the query	1 2 3 4 5		6
Staff knowledge of your business	1 2 3 4 5		6

Appendix 7
Sample communication research quantitative questionnaire

This is from a quantitative telephone interview with European opinion-formers including association member companies.

Q.54 Which, if any, X communication initiatives or activities are you aware of? **DO NOT READ OUT.**

   FIRST MENTION – **SINGLE CODE**
   OTHER MENTION – **MULTICODE**

   DEPTHS ONLY: ask respondents how they were made aware of these activities/initiatives?

Q.55 And which of these other communications initiatives or activities are you aware of?

   READ OUT ALL NOT MENTIONED AT Q54.
   MULTICODE

Q.56 Thinking now about general information sources produced by X, can you tell me whether you have received, consulted or attended any of the following? **READ OUT. MULTICODE**

ASK Q57 ONLY FOR THOSE ITEMS MENTIONED IN Q56

Q.57   And in your opinion how useful is each of these sources of information? Would you say that it was very useful, fairly useful, not very useful or not at all useful?

READ OUT ALL MENTIONED IN Q56. SINGLE CODE

	First Mention Q54	SPONT Q54	PRO- MPT Q55	Used Q56	Usefulness Q57				
	(408)	(409)	(410)	(411)	**Very**	**Fairly**	**Not very**	**Not at all**	
Newsletter	1	1	1	1	1	2	3	4	(412)
Fact sheets	2	2	2	2	1	2	3	4	(413)
Customer updates	3	3	3	3	1	2	3	4	(414)
Seminars	4	4	4	4	1	2	3	4	(415)
Briefings	5	5	5	5	1	2	3	4	(416)
Advocacy programmes	6	6	6	6	1	2	3	4	(417)
Joint working groups	7	7	7	7	1	2	3	4	(418)
Meetings and presentations to industry partners	8	8	8	8	1	2	3	4	(419)
Joint projects	9	9	9	9	1	2	3	4	(420)
Websites	0	0	0	0	1	2	3	4	(421)
	(422)	(423)	(424)	(425)					
Personal contact with X representative	1	1	1	11	1	2	3	4	(426)
Scientific or technical papers	2	2	2	2	1	2	3	4	(427)
Legislation documents	3	3	3	3		1	2	3	(428)
Other (specify)	4	4	4	4	1	2	3	4	(429)

Appendix 8
Principles of the Data Protection Act 1998

All processing of personal data must conform to the requirements of the 1998 UK Data Protection Act. There are eight key principles, one of which is 'Personal data shall not be transferred to a country or territory outside the European Economic Area unless that country or territory ensures an adequate level of protection for the rights and freedoms of data subjects in relation to the processing of personal data.'

The guiding principles of the Act are:

- Transparency – ensuring individuals have a very clear and unambiguous understanding of the purpose(s) for collecting the data and how it will be used.
- Consent – at the time that the data is collected, individuals must give their consent to their data being collected, and also at this time, have the opportunity to opt out of any subsequent uses of the data.

When collecting research data the purpose of the data collection must be transparent. Data collected only for market research purposes must only be used for that purpose. If data is to be collected for other purposes such as staff training this must be explained from the outset.

If a respondent's details are to be held on a database for a further interview, the respondent must be made aware of this at the initial interview and given the option not to be recontacted.

Appendix 9

The Market Research Society Code of Conduct

INTRODUCTION

The market research society

With over 8,000 members in more than 50 countries, The Market Research Society (MRS) is the world's largest international membership organization for professional researchers and others engaged in (or interested in) marketing, social or opinion research.

It has a diverse membership of individual researchers within agencies, independent consultancies, client-side organizations, and the academic community, and from all levels of seniority and job functions.

All members agree to comply with the MRS Code of Conduct, which is supported by the Codeline advisory service and a range of specialist guidelines on best practice.

MRS offers various qualifications and membership grades, as well as training and professional development resources to support these. It is the official awarding body in the UK for vocational qualifications in market research.

MRS is a major supplier of publications and information services, conferences and seminars and many other meeting and networking opportunities for researchers.

MRS is 'the voice of the profession' in its media relations and public affairs activities on behalf of professional research practitioners, and aims to achieve the most favourable climate of opinions and legislative environment for research.

The purpose of the code of conduct

This edition of the Code of Conduct was agreed by The Market Research Society to be operative from July 1999. It is a fully revised version of a self-regulatory code which has been in existence since 1954. This Code is based upon and fully compatible with the ICC/ESOMAR International Code of Marketing and Social Research Practice. The Code of Conduct is designed to support all those engaged in marketing or social research in maintaining professional standards. It applies to all members of The Market Research Society, whether they are engaged in consumer, business to business, social, opinion or any other type of confidential survey research. It applies to all quantitative and qualitative methods for data gathering. Assurance that research is conducted in an ethical manner is needed to create confidence in, and to encourage cooperation among, the business community, the general public, regulators and others.

The Code of Conduct does not take precedence over national law. Members responsible for international research shall take its provisions as a minimum requirement and fulfil any other responsibilities set down in law or by nationally agreed standards.

The purpose of guidelines

MRS Guidelines exist or are being developed in many of these areas in order to provide a more comprehensive framework of interpretation. These guidelines have been written in recognition of the increasingly diverse activities of the Society's members, some of which are not covered in detail by the Code of Conduct. A full list of guidelines appears on the Society's website, and is also available from the Society's Standards Manager.

One particular guideline covers the use of databases containing personal details of respondents or potential respondents, both for purposes associated with confidential survey research and in cases where respondent details are passed to a third party for marketing or other purposes. This guideline has been formally accepted by the Society, following extensive consultation with members and with the Data Protection Registrar/Commissioner.

Relationship with data protection legislation

Adherence to the Code of Conduct and the database Guidelines will help to ensure that research is conducted in accordance with the principles of data protection legislation. In the UK this is encompassed by the Data Protection Act 1998.

Data Protection Definitions

Personal Data means data which relates to a living individual who can be identified:

- from the data, or
- from the data and other information in the possession of, or likely to come into the possession of, the data controller

and includes any expression of opinion about the individual and any indication of the intentions of the data controller or any other person in respect of the individual.

Processing means obtaining, recording or holding the information or data or carrying out any operation or set of operations on the information or data, including:

- organization, adaptation or alteration;
- retrieval, consultation or use;
- disclosure by transmission, dissemination or otherwise making available;
- alignment, combination, blocking, erasure or destruction.

It is a requirement of membership that researchers must ensure that their conduct follows the letter and spirit of the principles of Data Protection legislation from the Act. In the UK the eight data protection principles are:

- **The First Principle**
  Personal data shall be processed fairly and lawfully.[1]
- **The Second Principle**
  Personal data shall be obtained only for one or more specified and lawful purposes, and shall not be further processed in any manner incompatible with that purpose or those purposes.
- **The Third Principle**
  Personal data shall be adequate, relevant and not excessive in relation to the purpose or purposes for which they are processed.
- **The Fourth Principle**

Personal data shall be accurate and, where necessary, kept up to date.

- **The Fifth Principle**

  Personal data processed for any purpose or purposes shall not be kept longer than is necessary for that purpose or those purposes.

- **The Sixth Principle**

  Personal data shall be processed in accordance with the rights of data subjects under this Act.

- **The Seventh Principle**

  Appropriate technical and organizational measures shall be taken against unauthorized or unlawful processing of personal data and against accidental loss or destruction of, or damage to, personal data.

- **The Eighth Principle**

  Personal data shall not be transferred to a country or territory outside the European Economic Area, unless that country or territory ensures an adequate level of protection for the rights and freedoms of data subjects in relation to the processing of personal data.

Exemption for Research Purposes

Where personal data processed for research, statistical or historical purposes are not processed to support decisions affecting particular individuals, or in such a way as likely to cause substantial damage or distress to any data subject, such processing will not breach the Second Principle and the data may be retained indefinitely despite the Fifth Principle.

As long as the results of the research are not published in a form, which identifies any data subject, there is no right of subject access to the data.

Code Definitions

- **Research**

  Research is the collection and analysis of data from a sample of individuals or organizations relating to their characteristics, behaviour, attitudes, opinions or possessions. It includes all forms of marketing and social research such as consumer and industrial surveys, psychological investigations, observational and panel studies.

- **Respondent**

  A respondent is any individual or organization from whom any information is sought by the researcher for the purpose of a marketing or social research project. The term covers cases where information is to be obtained by verbal interviewing techniques, postal and other self-completion questionnaires, mechanical or electonic equipment, observation and any other method where the identity of the provider of the information may be recorded or otherwise traceable. This includes those approached for research purposes whether or not substantive information is obtained from them and includes those who decline to participate or withdraw at any stage from the research.

■ **Interview**

An interview is any form of contact intended to provide information from a respondent.

■ **Identity**

The identity of a respondent includes, as well as his/her name and/or address, any other information which offers a reasonable chance that he/she can be identified by any of the recipients of the information.

■ **Children**

For the Purpose of the Code, children and young people are defined as those aged under 18. The intention of the provisions regarding age is to protect potentially vulnerable members of society, whatever the source of their vulnerability, and to strengthen the principle of public trust. Consent of a parent or responsible adult should be obtained for interviews with children under 16. Consent must be obtained under the following circumstances:

■ in home/at home (face-to-face and telephone interviewing);
■ group discussions/depth interviews;
■ where interviewer and child are alone together.

Interviews being conducted in public places, such as in-street/in-store/central locations, with 14 and 15 years olds may take place without consent if a parent or responsible adult is not accompanying the child. In these situations an explanatory thank you note must be given to the child.

Under special circumstances, a survey may waive parental consent but only with the prior approval of the Professional Standards Committee.

■ **Records**

The term records includes anything containing information relating to a research project and covers all data collection and data processing documents, audio and visual recordings. Primary records are the most comprehensive record of information on which a project is based; they include not only the original data records themselves, but also anything needed to evaluate those records, such as quality control documents. Secondary records are any other records about the Respondent.

- **Client**
  Client includes any individual, organization, department or division, including any belonging to the same organization as the research agency which is responsible for commissioning a research project.
- **Agency**
  Agency includes any individual, organization, department or division, including any belonging to the same organization as the client which is responsible for, or acts as, a supplier on all or part of a research project.
- **Professional Body**
  Professional body refers to The Market Research Society.
- **Public Place**
  A 'public place' is one to which the public has access (where admission has been gained with or without a charge) and where an individual could reasonably expect to be observed and/or overheard by other people, for example in a shop, in the street or in a place of entertainment.

PRINCIPLES

Research is founded upon the willing cooperation of the public and of business organizations. It depends upon their confidence that it is conducted honestly, objectively, without unwelcome intrusion and without harm to respondents. Its purpose is to collect and analyse information, and not directly to create sales nor to influence the opinions of anyone participating in it. It is in this spirit that the Code of Conduct has been devised.

The general public and other interested parties shall be entitled to complete assurance that every research project is carried out strictly in accordance with this Code, and that their rights of privacy are respected. In particular, they must be assured that no information which could be used to identify them will be made available without their agreement to anyone outside the agency responsible for conducting the research. They must also be assured that the information they supply will not be used for any purposes other than research and that they will not be adversely affected or embarrassed as a direct result of their participation in a research project.

Wherever possible respondents must be informed as to the purpose of the research and the likely length of time necessary for the collection of the information. Finally, the research findings themselves must always be reported accurately and never used to mislead anyone, in any way.

RULES

A. Conditions of membership and professional responsibilities

A.1   Membership of the professional body is granted to individuals who are believed, on the basis of the information they have given, to have such qualifications as are specified from time to time by the professional body and who have undertaken to accept this Code of Conduct. Membership may be withdrawn if this information is found to be inaccurate.

General Responsibilities

A.2   Members shall at all times act honestly in dealings with respondents, clients (actual or potential), employers, employees, subcontractors and the general public.

A.3   Members shall at all times seek to avoid conflicts of interest with clients or employers and shall make prior voluntary and full disclosure to all parties concerned of all matters that might give rise to such conflict.

A.4   The use of letters after an individual's name to indicate membership of The Market Research Society is permitted in the case of Fellows (FMRS) and Full Members (MMRS). All members may point out, where relevant, that they belong to the appropriate category of the professional body.

A.5   Members shall not imply in any statement that they are speaking on behalf of the professional body unless they have the written authority of Council or of some duly delegated individual or committee.

Working Practices

A.6   Members shall ensure that the people (including clients, colleagues and subcontractors) with whom they work are sufficiently familiar with this Code of Conduct and that working arrangements are such that the Code is unlikely to be breached through ignorance of its provisions.

A.7   Members shall not knowingly take advantage, without permission, of the unpublished work of a fellow member which is the property of that member. Specifically, members shall not carry out or commission work based on proposals prepared by a member in another organization unless permission has been obtained from that organization.

A.8 All written or oral assurances made by anyone involved in commissioning of conducting projects must be factually correct and honoured.

Responsibilities to Other Members

A.9 Members shall not place other members in a position in which they might unwittingly breach any part of this Code of Conduct.

Responsibilities of Clients to Agencies

A.10 Clients should not normally invite more than four agencies to tender in writing for a project. If they do so, they should disclose how many invitations to tender they are seeking.

A.11 Unless paid for by the client, a specification for a project drawn up by one research agency is the property of that agency and may not be passed on to another agency without the permission of the originating research agency.

Confidential Survey Research and Other Activities

(apply B.15 and Notes to B.15)

A.12 Members shall only use the term *confidential survey research* to describe research projects which are based upon respondent anonymity and do not involve the divulgence of identities or personal details of respondents to others except for research purposes.

A.13 If any of the following activities are involved in, or form part of, a project then the project lies outside the scope of confidential survey research and must not be described or presented as such:

(a) enquiries whose objectives include obtaining personal information about private individuals per se, whether for legal, political, supervisory (eg job performance), private or other purposes;

(b) the acquisition of information for use by credit-rating or similar purposes;

(c) the compilation, updating or enhancement of lists, registers or databases which are not exclusively for research purpose (eg which will be used for direct or relationship marketing);

(d) industrial, commercial or any other form of espionage;

(e) sales or promotional responses to individual respondents;

(f) the collection of debts;

(g) fund raising;

(h) direct or indirect attempts, including the framing of questions, to influence a respondent's opinions or attitudes on any issue other than for experimental purposes which are identified in any report or publication of the results.

A.14 Where any such activities referred to by paragraph A.13 are carried out by a member, the member must clearly differentiate such activities by:

(a) not describing them to anyone as confidential survey research and

(b) making it clear to respondents at the start of any data collection exercise what the purposes of the activity are and that the activity is not confidential survey research.

Scope of Code

A.15 When undertaking confidential survey research based on respondent anonymity, members shall abide by the ICC/ESOMAR International Code of Conduct which constitutes Section B of this Code.

A.16 MRS Guidelines issued, other than those published as consultative drafts, are binding on members where they indicate that actions or procedures *shall* or *must* be adhered to by members. Breaches of these conditions will be treated as breaches of the Code and may be subject to disciplinary action.

A.17 Recommendations within such guidelines that members should behave in certain ways are advisory only.

A.18 It is the responsibility of members to keep themselves updated on changes or amendments to any part of this Code which are published from time to time and announced in publications and on the web pages of the Society. If in doubt about the interpretation of the Code, members may consult the Professional Standards Committee or its Codeline Service set up to deal with Code enquiries.

Disciplinary Action

A.19 Complaints regarding breaches of the Code of Conduct by those in membership of the MRS must be made to The Market Research Society.

A.20 Membership may be withdrawn, or other disciplinary action taken, if, on investigation of a complaint, it is found that in the opinion of the professional body, any part of the member's research work or behaviour breaches this Code of Conduct.

A.21 Members must make available the necessary information as and when requested by the Professional Standards Committee and Disciplinary Committee in the course of an enquiry.

A.22 Membership may be withdrawn, or other disciplinary action taken, if a member is deemed guilty of unprofessional conduct. This is defined as a member:

(a) being guilty of any act or conduct which in the opinion of a body appointed by Council might bring discredit on the profession, the professional body or its members;

(b) being guilty of any breach of the Code of Conduct set out in this document;

(c) knowingly being in breach of any other regulations laid down from time to time by the Council of the professional body;

(d) failing without good reason to assist the professional body in the investigation of a complaint;

(e) having a receiving order made against him/her or making any arrangement or composition with his/her creditors;

(f) being found to be in breach of the Data Protection Act by the Data Protection Registrar.

A.23 No member will have his/her membership withdrawn, demoted or suspended under this Code without an opportunity of a hearing before a tribunal, of which s/he will have at least one month's notice.

A.24 Normally, the MRS will publish the names of members who have their membership withdrawn, demoted or are suspended or have other disciplinary action taken with the reasons for the decision.

A.25 If a member subject to a complaint resigns his/her membership of the Society whilst the case is unresolved, then such resignation shall be published and in the event of re-admission to membership the member shall be required to cooperate in the completion of any outstanding disciplinary process.

B. ICC/ESOMAR code of marketing and social research practice

General

B.1 Marketing research must always be carried out objectively and in accordance with established scientific principles.

B.2 Marketing research must always conform to the national and international legislation which applies in those countries involved in a given research project.

The Rights of Respondents

B.3 Respondents' cooperation in a marketing research project is entirely voluntary at all stages. They must not be misled when being asked for cooperation.

B.4 Respondents' anonymity must be strictly preserved. If the respondent on request from the Researcher has given permission for data to be passed on in a form which allows that respondent to be identified personally:
  (a) the Respondent must first have been told to whom the information would be supplied and the purposes for which it will be used, and also
  (b) the Respondent must ensure that the information will not be used for any non-research purpose and that the recipient of the information has agreed to conform to the requirements of the Code.

B.5 The Researcher must take all reasonable precautions to ensure that Respondents are in no way directly harmed or adversely affected as a result of their participation in a marketing research project.

B.6 The Researcher must take special care when interviewing children and young people. The informed consent of the parent or responsible adult must first be obtained for interviews with children.

B.7 Respondents must be told (normally at the beginning of the interview) if observation techniques or recording equipment are used, except where these are used in a public place. If a respondent so wishes, the record or relevant section of it must be destroyed or deleted. Respondents' anonymity must not be infringed by the use of such methods.

B.8 Respondents must be enabled to check without difficulty the identity and bona fides of the Researcher.

The Professional Responsibilities of Researchers

B.9 Researchers must not, whether knowingly or negligently, act in any way which could bring discredit on the marketing research profession or lead to a loss of public confidence in it.

B.10 Researchers must not make false claims about their skills and experience or about those of their organization.

B.11 Researchers must not unjustifiably criticise or disparage other Researchers.

B.12 Researchers must always strive to design research which is cost-efficient and of adequate quality, and then to carry this out to the specification agreed with the Client.

B.13 Researchers must ensure the security of all research records in their possession.

B.14 Researchers must not knowingly allow the dissemination of conclusions from a marketing research project which are not adequately supported by the data. They must always be prepared to make available the technical information necessary to assess the validity of any published findings.

B.15 When acting in their capacity as Researchers the latter must not undertake any non-research activities, for example database marketing involving data about individuals which will be used for direct marketing and promotional activities. Any such non-research activities must always, in the way they are organized and carried out, be clearly differentiated from marketing research activities.

Mutual Rights and Responsibilities of Researchers and Clients

B.16 These rights and responsibilities will normally be governed by a written Contract between the Researcher and the Client. The parties may amend the provisions of rules B.19–B.23 below if they have agreed this in writing beforehand; but the other requirements of this Code may not be altered in this way. Marketing research must also always be conducted according to the principles of fair competition, as generally understood and accepted.

B.17 The Researcher must inform the Client if the work to be carried out for that Client is to be combined or syndicated in the same project with work for other Clients but must not disclose the identity of such clients without their permission.

B.18 The Researcher must inform the Client as soon as possible in advance when any part of the work for that Client is to be subcontracted outside the Researcher's own organization (including the use of any outside consultants). On request the Client must be told the identity of any such subcontractor.

B.19 The Client does not have the right, without prior agreement between the parties involved, to exclusive use of the Researcher's services or those of his organization, whether in whole or in part. In carrying out work for different clients, however, the Researcher must endeavour to avoid possible clashes of interest between the services provided to those clients.

B.20 The following Records remain the property of the Client and must not be disclosed by the Researcher to any third party without the Client's permission:

(a) marketing research briefs, specifications and other information provided by the Client;

(b) the research data and findings from a marketing research project (except in the case of syndicated or multi-client projects or services where the same data are available to more than one client).

The Client has, however, no right to know the names or addresses of Respondents unless the latter's explicit permission for this has first been obtained by the Researcher (this particular requirement cannot be altered under Rule B.16).

B.21 Unless it is specifically agreed to the contrary, the following Records remain the property of the Researcher:

(a) marketing research proposals and cost quotations (unless these have been paid for by the Client). They must not be disclosed by the Client to any third party, other than to a consultant working for the Client on that project (with the exception of any consultant working also for a competitor of the Researcher). In particular, they must not be used by the Client to influence research proposals or cost quotations from other Researchers.

(b) the contents of a report in the case of syndicated research and/or multi-client projects or services when the same data are available to more than one client and where it is clearly understood that the resulting reports are available for general purchase or subscription. The Client may not disclose the findings of such research to any third party (other than his own consultants and advisors for use in connection with his business) without the permission of the Researcher.

(c) all other research Records prepared by the Researcher (with the exception in the case of non-syndicated projects of the report to the Client, and also the research design and questionnaire where the costs of developing these are covered by the charges paid by the Client).

B.22 The Researcher must conform to current agreed professional practice relating to the keeping of such records for an appropriate period of time after the end of the project. On request the Researcher must supply the Client with duplicate copies of such records provided that such duplicates do not breach anonymity and confidentiality requirements (Rule B.4); that the request is made within the agreed time limit for keeping the Records; and that the Client pays the reasonable costs of providing the duplicates.

B.23 The Researcher must not disclose the identity of the Client (provided there is no legal obligation to do so) or any confidential information about the latter's business, to any third party without the Client's permission.

B.24 The Researcher must, on request, allow the Client to arrange for checks on the quality of fieldwork and data preparation provided that the Client pays any additional costs involved in this. Any such checks must conform to the requirements of Rule B.4.

B.25 The Researcher must provide the Client with all appropriate technical details of any research project carried out for that Client.

B.26 When reporting on the results of a marketing research project the Researcher must make a clear distinction between the findings as such, the Researcher's interpretation of these and any recommendations based on them.

B.27 Where any of the findings of a research project are published by the Client, the latter has a responsibility to ensure that these are not misleading. The Researcher must be consulted and agree in advance the form and content of publication, and must take action to correct any misleading statements about the research and its findings.

B.28 Researchers must not allow their names to be used in connection with any research project as an assurance that the latter has been carried out in conformity with this Code unless they are confident that the project has in all respects met the Code's requirements.

B.29 Researchers must ensure that Clients are aware of the existence of this Code and of the need to comply with its requirements.

NOTES

How the ICC/ESOMAR international code of marketing and social research practice should be applied

These general notes published by ICC/ESOMAR apply to the interpretation of Section B of this Code in the absence of any specific interpretation which may be found in the MRS Definitions, in Part A of the MRS Code or in Guidelines published by the MRS. MRS members who are also members of ESOMAR will in addition be subject to requirements of the guidelines published by ESOMAR.

These Notes are intended to help users of the Code to interpret and apply it in practice.

The Notes, and the Guidelines referred to in them, will be reviewed and reissued from time to time. Any query or problem about how to apply the Code in a specific situation should be addressed to the Secretariat of MRS.

The Rights of Respondents

All Respondents are entitled to be sure that when they agree to cooperate in any marketing research project they are fully protected by the provisions of this Code and that the Researcher will conform to its requirements. This applies equally to Respondents interviewed as private individuals and to those interviewed as representatives of organizations of different kinds.

Note on Rule B.3

Researchers and those working on their behalf (eg interviewers) must not, in order to secure Respondents' cooperation, make statements or promises which are knowingly misleading or incorrect – for example, about the likely length of the interview or about the possibilities of being re-interviewed on a later occasion. Any such statements and assurances given to Respondents must be fully honoured.

Respondents are entitled to withdraw from an interview at any stage and to refuse to cooperate further in the research project. Any or all of the information collected from or about them must be destroyed without delay if the Respondents so request.

Note on Rule B.4

All indications of the identity of Respondents should be physically separated from the records of the information they have provided as soon as possible after the completion of any necessary fieldwork quality checks. The Researcher must ensure that any information which might identify Respondents is stored securely, and separately from the other information they have provided; and that access to such material is restricted to authorized research personnel within the Researcher's own organization for specific research purposes (eg field administration, data processing, panel or 'longitudinal' studies or other forms of research involving recall interviews).

To preserve Respondents' anonymity not only their names and addresses but also any other information provided by or about them which could in practice identify them (eg their Company and job title) must be safeguarded.

These anonymity requirements may be relaxed only under the following safeguards:

(a) Where the Respondent has given explicit permission for this under the conditions of 'informed consent' summarized in Rule 4 (a) and (b).

(b) Where disclosure of names to a third party (eg a Subcontractor) is essential for any research purpose such as data processing or further interview (eg an independent fieldwork quality check) or for further follow-up research. The original Researcher is responsible for ensuring that any such third party agrees to observe the requirements of this Code, in writing, if the third party has not already formally subscribed to the Code.

It must be noted that even these limited relaxations may not be permissible in certain countries. The definition of 'non-research activity', referred to in Rule 4(b), is dealt with in connection with Rule I5.

Note on Rule B.5

The Researcher must explicitly agree with the Client arrangements regarding the responsibilities for product safety and for dealing with any complaints or damage arising from faulty products or product misuse. Such responsibilities will normally rest with the Client, but the Researcher must ensure that products are correctly stored and handled while in the Researcher's charge and that Respondents are given appropriate instructions for their use. More generally, Researchers should avoid interviewing at inappropriate or inconvenient times. They should also avoid the use of unnecessarily long interviews; and the asking of personal questions which may worry or annoy Respondents, unless the information is essential to the purposes of the study and the reasons for needing it are explained to the Respondent.

Note on Rule B.6

The definitions of 'children' and 'young people' may vary by country but if not otherwise specified locally should be taken as 'under 14 years' and '14–17 years' (under 16, and 16–17 respectively in the UK).

Note on Rule B.7

The Respondent should be told at the beginning of the interview that recording techniques are to be used unless this knowledge might bias the Respondent's subsequent behaviour: in such cases the Respondent must be told about the recording at the end of the interview and be given the opportunity to see or hear the relevant section of the record and, if they so wish, to have this destroyed. A 'public place' is defined as one to which the public has free access and where an individual could reasonably expect to be observed and/or overheard by other people present, for example in a shop or in the street.

Note on Rule B.8

The name and address/telephone number of the Researcher must normally be made available to the Respondent at the time of interview. In cases where an accommodation address or 'cover name' are used for data collection purposes arrangements must be made to enable Respondents subsequently to find without difficulty or avoidable expense the name and address of the Researcher. Wherever possible 'Freephone' or similar facilities should be provided so that Respondents can check the Researcher's bona fides without cost to themselves.

The Professional Responsibilities of Researchers

This Code is not intended to restrict the rights of Researchers to undertake any legitimate marketing research activity and to operate competitively in so doing. However, it is essential that in pursuing these objectives the general public's confidence in the integrity of marketing research is not undermined in any way. This Section sets out the responsibilities which the Researcher has towards the public at large and towards the marketing research profession and other members of this.

Note on Rule B.14

The kinds of technical information which should on request be made available include those listed in the Notes to Rule B.25. The Researcher must not however disclose information which is confidential to the Client's business, nor need he/she disclose information relating to parts of the survey which were not published.

Note on Rule B.15

The kinds of non-research activity which must not be associated in any way with the carrying out of marketing research include: enquiries whose objectives are to obtain personal information about private individuals *per se*, whether for legal, political supervisory (eg job performance), private or other purposes; the acquisition of information for use for credit rating or similar purposes; the compilation, updating or enhancement of lists, registers or databases which are not exclusively for research purposes (eg which will be used for direct marketing); industrial, commercial or any other form of espionage; sales or promotional attempts to individual Respondents; the collection of debts; fund-raising; direct or indirect attempts, including by the design of the questionnaire, to influence a Respondent's opinions, attitudes or behaviour on any issue.

Certain of these activities – in particular the collection of information for databases for subsequent use in direct marketing and similar operations – are legitimate marketing activities in their own right. Researchers (especially those working within a client company) may often be involved with such activities, directly or indirectly. In such cases it is essential that a clear distinction is made between these activities and marketing research since by definition marketing research anonymity rules cannot be applied to them.

Situations may arise where a Researcher wishes, quite legitimately, to become involved with marketing database work for direct marketing (as distinct from marketing research) purposes: such work must not be carried out under the name of marketing research or of a marketing research organization as such.

The Mutual Rights and Responsibilities of Researchers and Clients

This Code is not intended to regulate the details of business relationships between Researchers and Clients except in so far as these may involve principles of general interest and concern. Most such matters should be regulated by the individual business. It is clearly vital that such Contracts are based on an adequate understanding and consideration of the issues involved.

Note on Rule B.18

Although it is usually known in advance what subcontractors will be used, occasions do arise during the project where subcontractors need to be brought in, or changed, at very short notice. In such cases, rather than cause delays to the project in order to inform the Client it will usually be sensible and acceptable to let the Client know as quickly as possible after the decision has been taken.

Note on Rule B.22

The period of time for which research Records should be kept by the Researcher will vary with the nature of the project (eg ad hoc, panel, repetitive) and the possible requirements for follow-up research or further analysis. It will normally be longer for the stored research data resulting from a survey (tabulations, discs, tapes etc) than for primary field records (the original completed questionnaires and similar basic records). The period must be disclosed to, and agreed by, the Client in advance. In default of any agreement to the contrary, in the case of ad hoc surveys the normal period for which the primary field records should be retained is one year after completion of the fieldwork while the research data should be stored for possible further analysis for at least two years. The Researcher should take suitable precautions to guard against any accidental loss of the information, whether stored physically or electronically, during the agreed storage period.

Note on Rule B.24

On request the Client, or his mutually acceptable representative, may observe a limited number of interviews for this purpose. In certain cases, such as panels or in situations where a Respondent might be known to (or be in subsequent contact with) the Client, this may require the previous agreement of the Respondent. Any such observer must agree to be bound by the provisions of this Code, especially Rule B.4.

The Researcher is entitled to be recompensed for any delays and increased fieldwork costs which may result from such a request. The Client must be informed if the observation of interviews may mean that the results of such interviews will need to be excluded from the overall survey analysis because they are no longer methodologically comparable.

In the case of multi-client studies the Researcher may require that any such observer is independent of any of the Clients.

Where an independent check on the quality of the fieldwork is to be carried out by a different research agency the latter must conform in all respects to the requirements of this Code. In particular, the anonymity of the original Respondents must be fully safeguarded and their names and addresses used exclusively for the purposes of back-checks, not being disclosed to the Client. Similar considerations apply where the Client wishes to carry out checks on the quality of data preparation work.

Notes on Rule B.25

The Client is entitled to the following information about any marketing research project to which he has subscribed:

(1) **Background**
- for whom the study was conducted;
- the purpose of the study;
- names of subcontractors and consultants performing any substantial part of the work.

(2) **Sample**
- a description of the intended and actual universe covered;
- the size, nature and geographical distribution of the sample (both planned and achieved); and where relevant, the extent to which any of the data collected were obtained from only part of the sample;
- details of the sampling method and any weighting methods used;
- where technically relevant, a statement of response rates and a discussion of any possible bias due to non-response.

(3) **Data Collection**
- a description of the method by which the information was collected;
- a description of the field staff, briefing and field quality control methods used;
- the method of recruiting Respondents; and the general nature of any incentives offered to secure their cooperation;
- when the fieldwork was carried out;
- (in the case of 'desk research') a clear statement of the sources of the information and their likely reliability.

(4) **Presentation of Results**
- the relevant factual findings obtained;
- bases of percentages (both weighted and unweighted);

- general indications of the probable statistical margins of error to be attached to the main findings, and the levels of statistical significance of differences between key figures;
- the questionnaire and other relevant documents and materials used (or, in the case of a shared project, that portion relating to the matter reported on).

The Report on a project should normally cover the above points or provide a reference to a readily available document which contains the information.

Note on Rule B.27

If the Client does not consult and agree in advance the form of publication with the Researcher the latter is entitled to:

(a) refuse permission for his name to be used in connection with the published findings and
(b) publish the appropriate technical details of the project (as listed in the Notes to B.25).

Note on Rule B.29

It is recommended that Researchers specify in their research proposals that they follow the requirements of this Code and that they make a copy available to the Client if the latter does not already have one.

CODELINE

Codeline is a free, confidential answer service to Market Research Society Code of Conduct related queries raised by market researchers, clients, respondents and other interested parties. The aim of Codeline is to provide an immediate, personal and practical interpretation and advice service.

Codeline is directly responsible to the MRS Professional Standards Committee (PSC) to which each query and its response is reported at PSC's next meeting. Queries from enquirers are handled by an individual member of the Codeline panel, drawn from past members of the PSC. As long as contact can be made with the enquirer, queries will be dealt with by Codeline generally within 24 hours. Where necessary, the responding Codeline member can seek further specialist advice.

Codeline's response to enquirers is not intended to be definitive but is the personal interpretation of the individual Codeline member, based on personal Code-related experience. PSC and Codeline panellists may highlight some of the queries and responses for examination and ratification by the PSC, the ultimate arbiter of the Code, at its next meeting. In the event that an individual Codeline response is not accepted by the PSC the enquirer will be notified immediately.

Enquirer details are treated as totally confidential outside the PSC but should 'Research' or any other MRS journal wish to refer to a particularly interesting or relevant query in 'Problem Page' or similar, permission is sought and obtained from the enquirer before anonymous publication and after that query's examination by PSC.

Codeline operates in the firm belief that a wide discussion of the issues arising from queries or anomalies in applying the Code and its associated guidelines within the profession will lead both to better understanding, awareness and application of the Code among members and to a better public appreciation of the ethical standards the market research industry professes and to which it aspires.

How to use codeline

Codeline deals with any market research ethical issues. To contact Codeline please phone or fax the MRS Secretariat who will then allocate your query to a Codeline panellist.

If you choose to contact MRS by phone, the MRS Secretariat will ask you to confirm by fax the nature of your query, whether or not the caller is an MRS member or works for an organization which employs an MRS member and a phone number at which you can be contacted. This fax will then be sent to the allocated panellist who will discuss your query directly with you by phone as soon as possible after receipt of your enquiry.

Please forward any queries about the MRS Code of Conduct and Guidelines, in writing to the:

MRS Secretariat, 15 Northburgh Street, London EC1V 0JR
Tel: 020 7490 4911 Fax: 020 7490 0608

NOTES

1   In particular shall not be processed unless at least one of the conditions in Schedule 2 is met, and in the case of sensitive data, at least one of the conditions of Schedule 3 is also met. (These schedules provide that in determining whether personal data has been processed fairly, consideration must be given to the basis on which it was obtained.)

Glossary

SELECTED ABBREVIATIONS

AMSRS	Market Research Society of Australia
ASBA	American Small Businesses Association
AURA	Association of Users of Research Agencies
B2B	business to business
B2C	business to consumer
BIG	Business Intelligence Group
BMRA	British Market Research Association
CAPI	computer-assisted personal interviewing
CATI	computer-assisted telephone interviewing
CAWI	computer-assisted web interviewing
CEO	chief executive officer
CFO	chief financial officer
COO	chief operating officer
CPG	consumer packaged goods
CRM	customer relationship marketing
DP	data processing
ESOMAR	European Society of Opinion and Market Research
FMCG	fast-moving consumer goods
HR	human resources
IFA	Intermediary Financial Adviser
IMRA	Industrial Marketing Research Association

IT	information technology
KPI	key performance indicator
MR	market research
MRS	Market Research Society
NAICS	North American Industrial Classification System
NPD	new product development
OTC	over the counter
OTS/H	opportunities to see or hear
PDA	personal digital assistant
PR	public relations
RFP	request for proposal
ROC	return on capital
ROI	return on investment
SIC	standard industry classification
SME	small or medium-sized enterprise
SOHO	small office home office

STATISTICAL TERMS

Census If we measure (interview) all members of the population then we call it a census. If we conduct a census then there are no statistical queries about the results. In consumer research it is very rare to conduct a census; this is less so in B2B research. If a company only has 20 clients, it might be perfectly reasonable to interview all 20.

Confidence Usually, when we conduct statistical tests, we want to know how 'good' our results are, or, more precisely, how well the results from the sample reflect the population. We do this by reporting two numbers: an error amount number and a confidence level. For example, if we were to select 1,000 people from the UK population of 60 million and ask them a question, then we would normally expect the result to be accurate to within ±3 per cent, with a confidence level of 95 per cent. This means that if we did a survey in which 50 per cent of the sample said they preferred Microsoft, then we would be 95 per cent sure that in the whole population between 47 per cent and 53 per cent of people prefer Microsoft. The 95 per cent confidence level means that if we were to conduct 100 projects, we would expect to be wrong about the error term in five cases (in those cases the error would be bigger than ±3 per cent).

Normal distribution The normal distribution is a very powerful statistical tool that allows us to easily calculate the likely error between a large sample and a large population. The normal distribution is based on an assumption that the sample is randomly selected, and that the element being measured is normally distributed, but these niceties are often ignored. In research, we typically choose a confidence level of 95 per cent, but this can be replaced by 90 per cent or even 80 per cent – it is a matter of choice.

Population The complete set of cases we are interested in. The population for a particular study may be all the men in the UK, all business owners in Nottinghamshire, or all malt whisky distillers in Scotland.

Random sampling A random or probability sample is one in which each individual or unit has a known (and non-zero) chance of inclusion: that is, a calculable a priori selection probability. It is rarely used in B2B.

Quota sampling In advance, setting a figure (or target) on the number of interviews with a type(s) of respondent group(s) that must be secured and then, as fieldwork is in progress, checking that we are getting the right people and in the right numbers.

Sample We conduct research to try to understand a population, but we usually do so by interviewing a subset of the population, and hoping that results of this subset are very similar to what we would have got if we had interviewed the whole population. The term 'sample' implies that the people are selected in a way that means that they are reasonably likely to be representative of the population. For example, we might select them randomly, or we might select them to match certain quotas (for example, 50 per cent male, 50 per cent female). Most conventional statistics are based on an assumption that the sample was drawn (that is, selected) randomly.

Sampling error Even when a sample is selected properly, it will not perfectly reflect the population. For example, if we have a population of 2 million cappuccino drinkers of whom 1 million are male and 1 million are female, and if we select 100 of them at random, then it is very unlikely that we will have exactly 50 men and 50 women. In fact, we can use statistics to tell us that the chance of getting exactly 50 men is about 8 per cent; if we were to repeat the process 100 times, we would expect to get exactly 50 men 8 times, and 92 times we would expect to get a larger or smaller number. The difference that occurs between the population data and the sample is called the sampling error.

Formula

The confidence values using the t-test are given by:

$$\pm \text{ values} = t * \frac{\sigma}{\sqrt{N}}$$

Data processing terms

Banner/breaks/sample breakdowns/sample cells   These are the categories/demographics/subgroups for which responses are analysed in addition to the total sample. They appear at the top of the printout.

Tab/stub/side head   The term for items listed on the left-hand side of tables which represent answers, whether these are categories, numerics, pre-coded responses, and codes used for open-ended questions.

BUSINESS TERMS

Proprietary   Owned or licensed by a particular company (used in reference to market research techniques). Non-proprietary techniques are publicly available and free for use by anyone.

SIC or SIC code   Standard Industry Classification, typically used by governments and other agencies to classify types of businesses into categories (and sub-categories – the level of specificity that is available varies depending on the industry category).

Sugging   Selling under the guise of market research.

TECHNOLOGY TERMS

These are some useful terms for B2B online research (Source: Research in business (thanks to Marc Brenner, *Research* magazine and Darren Noyce, SKOPOS), March 2004):

Automatic routing   Respondents to an online survey are automatically taken to the next relevant question, based on their previous answer.

Bulletin board   An online area where, according to themes or topics, messages and responses are posted for the purpose of communication or debate. Useful for loosely ongoing qualitative projects and where respondents might enjoy conferring.

Chatroom   Similarly, an online area where you can chat with other people but in real time. Again useful for online qualitative research.

E-mail invite   An e-mail sent to potential respondents allowing them to click a hotlink and directly access a survey. Can include passwords needed once the respondent enters the survey site.

Grid question   A type of online survey question comprising a series of statements or scales for evaluation and rating.

Partial complete   Where a respondent does not get to the end of an internet survey. The answers that have been given may or may not be included in the final data set.

Pop-up survey   A survey that 'pops up' in its own window.

Radio button   Used in online questionnaires, this allows the respondent to choose only one option from a list of possible answers.

TAWI   Telephone-assisted web-based interviewing. A hybrid method where interviewers from call centres or telephone interviewers might be used to guide a respondent through an online or web-based survey.

XML   eXtensible Markup language. A more dynamic successor to HTML. XML is used for transferring data to the web. It is also used for data exchange between B2B websites.

References and further reading

Ambler, Tim (2000) *Marketing and the Bottom Line: The new metrics of corporate wealth*, FT Prentice Hall, London

Bedbury, Scott (2002) *A New Brand World*, Penguin, New York

Brace, Ian (2004) *Questionnaire Design: How to plan, structure and write survey material for effective market research*, Kogan Page, London

Churchill, Gilbert (1999) *Marketing Research: Methodological foundations*, Dryden, Fort Worth, Texas

De Chenatony, Leslie (2001) *From Brand Vision to Brand Evaluation*, Butterworth-Heinemann, Oxford

Denzin, Norman and Lincoln, Yvonna (eds) (1994) *Handbook of Qualitative Research*, Sage, Thousand Oaks, CA

Douglas, Susan and Craig, C Samuel (1983) *International Marketing Research*, Prentice Hall, Englewood Cliffs, NJ

Economist (2003) *Economist Brands and Branding*, Bloomberg Press, Princeton, NJ (Specialist authors have prepared individual chapters. Three main themes are covered: the case for brands, best practice in branding (including case studies of visual and verbal identity, communications, and brand 'protection') and the future for brands (including globalization, opportunities in South-East Asia, and social responsibility). Chapters by Rita Clifton and John Simmons, Chuck Bryner, Shaun Smith, Tony Allen and John Simmons, and Jan Lindemann.)

Ferguson, George (1976) *Statistical Analysis in Psychology and Education*, McGraw-Hill, New York

Gilmore, Richard (2004) Doctors eat ice cream, too, paper for Market Research Conference, Market Research Society, London

Gordon, W (1999) *Goodthinking: A guide to qualitative research*, Admap, Henley on Thames

Groth, Robert (1997) *Data Mining: Building competitive advantage*, Prentice Hall, Englewood Cliffs, NJ

Hague, Paul, Hague, Nick and Morgan, Carol-Ann (2004) *Market Research in Practice: A guide to the basics*, Kogan Page, London

Hammersley, M and Atkinson, P (1995) *Ethnography: Principles in practice*, Routledge, London

Harvard Business Review (2001) Special edition on CRM, *Harvard Business Review*

Iacobucci, Dawn (ed) (2001) *Kellogg on Marketing*, Wiley, New York (This has three chapters specifically devoted to learning about the customer and the market place, addressing qualitative and quantitative market research techniques and applications, and each chapter contains a large reference list.)

Kantar Group (1995) Market research industry, *Economist*, 22 July, pp 60–63 (a study of the worldwide market research industry)

Kish, Leslie (1965) *Survey Sampling*, Wiley, New York

Krishamurthi, Lakshman (2001) Pricing strategies and tactics, in Dawn Iacobucci (ed), *Kellogg on Marketing*, Wiley, New York

Lenskold, James (2003) *Marketing ROI*, McGraw-Hill, New York

Leonard, Dick (2002) *Guide to the European Union*, Economist books [Online] www.bloomberg.com/economistbooks

Ling, John and Stuart, Mark (eds) (2003) *Marketing Research and Information*, CIM Publishing, London

Macer, Tim (2004) Quoted in research in business, integrating MR and technology supplement, *Research*, March

Macfarlane, Phyllis (1991) Sample design in selection and estimating, in *Researching Business Markets*, ed K Sutherland, pp 141–62, Kogan Page, London

Mandel, Michael (1997) Vital statistics for the real-life economy, *BusinessWeek*, 29 Dec, p 42

Market Research Society (2004) Research in business – integrating MR and technology, supplement for *Research*, sponsored by ORC International, March

McGivern, Y (2003) *The Practice of Market and Social Research: An introduction*, FT/Prentice Hall, London

McKinsey (2004) Guide to doing business in China, *McKinsey Quarterly* [Online] www.mckinseyquarterly.com (accessed June 2004)

Meijer, Wander (1999) Marketing research in Europe: it's the economy, stupid!, *Quirks Marketing Research Review* [Online] www.quirks.com (November) (accessed June 2004)

Morrison, Terri, Conaway, Wayne A and Borden, George A (1994) *Kiss, Bow or Shake Hands: How to do business in sixty countries*, Adams Media Corporation, Avon, MA

MrWeb (2002) B2B research skills – how are they different, *MrWeb Newsletter*, July

Nail, Jim (2002) Mastering marketing management, research report, Forrester Research, Cambridge, MA, September

Oechsle, S and Henderson, T (2000) Identity: an exploration into purpose and principles at Shell, *Corporate Reputation Review* **3**, pp 75–77

Poynter, Ray (2004) Small samples and small populations: a guide to good practice, BIG Conference paper, 19–21 May 2004, Chepstow

Rawnsley, Alan (ed) (1978) *A Manual of Industrial Marketing Research*, Wiley, Chichester

Reynolds, Janice (2002) *A Practical Guide to CRM*, Osborne McGraw-Hill, London

Rubin, H and Rubin, I (1995) *Qualitative Interviewing: The art of hearing data*, Sage, London

Sherry, John and Kozinets, Robert (2001) Qualitative inquiry in marketing and consumer research, in Dawn Iacobucci (ed), *Kellogg on Marketing*, Wiley, New York

Smela, Barbara (2002) Global research: what you need to know to be successful, *Quirks Marketing Research Review* [Online] www.quirks.com (November)

Sopp, Leslie (2004) Quoted in research in business integrating MR and technology supplement, *Research*, March

Stoll, Martin (2004) Advanced qualitative methods for researching the business consumer, BIG Conference paper, 19–21 May 2004, Chepstow

Sutherland, Ken (ed) (1991) *Researching Business Markets: The IMRA handbook of business-to-business marketing research*, Kogan Page, London

Wills, Steve (2004) A fundamental rethink on customer insight, BIG Conference paper, 19–21 May 2004, Chepstow

Wilson, Alan (2002) *Marketing Research: An integrated approach*, FT Prentice Hall, London

Wilson, Aubrey (1973) *The Assessment of Industrial Markets*, Associated Business Programmes, London

Index

ad hoc projects   55, 59, 172, 235
advertising   195–97
   market communications and
      198–200
   tracking   198
advertising and communications
   research   172
AIMRI (international, mainly
   Europe)   238, **240**
Ama (United States)   238, **240**, 243
Americas Marketing Pocket Book   71
AMSRS (Market Research Society of
   Australia)   6–7, 73
anonymity   90
Arf (United States)   238, **240**
Asia-Pacific   40
Asian regional review   215
   B2B focus   215–16
   environment   216–17
   international   215
   market size   215
   type of work   216
Association of Qualitative
   Researches (AQR)   161
Association of Users of Research
   Agencies (AURA)   105
attitudinal questions   114, 118–21
Australia   6–7, 30
   ASIC code   30, 219
   BIS conducts syndicated studies in
      B2B markets   60
   'early adopters'   218
   hub to coordinate Asia   213
   Market Research Society website
      72
Australian Bureau of Statistics
   219

B2B and B2C research,
   companies that typically undertake
      17
   major differences   12–13
   reasons for simultaneous research
      14
B2B client   221–22
   how to choose a B2B research
      supplier   226–28

preparing B2B research briefs
   225–26
responsibilities of   222–24
skills of   225
B2B interviewing, guidelines for
   88–89, 106
B2B research,
   appeal of   19
   borderline sectors of   18
   companies that undertake   17
   definition   3–5, 10
   experienced researchers have 'rule
      of thumb' for pricing   160
   history   5
   'how many' need we speak to
      11, 20
   how to count
      customer/respondent is
      perennial problem in   23
   learning often done 'on the job'
      237
   more expensive than consumer
      research   163–64
   role of technology growing in
      47
   screening for eligibility important
      35
   services and   31
   set of critical questions   20–21
   size of sector   5–7
   syndication not very common   60
   users of   16–19
   variation in size of samples for
      22, 32–35
   variety with different markets and
      new subjects   11
   'what' of research different in B2B
      context   12
   what to do to get fully *into*   51
   what to do when no databases are
      available   25
   when reporting think of the 'big
      picture'   159
B2B research specialist industry
   bodies (UK)   239
B2B researcher   228–29
   B2B recruiters and   234

302

case study: summary of B2B
    considerations for   229–30
fieldworker (telephone
    interviewer)   233–4
other roles for   234
projects in different stages   231–32
research executives as   230–31
B2C research,
    definition   3, 10–11
    finance, most business with
        ultimate consumer   17–18
banner specification   144–50, 297
Bedbury, Scott, *A New Brand World*
    (2002)   203, 206
behavioural questions   117–18
BIG (Business Intelligence Group)
    5, 236, 239, **241**
BIG conference   34, 94, **241**
BlackBerry   14, 53
Bloomerce, internet panel for
    European coverage   60
bought-in lists, problems of   25
brainstorming   4, 42, 79–81, 167
brand image and supplier reputation
    32
branding and corporate reputation
    16, 203–04
Brands and Branding   206
briefing, suggestions for   134–37
briefing paper   135–37
British Library   73
British Market Research Association
    (BMRA)   6
bubble diagrams   94
Burke Institute   237
business competition   48
business problems B2B research
    addresses   15
    research using external
        respondents   15–16
    research using internal respondents
        16

Canadian regional review   214–15
CASRO (United States and
    elsewhere)   238, **240**
'Category Six' research   244–45
CATI   32, 55, 131
CATI or CAPI (computer assisted
    telephone/personal
    interviewing) systems   32
CD ROM   105, 152
CEO (chief executive officer)   8, 11
CFO (chief financial officer)   8
challenges faced by B2B research,

negatives   48
other issues   48–49
Chartered Institute of Marketing
    (CIM)   113
charting   153–55, 156–59
China   40, 216
CIA's *World Fact Book*   71
client feedback reports   153
client lists, provided on paper or
    Excel spreadsheets or exportable
    formats   24–25
'coding frame', definition   143
communication channels   131
communications research, normal
    framework for   201
competitive analysis   44, 178
computer tables (cross-tabulations)
    and multivariate analysis   143–44
computer-assisted personal
    interviewing (CAPI)   32, 44, 123
Confirmit (questionnaire design
    software)   126, 130
conjoint or trade-off analysis,
    sometimes used in B2B   110
consolidation of companies   48
consumer research, predictable and
    'standard' pricing   160
COO (chief operating officer)   8
corporate finance   92
corporate name, primary brand
    name   203
corporate reputation research   205
cost, limiting factor on project size   11
costing,
    considerations from agency side
        164–65
    containing project costs   165
    factors influencing costs   161
    factors to take into account
        161–63
    implications   163–64
    first considerations   160–61
CPG (consumer packaged goods)   4
Crawford's Directory of City
    Connections   26–27
Curtis, Laurence (CEO of Research
    Business International)   6
customer relations management
    (CRM)   43, 74, 189–92, 193
customer satisfaction   18, 172
customer satisfaction/ customer
    relations management research
    179, 189–92
    measurement techniques and
        models   192–95

reporting for B2B   195–**96**

data mining   74–75
Data Monitor research report   72
data protection legislation and
     'licence to operate'   48
decision making, key criteria for   15
decision making questions   114,
     121–22
Dentrite International   43
desk research   4, 41, 44, 49, 61, 84,
     180
   another type: data mining
        74–75
   'backdrop' to qualitative or
        quantification research   69–70
   process   70–71
   resources for   71–72
      online sources   73–74
      research reports available
           72–73
   summary of what to consider
        when conducting   76
   validating data from   76
developed nations, trend from
     manufacture to technology
     179
diaries, used in consumer research
     112
differences between B2B and
     consumer research,
   content differences   12–13
   sample and size differences   10–12
Direct Mail Information Service   112
Direct Marketing Guidelines   245
Direct Selling Directive   245
drawing or other non-verbal
     techniques   94
Duck, Maureen (researcher at
     Financial Times)   226
Dun & Bradstreet (D&B)   27

e-communications and e-interactions
     199
e-learning, surveying via in-depth
     qualitative interviews   34
e-mail surveys   141
E-Tabs Lite Reader   47
Efamro (Europe)   238, 244
electronic analysis   97
Emotional Values   208–**09**
employee research/climate studies
     16
energy companies and utilities   169,
     174

EphMRA (European Pharmaceutical
     Market Research Association)
     242
ESOMAR   5–6, 43, 238–**40**, 242–44
ethics in B2B research,
   codes of conduct   242–43
   data protection   243–45
ethnography, useful on rare occasions
     95
Euromonitor research report   72–73
Europe   10, 140
European Society of Opinion and
     Market Research *see* ESOMAR
European Union Directives   244
evaluation of quality, customer
     service, supplier reputation
     114, 122–23

face-to-face interviewing   55, 59, **87,**
     141
factual questions   114, 116–18
field interviewers, quantitative
     interviews and   55–**56**
fieldwork, longer should be allowed
     for more difficult   140–41, 162
Financial Reputation   208–**09**
financial services   169, 171–72
FMCG (fast-moving consumer
     goods)   4–5, 18, 160
focus groups   54–5, 78–9, **87,** 217
France   **140,** 217
'free found' (companies sourced and
     found by researcher)   8, 25–26

Gabor Granger pricing technique   188
gatekeepers   10,169, 233
General Packet Radio Service (GPRS)
     53
Germany   **140,** 163, 217–18
Glossary   34, 153, 294–98
government statistics   26
grossing up or 'estimation', scaling-
     up or extrapolation   38
Guide to the European Union   218

how B2B research compliments other
     research, case study: telecoms
     company   13–14
HR (human resources)   8, 11
hypothetical situations   93–94

Iacobucci, Dawn, 'Services marketing
     and customer service' (chapter)
     31
IBM, 'spirit and letter of IBM'   206–07

ICC/ESOMAR International Code of marketing and Social Research 242

image tracking 18

IMRA/MRS code of conduct (revised in 1983) 242

in-depth interviews ('one on one'), conducted by telephone or in person 77–78

incentives,
B2B interviews and 85–87
costing and 162
quantitative B2B research and 141–42

independent advice 93

India 40, 216

Industrial Marketing Research Association (IMRA), change to BIG 5

information technology see (IT)

insight **101–04**

intensive care units (ICU) 33

Inter-Departmental Business Register (IDBR) 26

Intermediary Financial Advisers (IFAs), B2C and 18

internet – web or e-mail 55

internet and online research 10, 126–28

interviewing experts, may be quicker route to enlightenment 59

interviewing software 44

Ipa (UK) 239–**41**

IT 5, 8, 17

IT and telecoms 13, 169–171, 229

Japan 140, 215–16

Key British Enterprises (KBE) 27

key interviews 11

Key Note research report 72

key titles in companies 8–9

Krishamurthi, Lakshman 188

languages, piloting international B2B study in different 134, 233

Lenskold, James 43

Lindemann, Jan, Brands and Branding, chapter 'Brand evaluation' 203

lists 108
vary in terms of information about each listing 27–8
logistics issues 8

Macfarlane, Phyllis, Researching Business markets(1991) 20

McGivern, Yvonne, The Practice of Market and Social Research (2003) 97–98

McKinsey Consulting report, 'guide to doing business in China' 217

manufacturing/industry/chemicals 169, 173–74
typical studies 174

'marked up' questionnaire, useful for pre-data entry 142

market research organizations 237–8, **240**

Market Research Society 43

Market Research Society (MRS) 236

market segmentation, segmentation philosophy in marketing plan 177

market sizing and assessment 15

marketing and communications 16

Marketing Pocket Book 71

Marketing Research and Information 113

Market sizing/market configuration research 179, 184–86

MBA Marketing Research courses 237

MEP in Brussels, interviewing 78, 89

milestones for a company 'CV' 94

Mintel 72

MRI scanners 22

MRS Professional Standards Committee and Codeline 244

MRS (UK and Elsewhere) 239, 242, 245

Municipal Year Book (MYB) 26

Nail, Jim (Mastering Marketing Management) 43

Netto 19

neurolinguistic programming (NLP) 42

new product development see NPD

NOP World, omnibuses and 59–60

North American Industrial Classification System (NAIS) 30–31

'nose test' 99

NPD 19, 50, 61–62, 65–66, 111, **182**, 216
innovation and 179–83
questions 114, 122–**23**

Office of National Statistics 26

omnibus, subscription quantitative survey to which client questions can be added   57
'one to one' personal interviewing techniques   11, 55
other sectors engaging in B2B research   176–77
'other specify' items, post-coded after interviewing   112
'other specify' responses   143
overviews of respondents, sectors, applications,
    advertising and marketing communications research   195
    advertising and market communications   198–99
    advertising research   195–97
        case study: development of advertising to bolster corporate image re social responsibility   197
        case study: role of qualitative research in communications research   200
        marketing communications: evaluating e-communications and e-interactions   199
        measurement techniques and models   198
    applications
        case study: segmentation study of small and medium enterprises   177–78
        combining research topics in B2B research   177
    business respondent   166–67
        approaching the   168–69
        case study: brainstorming session with pharmaceutical marketing executives   167
    change in emphasis   179
    common research areas   179
        case study: NPD research with plumbers and fitters and consumers in household appliances   182–83
        new product development and innovation   179–82
    corporate image and branding research
        case study: developing a brand identity   209–10

corporate image research   205–07
    keeping up to date   207–08
    principles   203–05
    reporting   208–09
customer satisfaction/customer relations management (CRM) research   189–90
    case study: customer satisfaction for pharmaceutical company   194
    case study: using market research to support a business case – re-tendering for government contract   190–92
evaluating written and visual communications   200–01
    case study: tracking effectiveness of public relations campaigns in the finance industry   202–03
market sizing/market configuration research   184–86
pricing   186–87
    case study: pricing research of government service for farmers   187–89
sectors   169
    energy companies and utilities   174–75
    financial services   171–72
    IT and telecoms   169–71
    manufacturing/industry/chemicals   173–74
    pharmaceutical   175–76
    professional services   175
    transport   172–73
sectors other   176–77

paired interviews   55, 77–78
panels   57, 60, 131–33
Pareto principle   12
PBIRG (Pharmaceutical Business and Intelligence Research Group)   242
Pearson Education Year Book   26
pen and paper analysis   97
people researched in B2B work, centre of influence   9
    defining B2B respondent   7
    titles   7–9
performance assessment and tracking   15

personal organizers (PDAs), Palm
     Pilot or BlackBerry   14
personification   93
pharmaceutical sector, borderline
     case of B2B   18
pharmaceutical   175–76
piloting questionnaires
     31, 111, 134
Pitts, Kate (futurist if Royal Mail,
     UK)   43, 76
Plain man's Guide to Data Protection
     244
positioning   92
post-quantitative qualitative work,
     refine a concept in action   65
PowerPoint presentation   104, 152
Poynter, Ray   33, 130
     2004 BIG Conference Article of
          Virtual Surveys   34
practical aspects, B2B interviewing
     86–87
pre-coded questions   112
pricing   179
     principles   186–89
     reporting techniques for pricing
          research   189–90
process management   44
professional services   169, 175
profiling   38–39
publications, used for reference   153
Push Wap   53
putting the study into action,
     deciding on the sample frame
          23–24
     generating the sample   29
     sourcing the sample: lists
          24–28

qualitative B2B interviewing
     50, 53, 82
     'dont's' to bear in mind   90
     'warming' and recruiting
          83–85
qualitative data analysis packages   97
qualitative research   4, 59, 69, 106, **182**
     analysis and reporting
          analysis methods   96–98
          reporting   100
     attribution or to reveal the
          respondent and transparency
          to reveal the client   90–91
     B2B interviewing and moderating,
          practical aspects   86–87
     case study: creative
          brainstorming   80

case study: creative
     brainstorming in practice
     in B2B   80–81
choice/decision making process
     101
insight in analysis and reporting
     101–03
     case study: customer insight
          103–04
     reporting requirements of
          clients   104–05
main types
     creative brainstorming or
          strategy sessions   79
     focus groups   78–79
     in-depth interviews   77–78
process   81–82
     best practices   87–89
     case study: personal interview
          with member of European
          parliament   89–90
     incentives   85–86
     recruiting   82–85
useful interviewing techniques   91
     direct questioning   92–93
     projective (and other) tech-
          niques   93–95
Quality Assurance in company, who
     is in charge   8, 11
quality assurance/productivity
     studies   16
quantitative brand health and
     corporate image tracking   172
quantitative research   4, 59, **63**–65,
     69, **182**
     administering questionnaires:
          fieldwork issues   133
     briefing   134–37
     case study: how incentives can
          rebound – personal story
          141–42
     data analysis   143–46
     example of banner and stub
          147–51, 297
     fieldwork duration   140–41
     interviewing and project
          management quality
          134
     piloting questionnaires   134
     pre-contact   137–38
     pre-data entry   142–43
     requirement for more than one
          respondent   138–39
     response rates   139–40
     stimulus materials   138

design issues and project
management relevant to
particular B2B methods   123
case study: BusinessWeek and
its online reader panel
131, 133
case study: online staff survey
128–30
case study: web-based research
management tool   130
multi-mode approach   131
online surveys and technological research solutions
126–28
panels   131–32
self-completion questionnaires
123–26
process   107–08
data specs, code frame and
statistical analysis   109
data tables   109
preparation into field and
fieldwork   108–09
questionnaire design
general principles   110–13
route map for a B2B questionnaire
design and content   113
types of questions   114–23
quantitative surveys, internet and
telephone methodologies
replacing face-to-face
interviewing   59
questionnaire, key things   110–11
quota sampling   31–32, 161, 296

'reality check' for reporting   98–99
References and further reading
299–301
regional review of Australia   218
environment   219
type of work and B2B focus   219
regional review of Europe   217
environment   218
type of work and B2B focus   217
regional review of Great Britain,
B2B focus   212
environment   212
international research   212
market size   211
type of work   212
reporting, B2B customer satisfaction
research   195
reporting mechanisms   44
reporting for quantitative research,
formats   152–53

hints   152
reputation research, framework
208–09
request for proposal (RFP)   20, 108,
161, 163, 221–22
Research magazine, integrating MR
and technology   131
research overload   48
research providers, business
syndicates and business
omnibuses   59
research report,
framework or template   96
'nose test' and   99
'reality check'   98
think visually and
diagrammatically   99–101
'research snapshot' idea   105
research supplier (agency), what to
include when costing   164
Research Support & Marketing
(RSM)   141
respondents   7–8, 10, 21–22, 108,
161
care must be taken to prevent
identification   243
consideration of   90–91
corporate reputation study and   8
as 'gate keepers'   169, 233
how should they be addressed
220
may need more than one
individual as   138–39
pre-contact with   137–38
understanding the business as
individuals   168
'warming' of may help reduce
costs   165
response and contact records,
important research results in
themselves   36
return on capital (ROC)   41
return on investment (ROI)
41, 43
Reuters   73–74
RIVA Training Institute, B2C and B2B
research   237
role/context   92
Royal Mail Information Centre,
Infobank   72
Russia   40

salience   92
sample frame,
evaluation of   30–31

five key elements 23–**24**
generating, rule of thumb 29
main sources 28
sample size,
    error related to **36**, 296
    factors for decision 32–33
sampling for B2B research,
    case study; multinational
        quantitative corporate
        reputation project 29
    deciding on the sample frame
        23–24
    defining business universe or
        population to be covered
        20–21
    evaluation of sample frame
        30–31
    generating the sample 29
    quotas or stratification of sample
        31–32
    research practices related to,
        screening 35–37
    selection of sample size 32–34
    sizing the available respondent
        group 21–22
    small can sometimes be great; big
        can sometimes be greater
        34–35
    sourcing the sample: lists
        24–29
    weighting and grossing up
        grossing up 38
        profiling 38–39
        weighting 37–**39**
sampling characteristics of business
    markets,
    defining business universe or
        population to be covered
        20–21
    sizing the available respondent
        group 21–22
Scandinavia 163, 217
screening and classification questions
    114–16
segmentation of customers and 16,
    172
SIC codes (UK) 25, 30, 75, 297
SMEs 125–26
    questions relating to mobile
        telephony 66–**67**
SOHO (small office home office
    sectors) 14, 28
Sopp, L. (recent Chairman of AURA)
    105
spam (unsolicited e-mail) 162–63

specialist agencies, higher charges
    165
specialists, available to do desk
    research 72
'stand alone' quantitative report
    152
Stoll, Martin (Ipos Insight) 94–95
stratification, useful where universe
    or population known 32
'sugging' (selling under guise of
    market research) 243, 297
survey design and analysis 44
SWOT analysis 208

Target 19
'target weighting' techniques 37–38
telephone directories, international
    B2B telephone fieldwork agencies
    and 28
telephone interviewing 55, 67–68,
    87, 138, 141, 233
Tesco 19
tracking studies 42, 55, 59–60, 207,
    235
training, no body dedicated to in B2B
    market research 236
transcripts of interviews for analysis
    97
transparency 91
transport 169
    typical studies 173
trends, envisaged by respondent 93
trends in B2B research,
    case study: using technical terms
        52–53
    conflicting demands 42–43
    ensuring a strong B2B market
        research offering
        positioning B2B research 51–52
        selling tips 52
    implications of current trends,
        research market place
        changes 49–50
    market-driven trends 40–41
    our knowledge base and how we
        conduct business 50–51
    research-driven trends 41–42
    specific trends and issues,
        technological advance and its
        effect on B2B research 44
    technological advance and its
        effect on, case study:
        questions on clients internal
        use of technology 44–45
    technology and research 45

case study: new and efficient
      methods of data capture
      47
   case study: touch–screen
      technology for business
      surveys 46
technology-driven trends 42

UK 18, 217
   BMRA and size of business
      research market 6
   Data Protection Act (1998) 244
   directories 27
   hub to coordinate Europe and
      Singapore 212–13
   Independent Consultants Group
      (ICG) 72
   response rates to questionnaires
      140
United States 18
   B2B share 6, 213
   data mining labelled as 'customer
      discovery' 74
   internet service of D&B's sales and
      marketing arm Zapdata 27
   market for e-commerce 42
   no exclusively B2B agencies 48
   relationship modelling 214
   Research Strategies' Executive
      Omnibus 60
   SIC codes being replaced by NAIS
      30
   Survey Sampling International
      (SSI) 60, 132
   training included in more general
      research training 237
United States regional review,
   B2B focus 213–14
   environment 214
   market share 212
   type of work 213
'universe or population' 20–**22**, 59,
   161, 296
unweighted bases on tables, to
   indicate reliability of data 38
upfront screening questions 36–37

video conferencing 22, 42, 165

web-based reporting 105, 153, 156
weighting, how it can be used
   37, **39**
what works and does not work 54
   addressing business issue using
      qualitative or quantitative
      approach 66–67
   another methodological note
      67–68
   case study: benefits of and
      drawbacks to iterative
      research in NPD 65–66
   case study: desk research assists
      NPD in unknown market
      61–62
   choice of qualitative versus
      quantitative 62–**63**
      qualitative 62–**63**
   deciding on the approach,
      principles 60–**61**, 64
   key categories of research **56**
   omnibus 57
      case study: using the media to
         canvass business opinion
         via the CNN time opinion
         poll 58
   panel research 57
   primary versus secondary and
      qualitative versus
      quantitative research
      55–**56**
   relative use of these approaches in
      B2B research 58–60
   useful descriptions of types of
      research 55
      ad hoc versus tracking/moni-
         toring studies 55
      interviewing methodologies
         55
   using qualitative and quantitative
      research together 64–65
workshops for reporting 153,
   155–56
World Markets Analysis 74
written and visual communications,
   evaluation 200–01

Yellow Pages 26